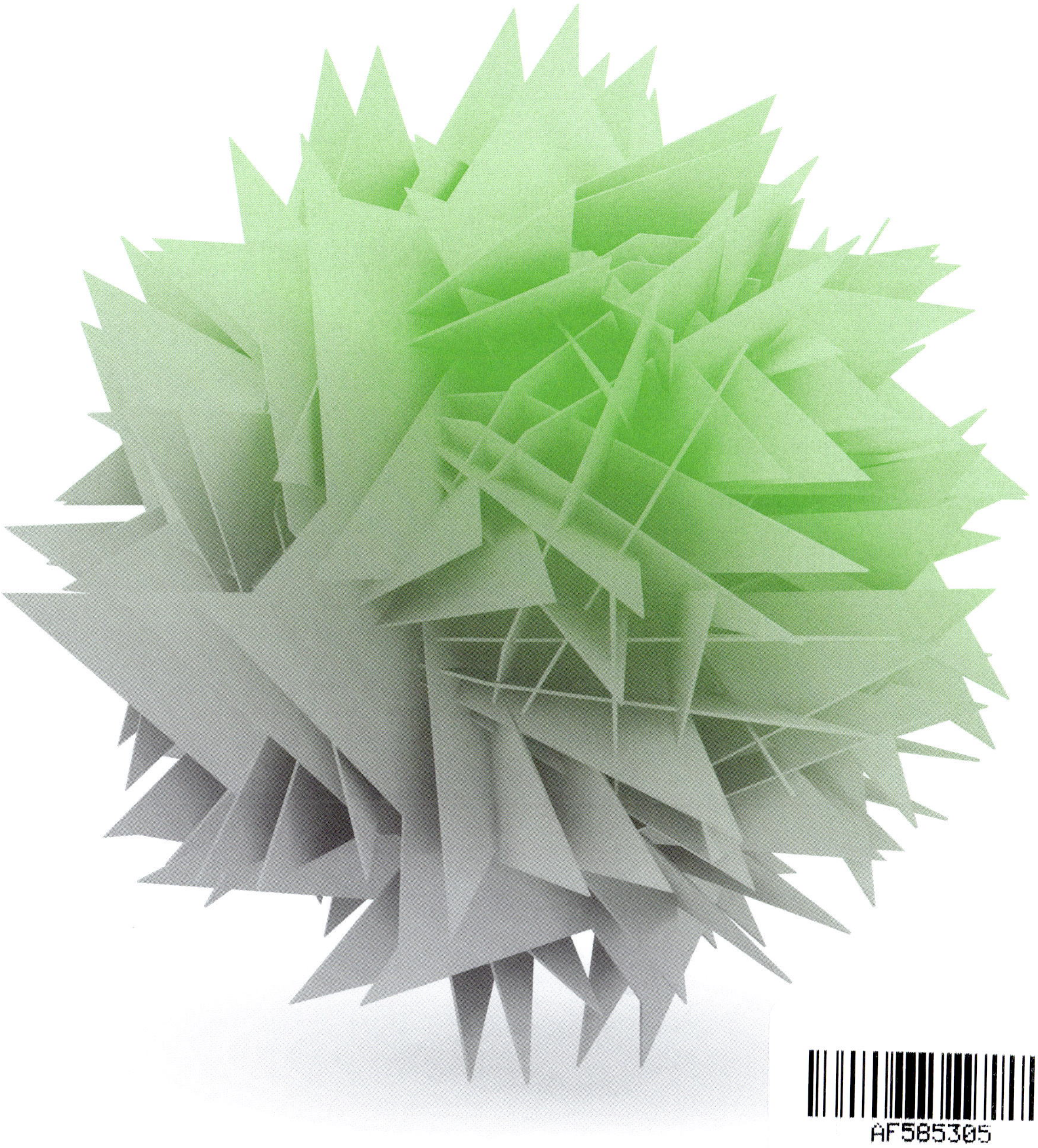

AF585305

GEOMETRY

Walker Maths Essentials: Geometry 4+
1st Edition
Charlotte Walker
Victoria Walker

Cover design: Cheryl Rowe, Macarn Design
Text designer: Cheryl Rowe, Macarn Design
Production controller: Siew Han Ong

Any URLs contained in this publication were checked for currency during the production process. Note, however, that the publisher cannot vouch for the ongoing currency of URLs.

Acknowledgements
Cover photo courtesy of Shutterstock.

We wish to thank the Boards of Trustees of Darfield and Riccarton High Schools for allowing us to use materials and ideas developed while teaching. Our thanks also go to all past and present colleagues, especially Kath Wilson, who have generously shared their experience and ideas.

© 2022 Cengage Learning Australia Pty Limited

Copyright Notice
Copyright: This book is not a photocopiable master. No part of the publication may be copied, stored or communicated in any form by any means (paper or digital), including recording or storing in an electronic retrieval system, without the written permission of the publisher. Education institutions that hold a current licence with Copyright Licensing New Zealand, may copy from this book in strict accordance with the terms of the CLNZ Licence.

For product information and technology assistance,
in Australia call **1300 790 853**;
in New Zealand call **0800 449 725**

For permission to use material from this text or product, please email
aust.permissions@cengage.com

National Library of New Zealand Cataloguing-in-Publication Data
A catalogue record for this book is available from the National Library of New Zealand

978 0 17 044753 9

Cengage Learning Australia
Level 7, 80 Dorcas Street
South Melbourne, Victoria Australia 3205

Cengage Learning New Zealand
Unit 4B Rosedale Office Park
331 Rosedale Road, Albany, North Shore 0632, NZ

For learning solutions, visit **cengage.co.nz**

Printed in China by 1010 Printing International Limited.
3 4 5 6 7 26 25

CONTENTS

Glossary

Make your own glossary of key terms:

Term	Definition	Picture/Example
Degrees		
Equilateral triangle		
Isosceles triangle		
Scalene triangle		
Quadrilateral		
Acute angle		
Right angle		
Obtuse angle		
Straight angle		
Reflex angle		

PHOTOCOPYING OF THIS PAGE IS RESTRICTED UNDER LAW.
ISBN: 9780170447539

Term	Definition	Picture/Example
Polygon		
Regular		
Irregular		
Symmetrical		
Two-dimensional (2D)		
Three-dimensional (3D)		
Complementary angles		
Supplementary angles		
Translation		
Reflection		
Rotation		
Enlargement		

ISBN: 9780170447539 PHOTOCOPYING OF THIS PAGE IS RESTRICTED UNDER LAW.

Shapes

Polygons

A polygon is a single shape that:
- is two-dimensional, or 2D (flat)
- has three or more straight sides, and
- is closed (has no gaps).

Examples:

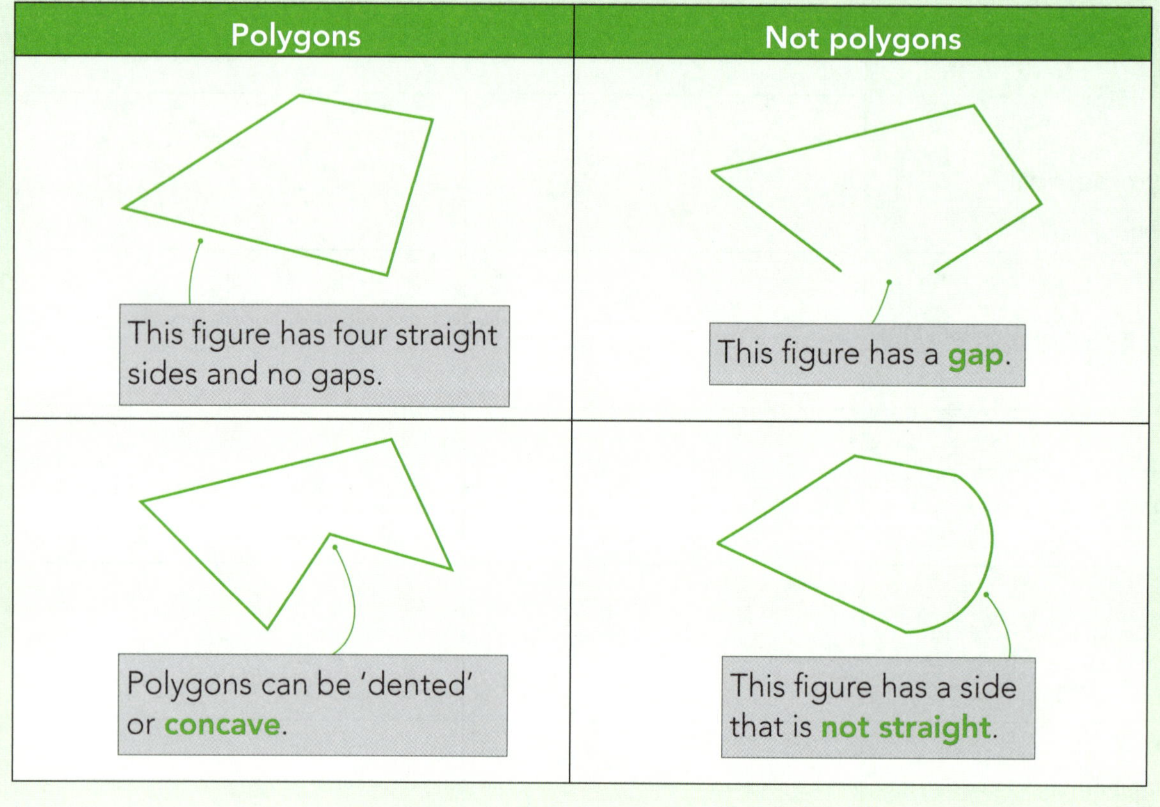

Circle the correct statement for each of these shapes.

1

Polygon   Not a polygon

2

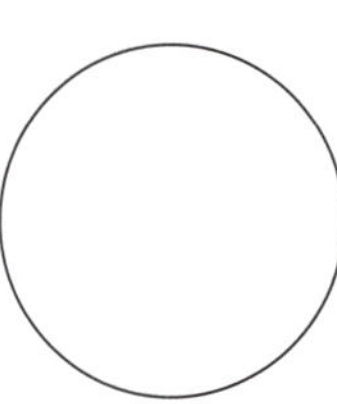

Polygon   Not a polygon

3

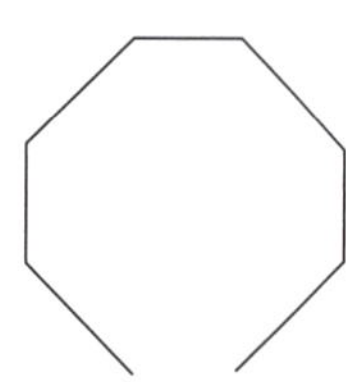

Polygon   Not a polygon

4

Polygon   Not a polygon

PHOTOCOPYING OF THIS PAGE IS RESTRICTED UNDER LAW. ISBN: 9780170447539

5

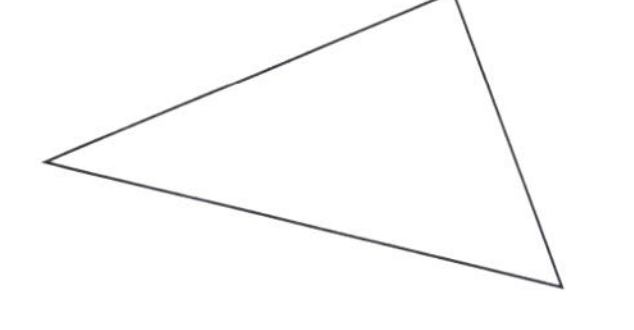

Polygon Not a polygon

6

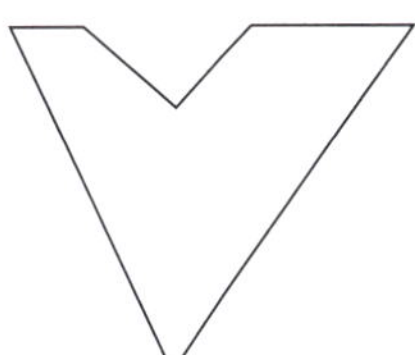

Polygon Not a polygon

7 Select the correct name for each polygon, and write it in the table.

Number of sides	Name	Diagram
3	______	
4	______	
5	______	
6	______	
7	______	
8	______	
9	______	
10	______	

Octagon

Hexagon

Triangle

Decagon

Quadrilateral

Heptagon

Pentagon

Nonagon

ISBN: 9780170447539 PHOTOCOPYING OF THIS PAGE IS RESTRICTED UNDER LAW.

Shape language

- **Triangle**: a closed shape with exactly three straight sides.
- **Quadrilateral**: a closed shape with exactly four straight sides.
- **Regular**: a shape with all sides and angles equal.
- **Irregular**: a shape with two or more unequal sides or angles.
- **Isosceles**: a triangle or trapezium with two equal sides.
- **Two-dimensional** (2D): a shape that has width and length but no thickness.
- **Symmetrical (reflective)**: a shape which can have a fold line that cuts the shape into two equal halves.

Example:

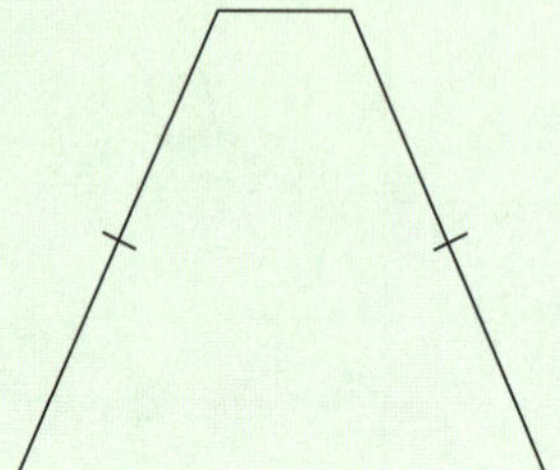

This shape can be described using these words: **2D**, **quadrilateral**, **isosceles**, **trapezium**, **polygon**, **symmetrical**.

You could **not** use these words to describe this shape: **regular**, **triangle**.

✗

Highlight the word(s) that can be used to describe these shapes.

1

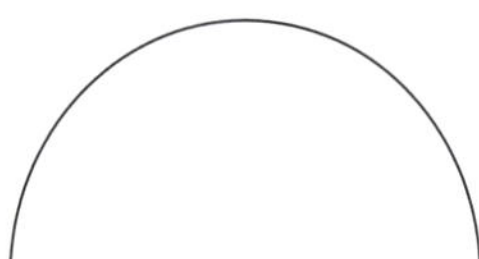

polygon quadrilateral symmetrical 2D

2

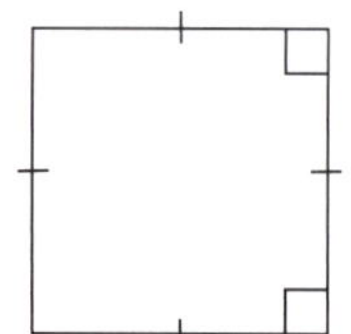

polygon regular quadrilateral irregular

3

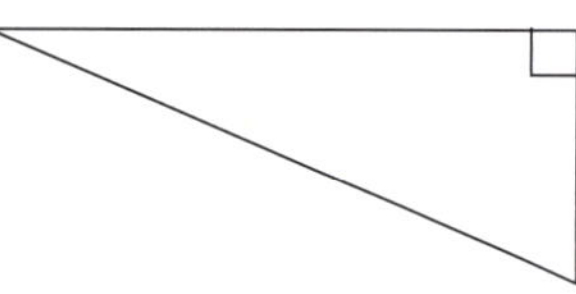

2D symmetrical polygon regular

4

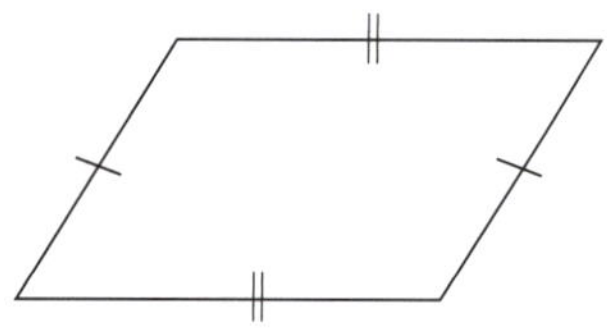

symmetrical polygon regular quadrilateral

PHOTOCOPYING OF THIS PAGE IS RESTRICTED UNDER LAW.
ISBN: 9780170447539

5

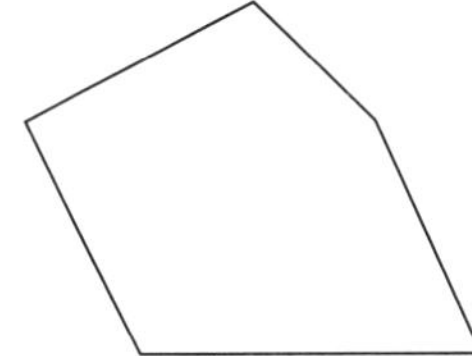

pentagon quadrilateral irregular regular

6

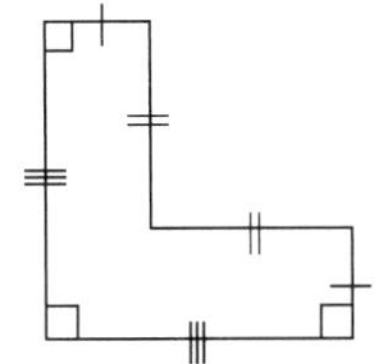

polygon regular symmetrical hexagon

7

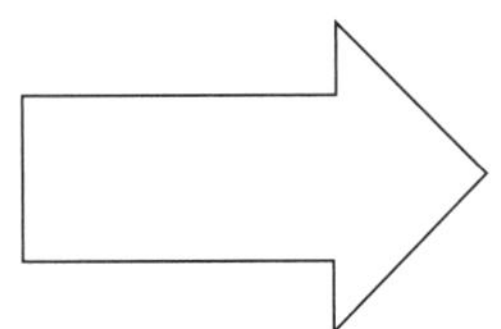

heptagon regular 2D polygon

What words can be used to describe these shapes?

8

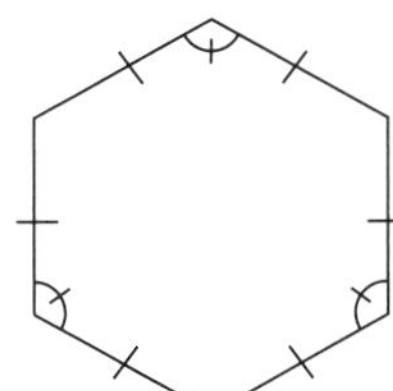

____

9

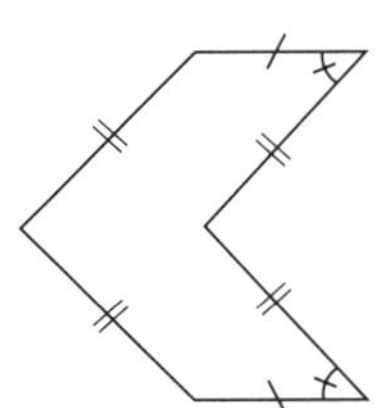

____

10

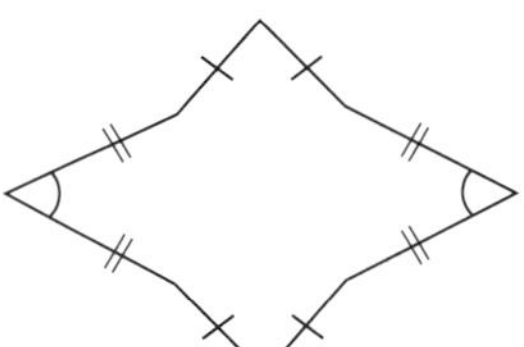

____

11

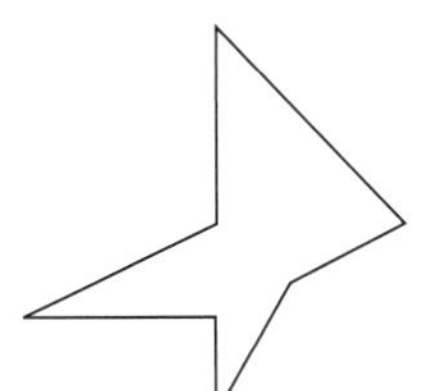

____

ISBN: 9780170447539 PHOTOCOPYING OF THIS PAGE IS RESTRICTED UNDER LAW.

Naming 2D shapes

- Here are some shapes with names that are useful.

Example:

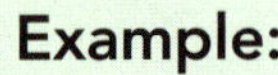

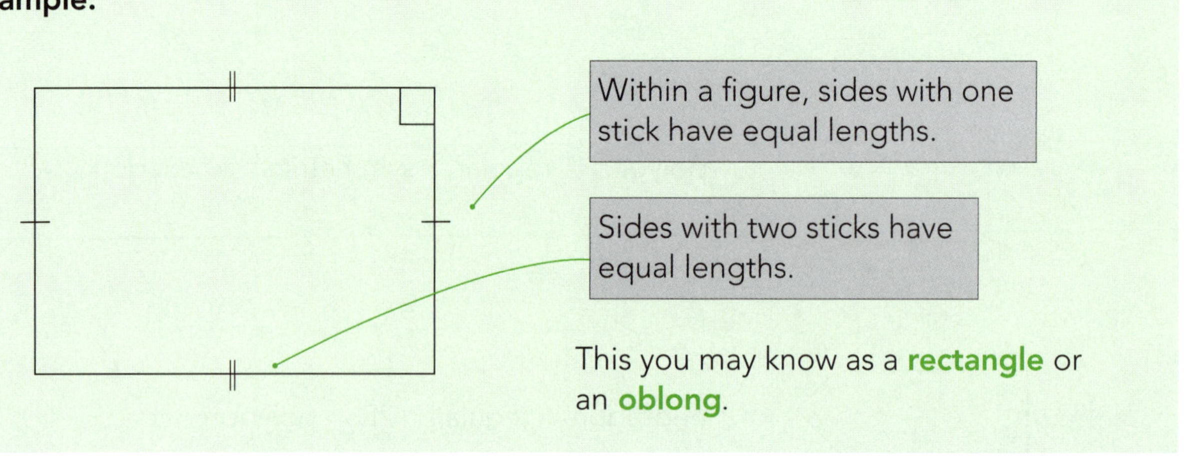

This you may know as a **rectangle** or an **oblong**.

Use the terms in the box to match them to the shapes below. You will have to use a term twice.

square	circle	trapezium	parallelogram
decagon	rhombus	equilateral triangle	oval
right-angled triangle	pentagon	right-angled isosceles triangle	hexagon
octagon	rectangle	isosceles triangle	nonagon
semicircle	heptagon	isosceles trapezium	kite

1

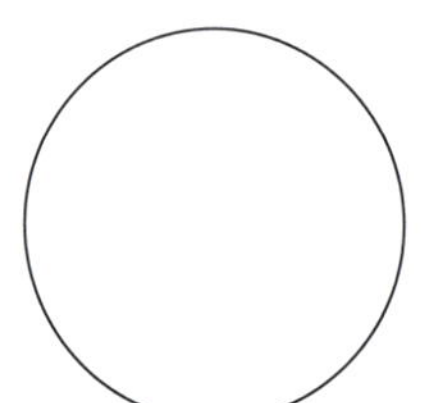

____

2

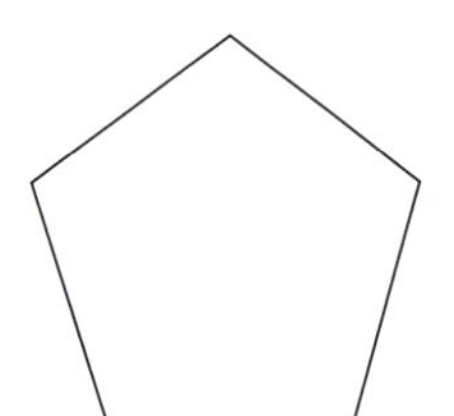

____

3

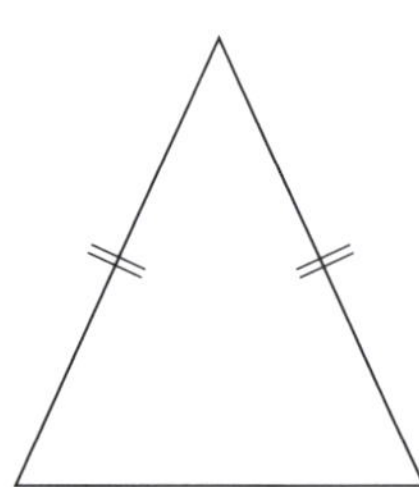

____

4

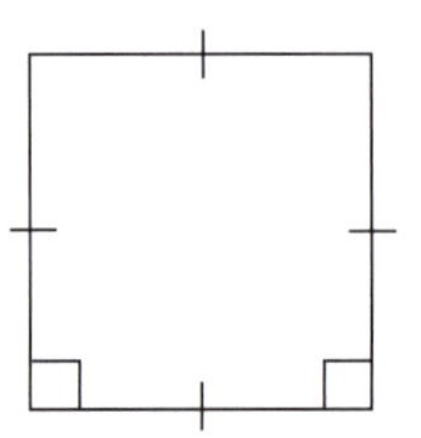

____

5

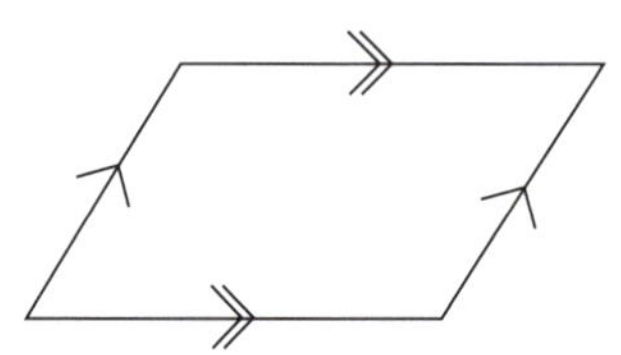

____

6

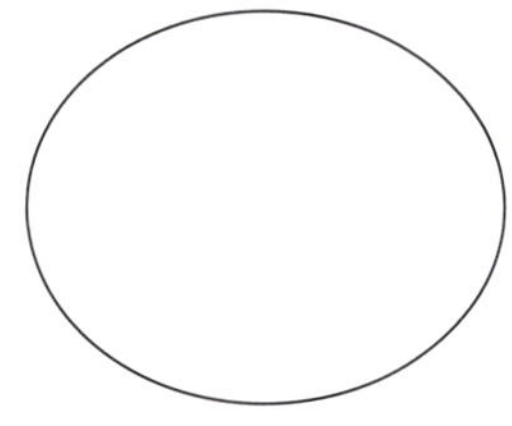

____

PHOTOCOPYING OF THIS PAGE IS RESTRICTED UNDER LAW. ISBN: 9780170447539

7

8

9

10

11

12

13

14

15

16

17

18

19

20

21

ISBN: 9780170447539 PHOTOCOPYING OF THIS PAGE IS RESTRICTED UNDER LAW.

Challenge 1

This diagram is made up of squares. The smallest squares are 1 unit square, and the largest is 8 units square. How many squares are there in this picture? You may find the table helpful.

Square size	Number
1 x 1	
2 x 2	
3 x 3	
4 x 4	
5 x 5	
6 x 6	
7 x 7	
8 x 8	
Total:	

How many triangles are in this figure? You may like to colour or code each shape and make a list to help you.

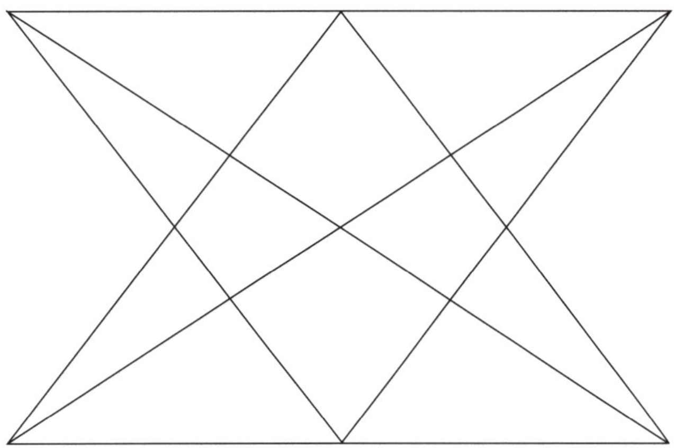

Triangle shape	Number
Total:	

PHOTOCOPYING OF THIS PAGE IS RESTRICTED UNDER LAW.
ISBN: 9780170447539

Angles

Types of angles

Name	Picture	Description
Acute angle		An angle between 0° and 90°.
Right angle		An angle that is 90°.
Obtuse angle		An angle between 90° and 180°.
Straight angle		An angle that is 180°.
Reflex angle		An angle between 180° and 360°.

Write down the name of each type of angle.

1

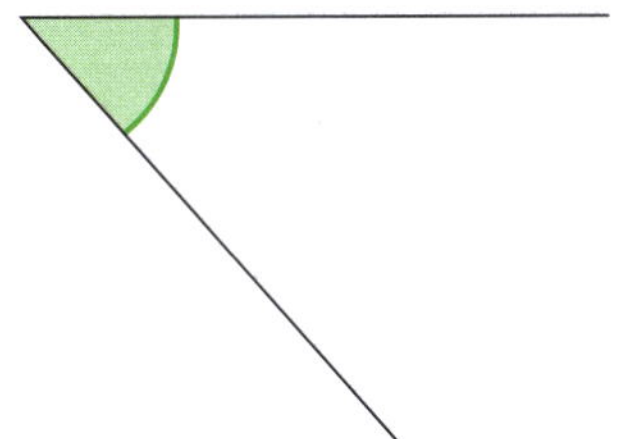

____

2

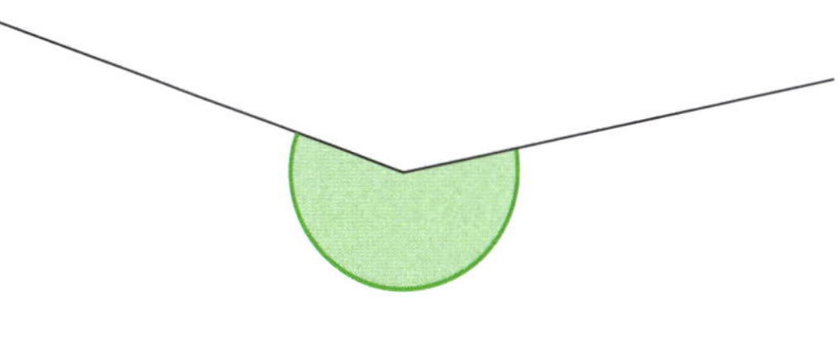

____

ISBN: 9780170447539 PHOTOCOPYING OF THIS PAGE IS RESTRICTED UNDER LAW.

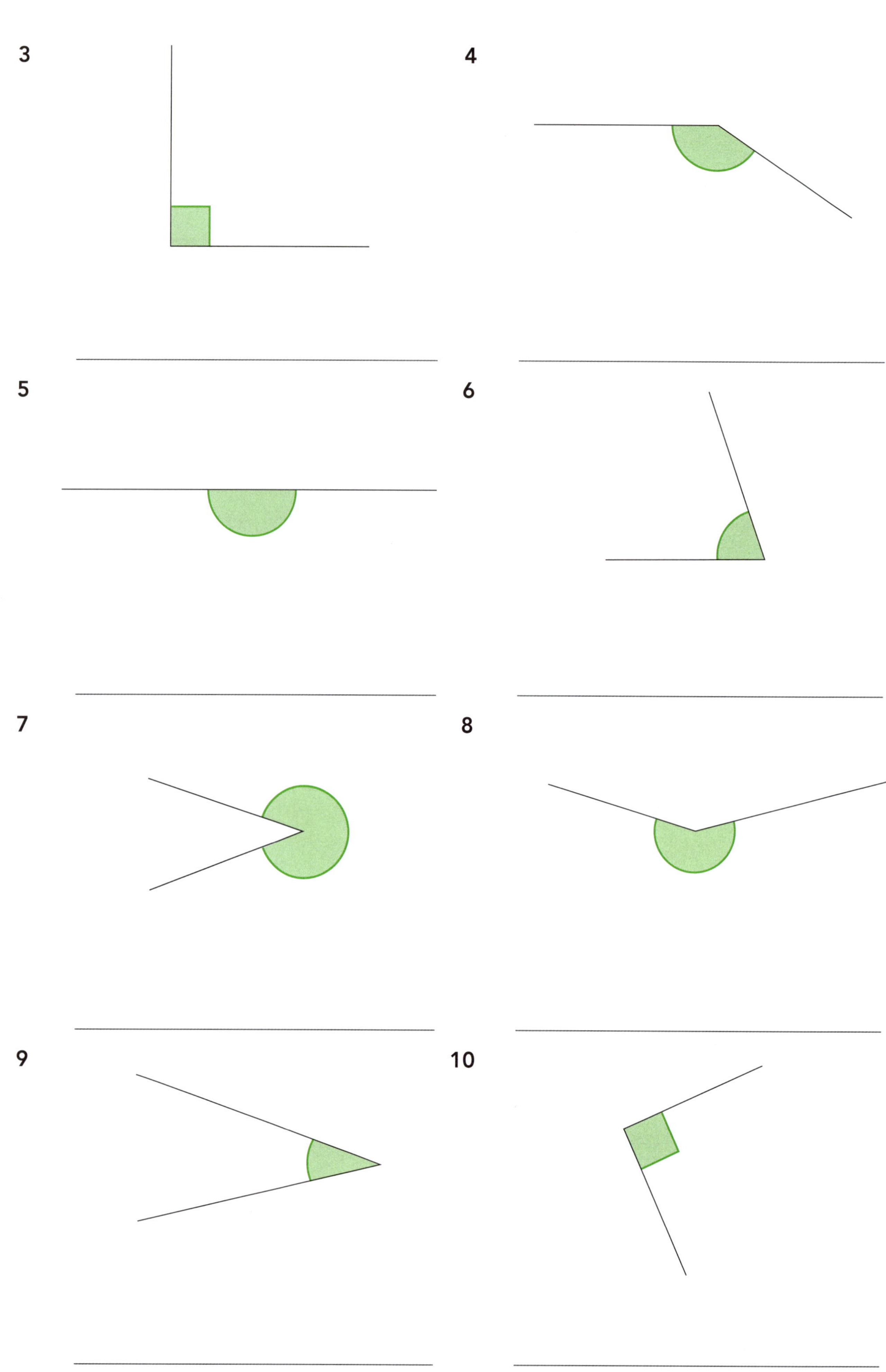

PHOTOCOPYING OF THIS PAGE IS RESTRICTED UNDER LAW. ISBN: 9780170447539

Naming angles

- Angles can be named in two ways.

1 Using the **three** letters **outside** each vertex.

This angle is ∠D**E**F or ∠F**E**D.

Notice that the middle letter (**E**) is at the angle.

F E D

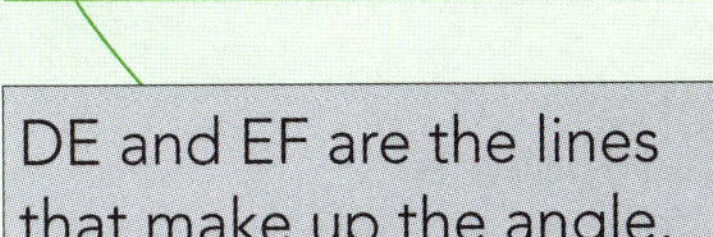

2 Using the **one** letter **inside** the angle.

This angle is ∠*y*.

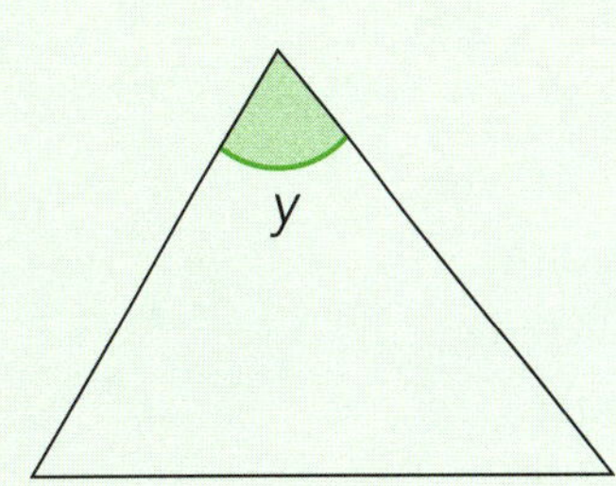

Match the angle names to the angles in the diagrams.

∠CBA	∠CAD	∠a	∠CAB
∠DAB	∠BCA	∠b	∠CDA

1

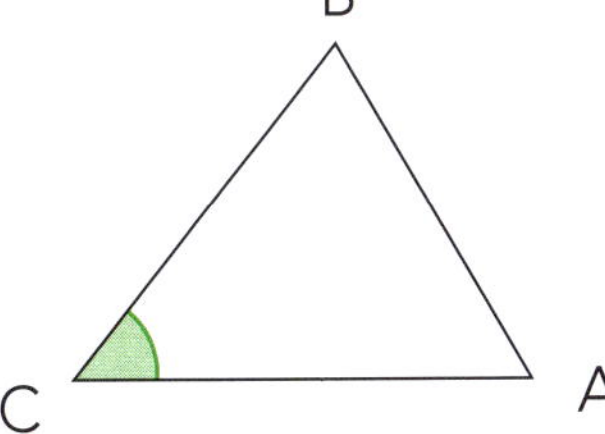

____

2

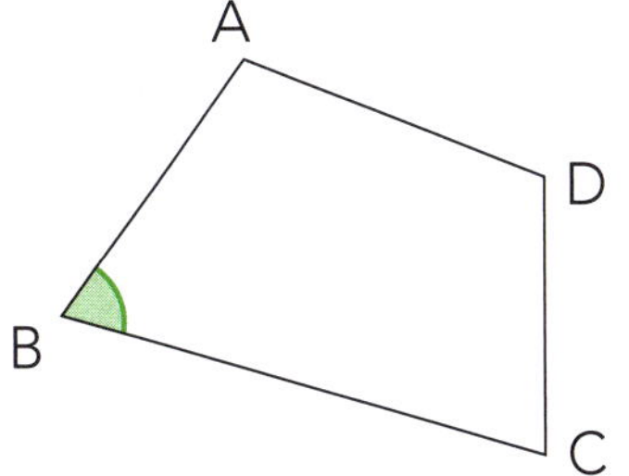

____

3

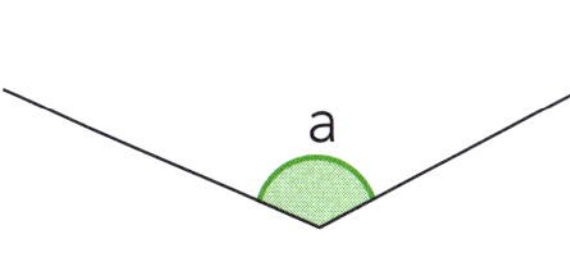

____

4

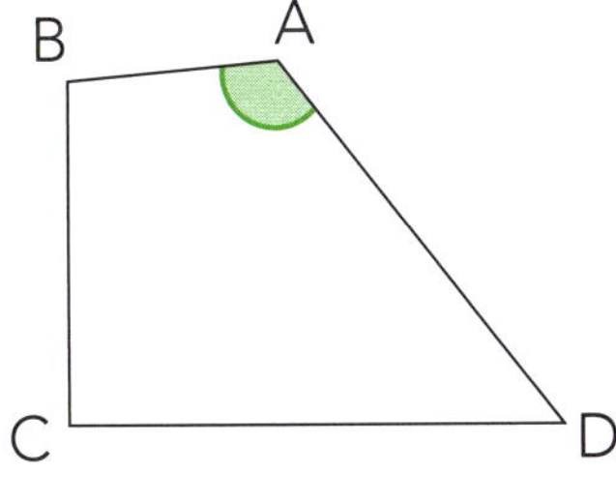

____

5

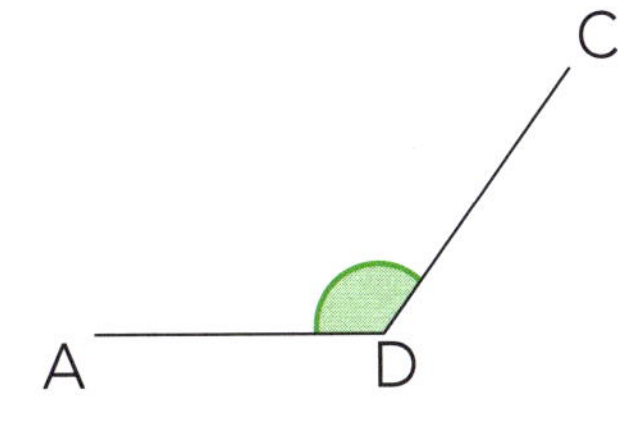

____

6

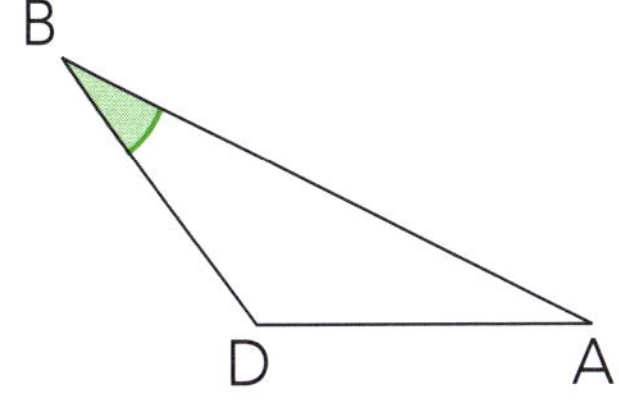

____

ISBN: 9780170447539 PHOTOCOPYING OF THIS PAGE IS RESTRICTED UNDER LAW.

Measuring acute and obtuse angles

Measuring angles is most commonly done with a protractor.

- Find **zero** on the scale to make sure that you read in the **correct** direction.
- **Think** about your answer. Does it seem reasonable?

Examples:

1

The inside scale reads **135°**. Notice that the outside scale shows 1° marks. You can use these to help your accuracy.

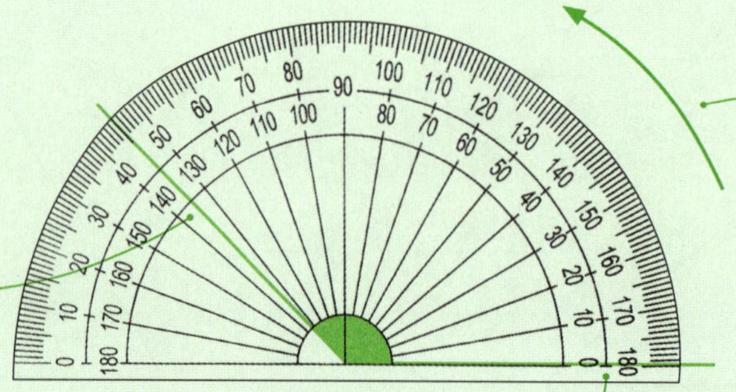

Because of the location of 0, in this case you need to read in an **anticlockwise** direction. ∴ you need to read the **inside scale**.

You must start to measure your angle from **0**.

2

The outside scale reads **71°**.

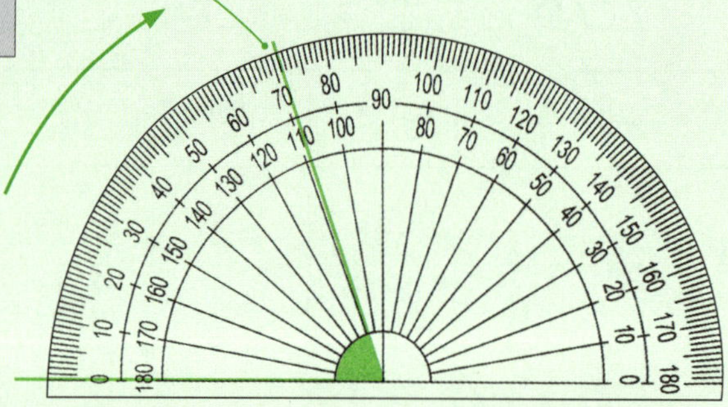

Write down the size of these angles.

1

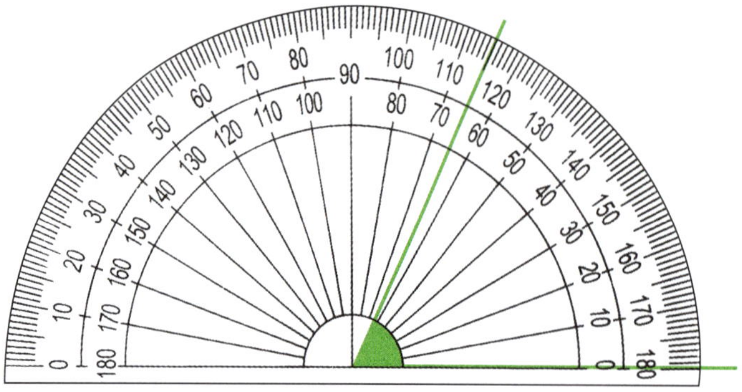

PHOTOCOPYING OF THIS PAGE IS RESTRICTED UNDER LAW. ISBN: 9780170447539

2

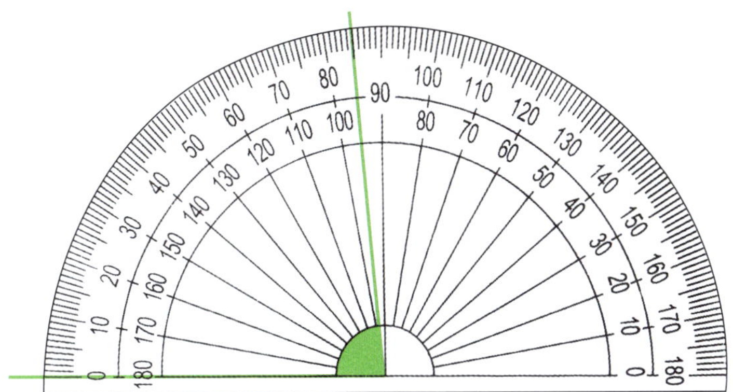

____

3

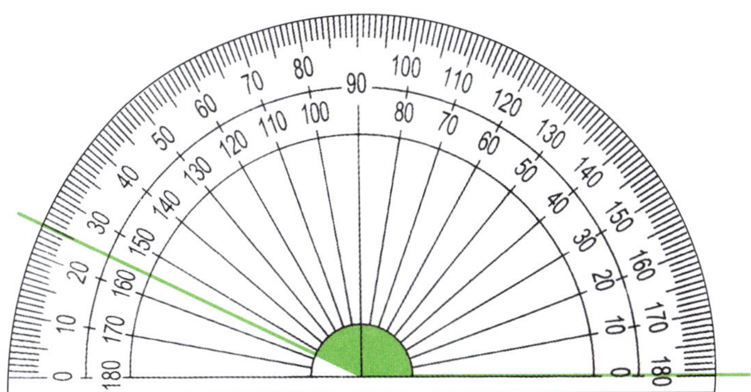

____

4

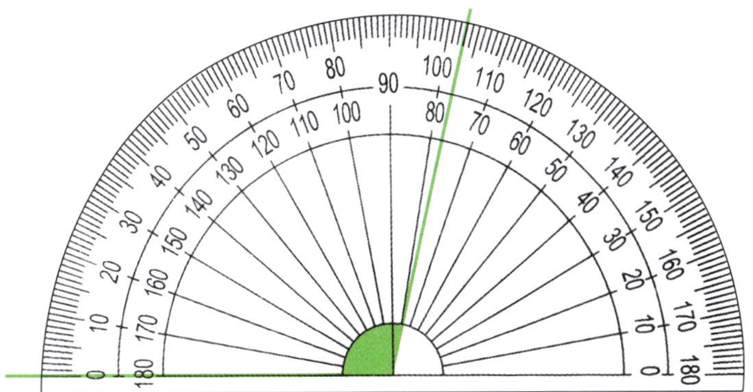

____

5

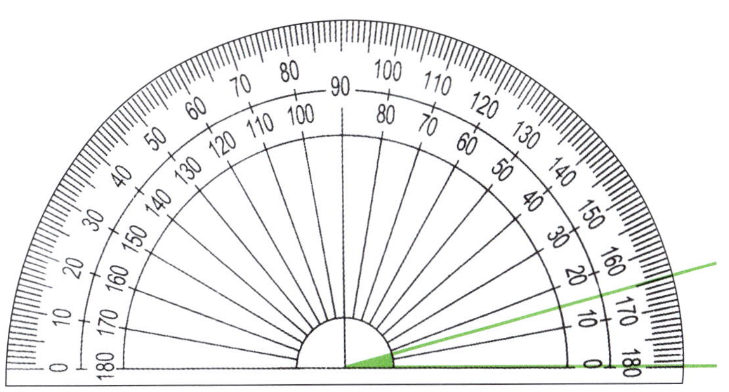

____

ISBN: 9780170447539 PHOTOCOPYING OF THIS PAGE IS RESTRICTED UNDER LAW.

Measuring reflex angles

- Find **zero** on the scale to make sure that you read in the **correct** direction.
- **Think** about your answer. Does it seem reasonable?

Examples:

1

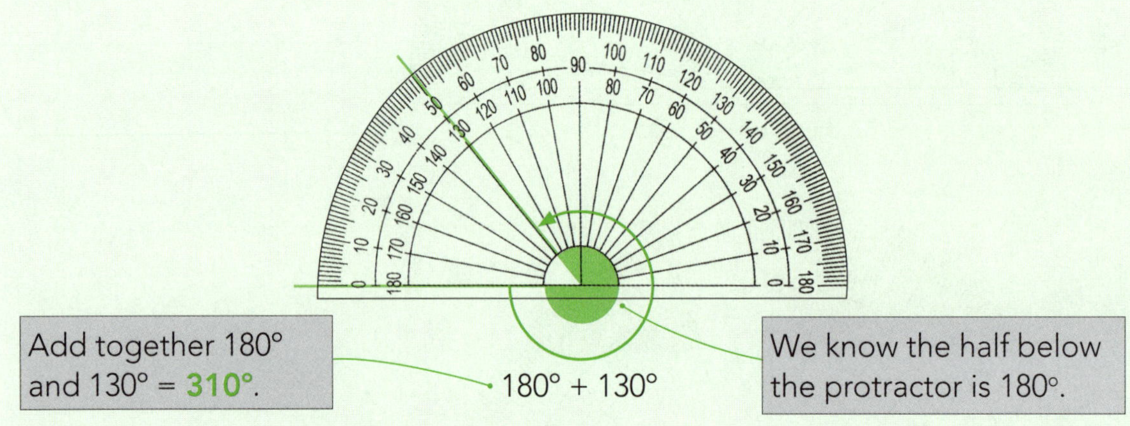

2 Using a 360° protractor:

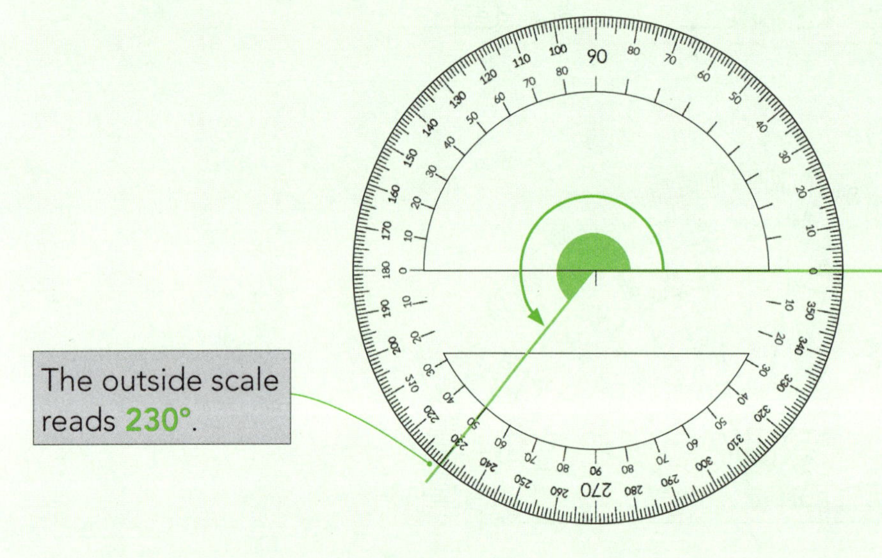

Write down the size of these angles.

1

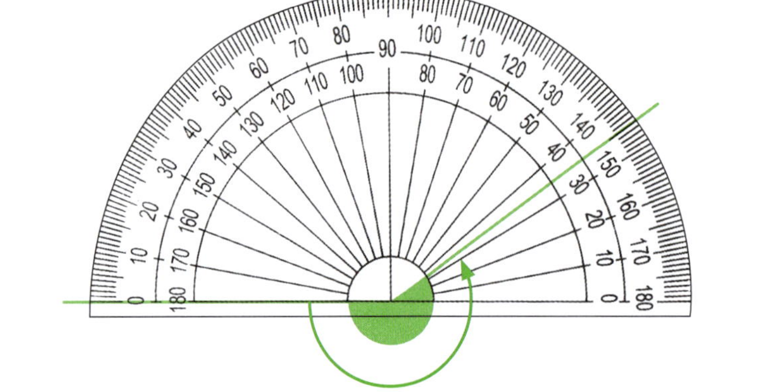

____

____

PHOTOCOPYING OF THIS PAGE IS RESTRICTED UNDER LAW. ISBN: 9780170447539

2

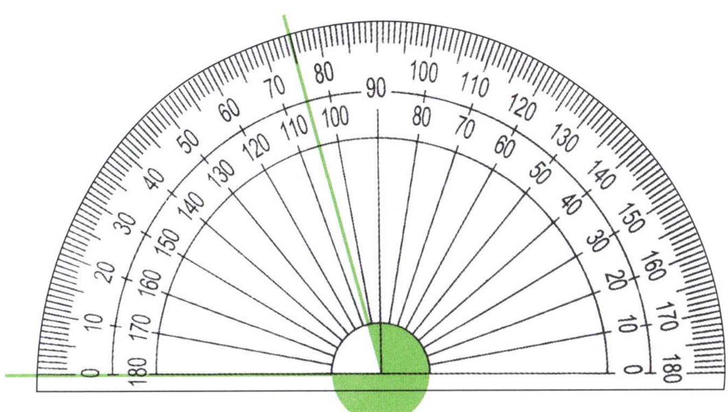

____

____

3

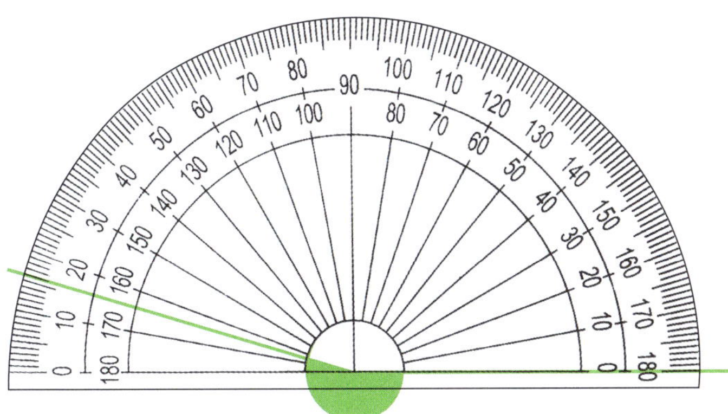

____

____

4

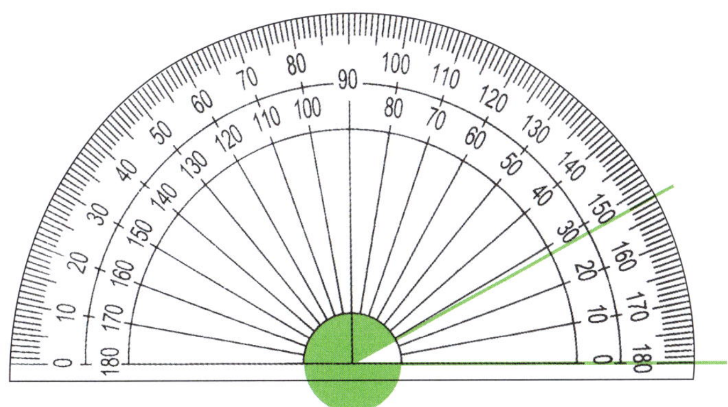

____

____

5

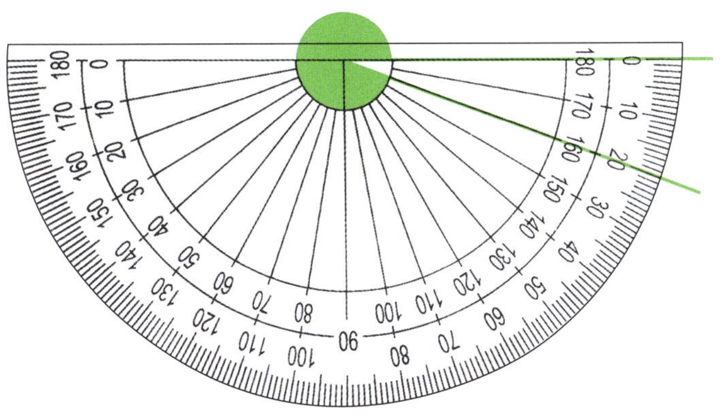

____

____

Estimating angles

Match each angle with the most appropriate picture.

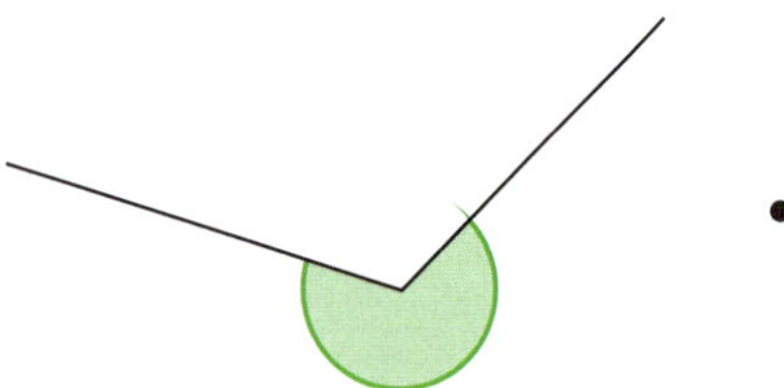	•	• 100°
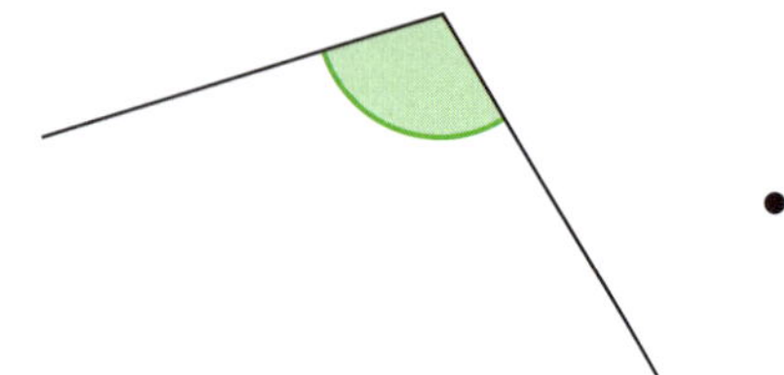	•	• 53°
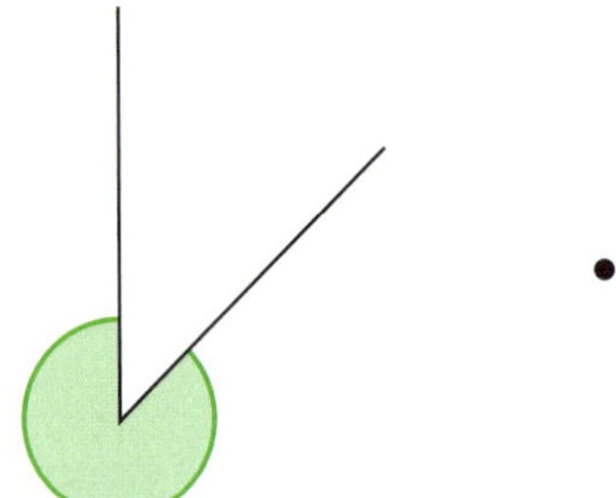	•	• 198°
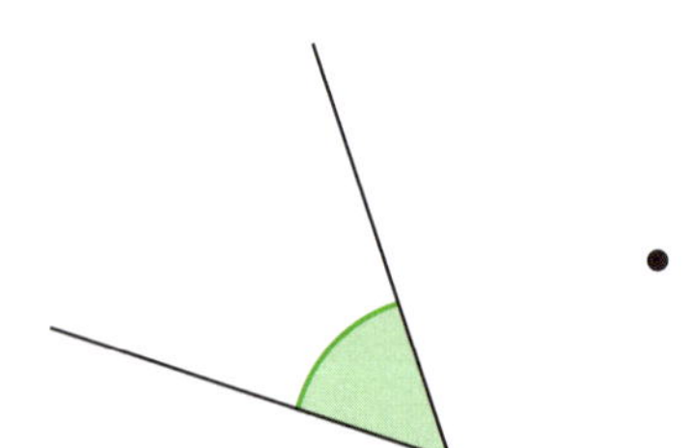	•	• 225°
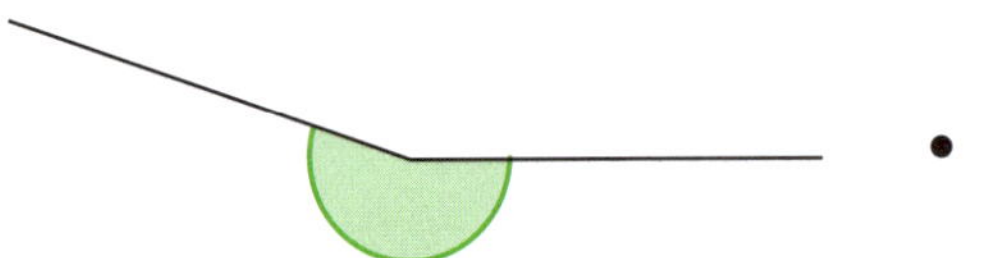	•	• 315°

PHOTOCOPYING OF THIS PAGE IS RESTRICTED UNDER LAW.
ISBN: 9780170447539

Angles on a line

- Angles on a line **add to 180°** and are known as **supplementary** angles.
- Angles that **add to 90°** are known as **complementary angles**.

Notice that this is an 'e'. Something complimentary is free.

Examples:

1 Find the value of x.

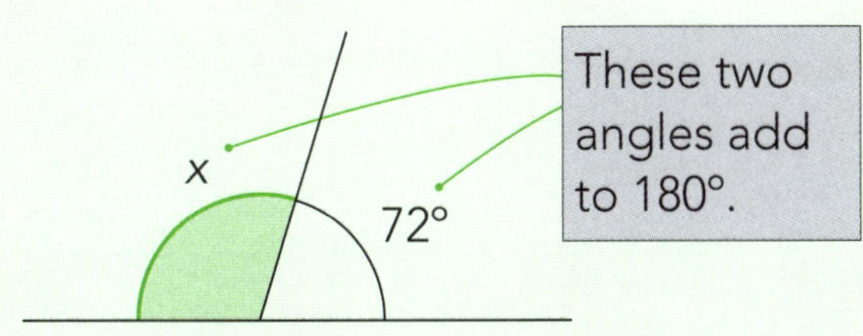

$x + 72° = 180°$
$x = 180° - 72°$
$x = 108°$

2 Find the value of y.

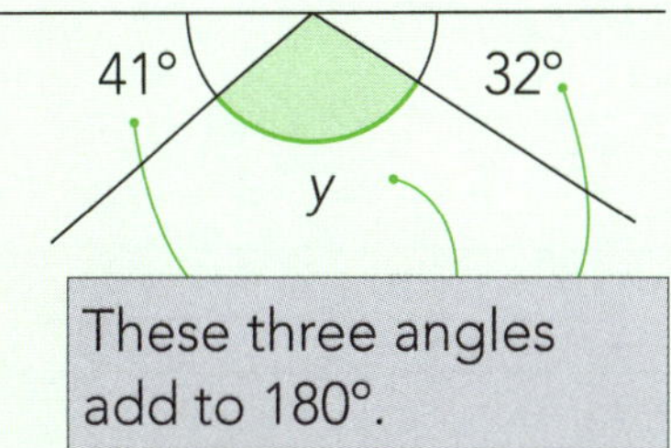

$41° + y + 32° = 180°$
$y = 180° - 41° - 32°$
$y = 107°$

Calculate the size of the missing angles.

1

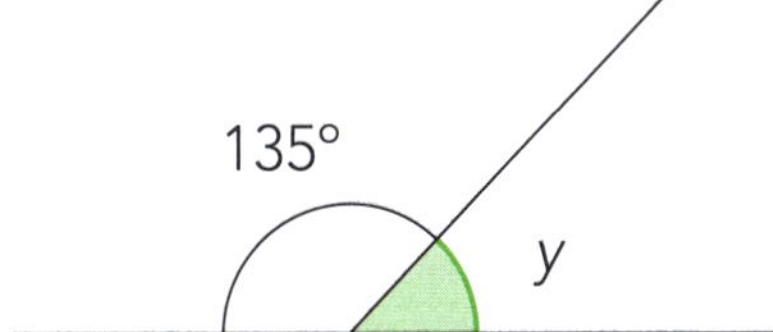

2

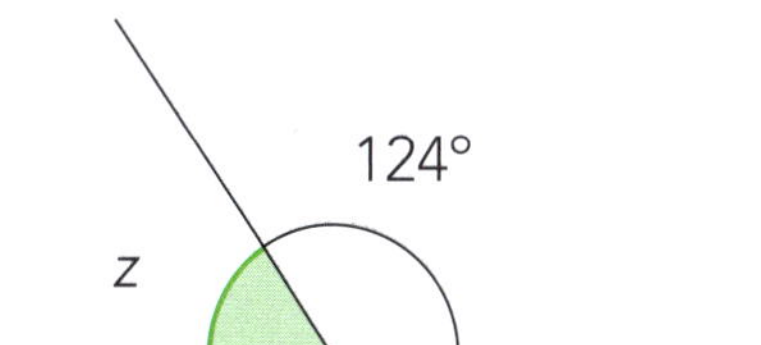

3

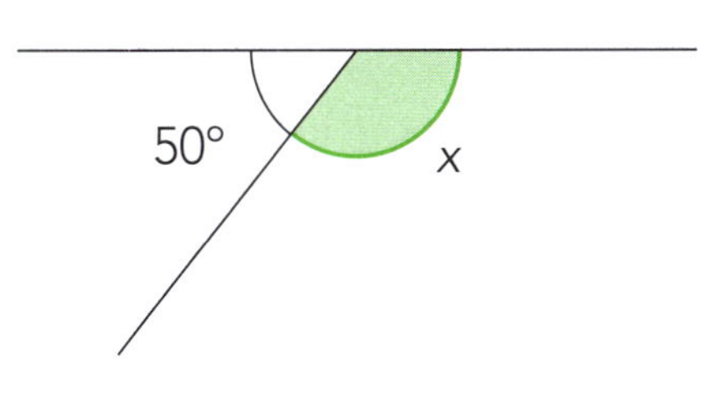

4

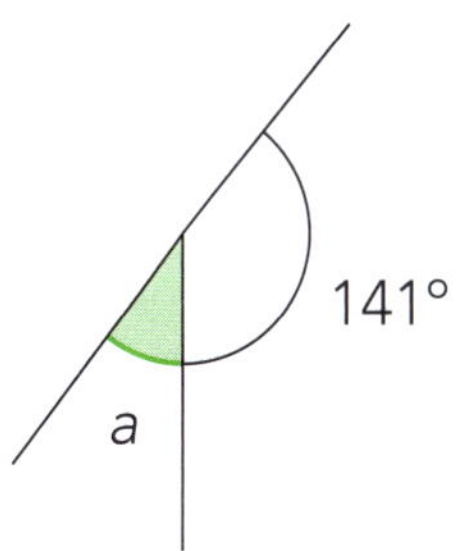

ISBN: 9780170447539 PHOTOCOPYING OF THIS PAGE IS RESTRICTED UNDER LAW.

5

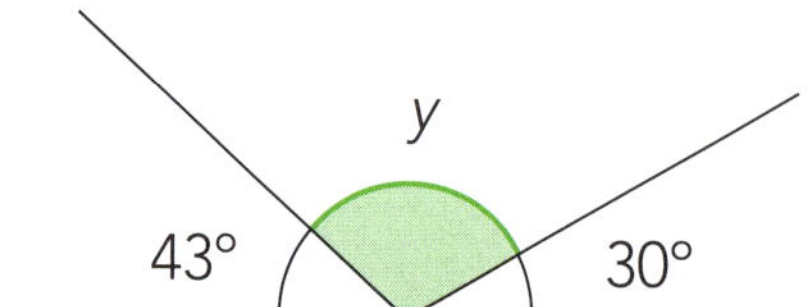

6

50°
z
33°

7

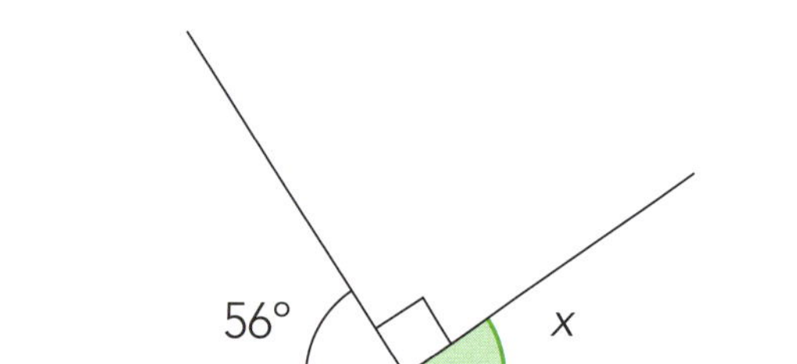

8

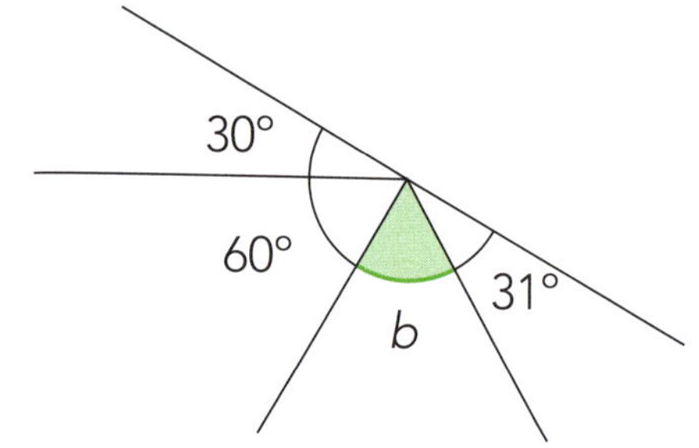

9 Angles AEB and CED are equal. ∠BEC = 80°.

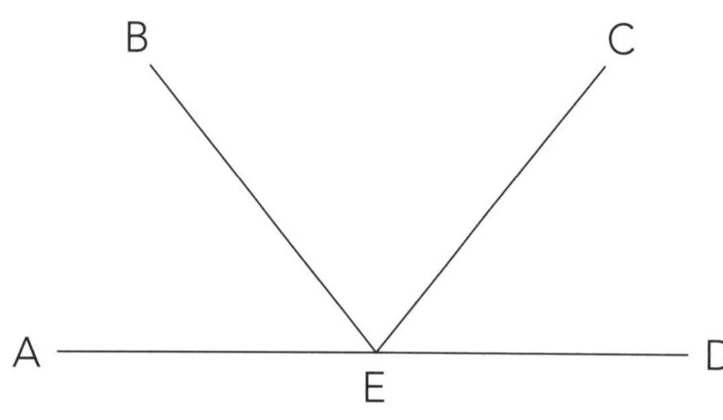

Calculate the size of ∠AEB.

10 ∠QTR is double ∠PTQ. ∠RTS = 93°.

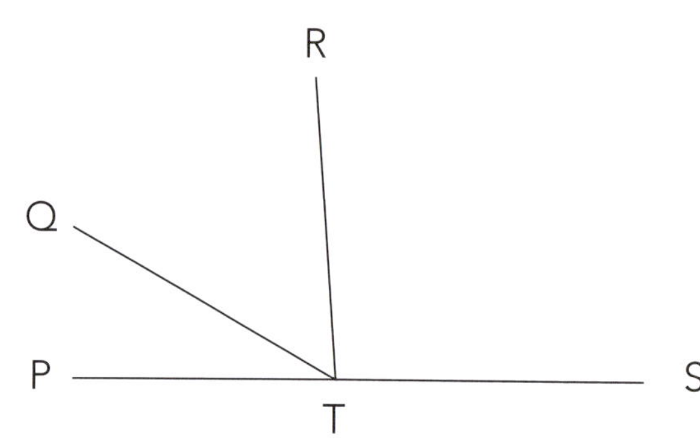

Calculate the size of ∠PTQ.

PHOTOCOPYING OF THIS PAGE IS RESTRICTED UNDER LAW. ISBN: 9780170447539

Angles at a point

- Angles at a point **add to 360°**.
- 360° is also called a **full rotation**.

Examples:

1 Find the value of x.

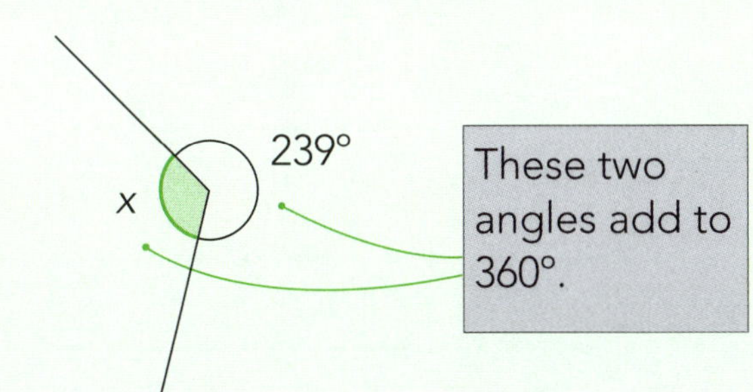

$x + 239° = 360°$
$x = 360° - 239°$
$x = 121°$

2 Find the value of y.

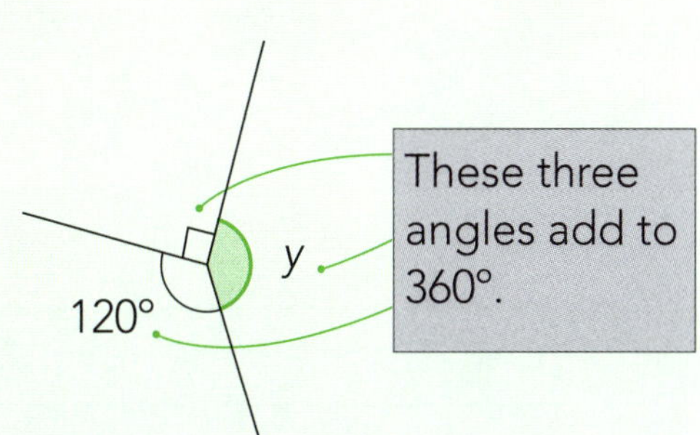

$120° + 90° + y = 360°$
$y = 360° - 120° - 90°$
$y = 150°$

Calculate the size of the missing angles.

1

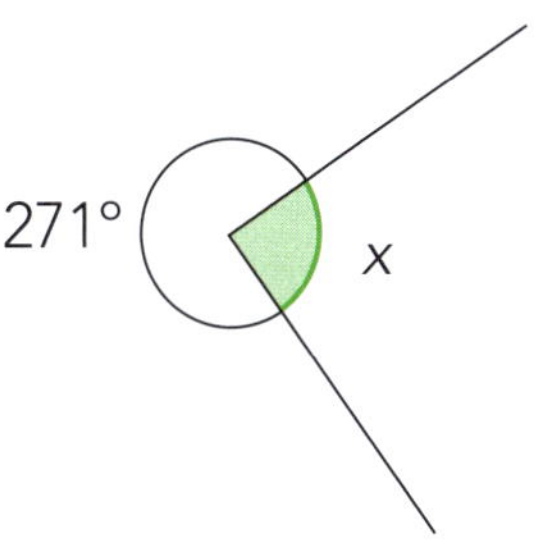

2

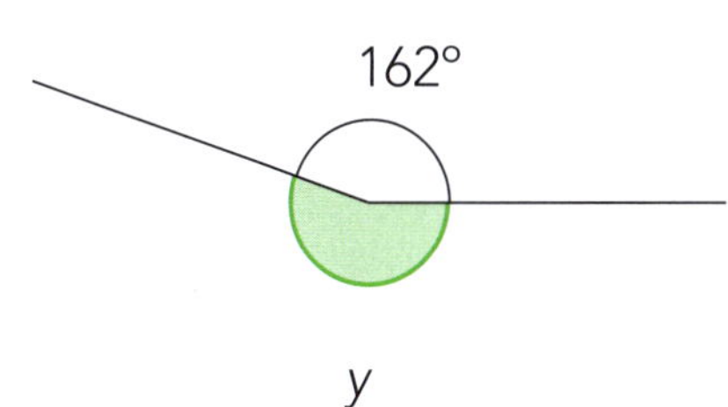

3

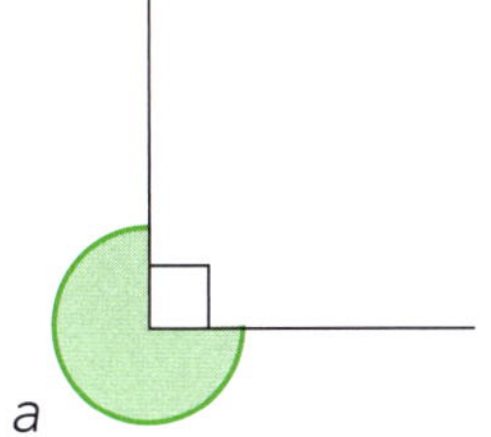

4

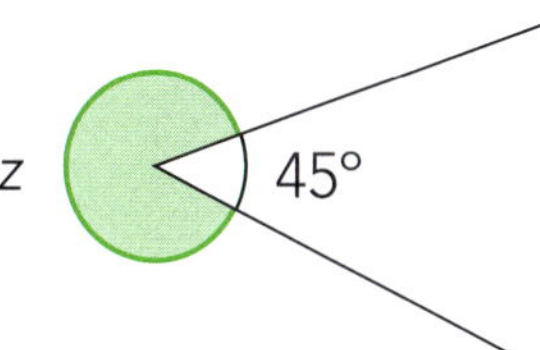

5

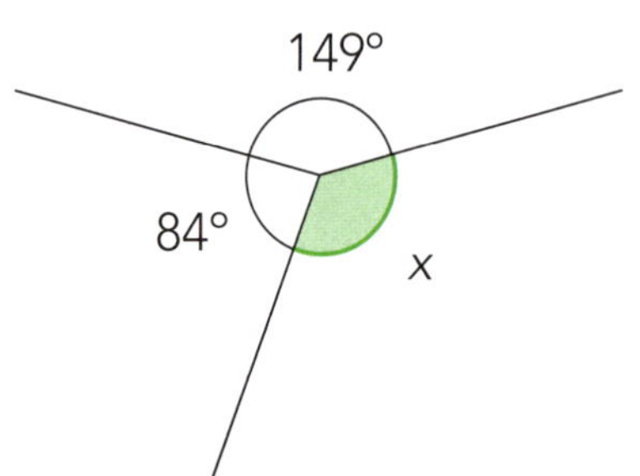

6

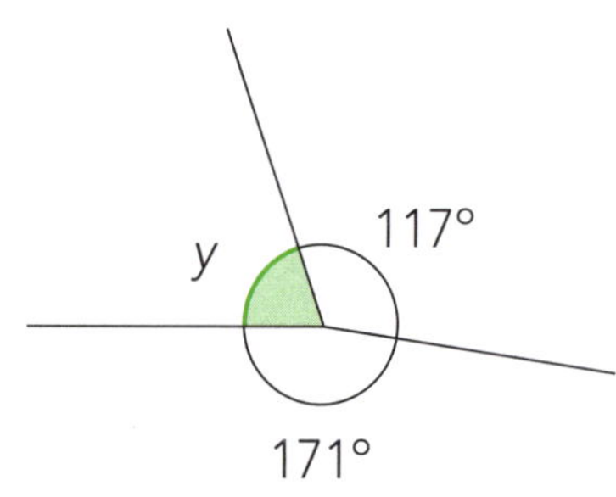

7 ∠PSQ = 37° and ∠QSR = 78°.

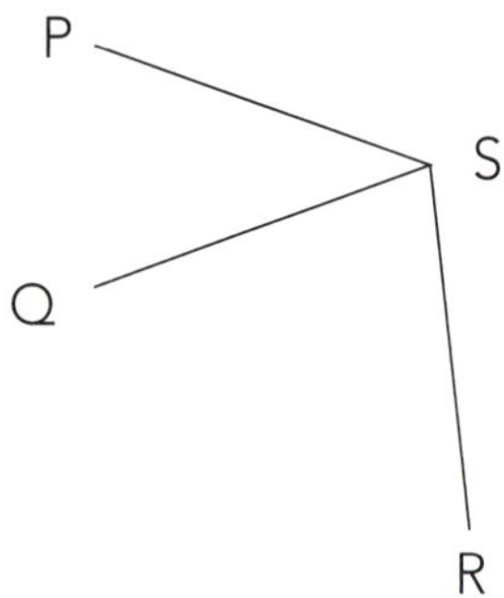

Calculate the size of reflex ∠PSR.

8 ∠WZY is a right angle and ∠YZX = 122°.

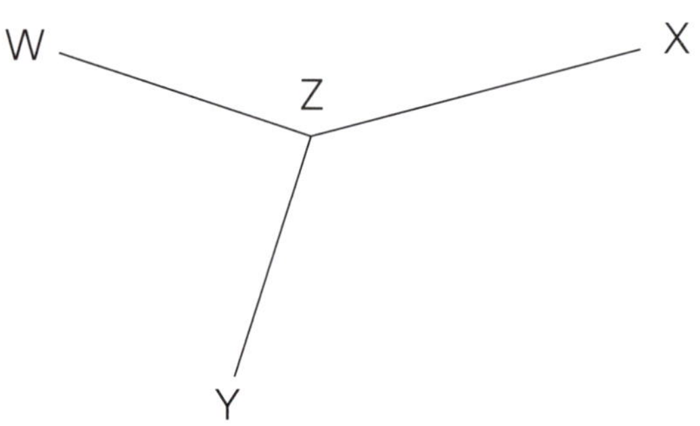

Calculate the size of ∠WZX.

9

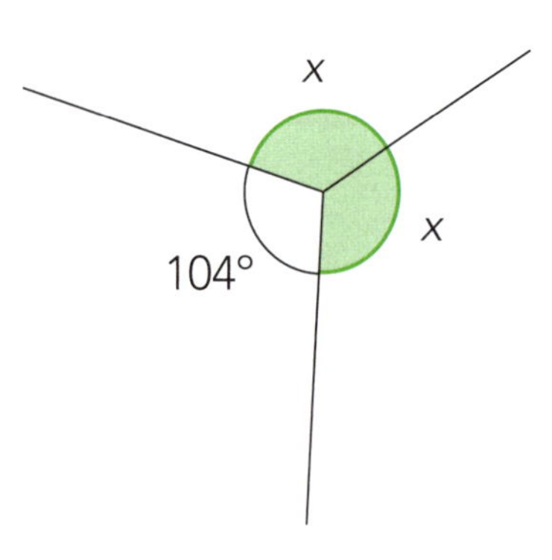

10

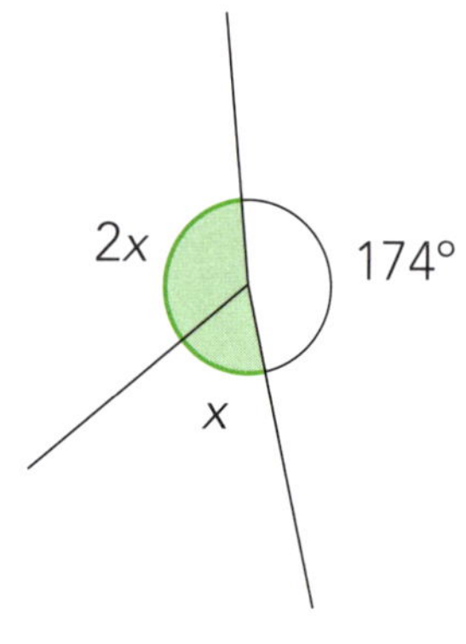

PHOTOCOPYING OF THIS PAGE IS RESTRICTED UNDER LAW. ISBN: 9780170447539

Vertically opposite angles

- Vertically opposite angles are **equal**.
- Notice that these do **not** have to be vertical. They can be at any orientation.

Examples:

1 Find the value of y.

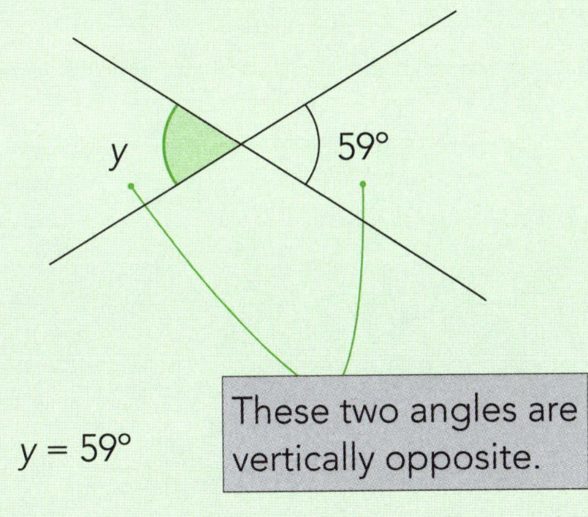

$y = 59°$

These two angles are vertically opposite.

2 Find the value of z.

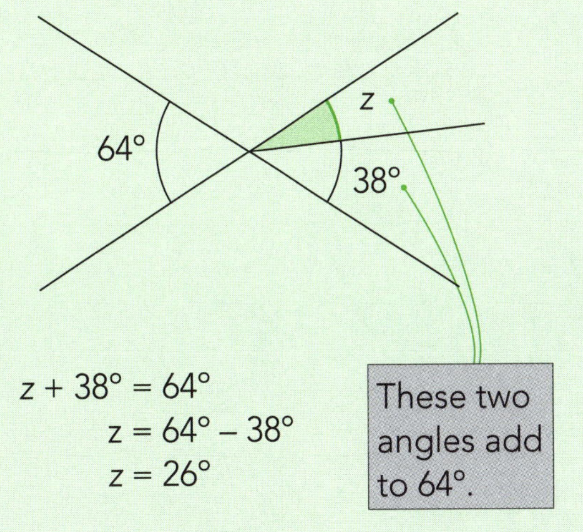

$z + 38° = 64°$
$z = 64° - 38°$
$z = 26°$

These two angles add to 64°.

Calculate the size of the missing angles.

1

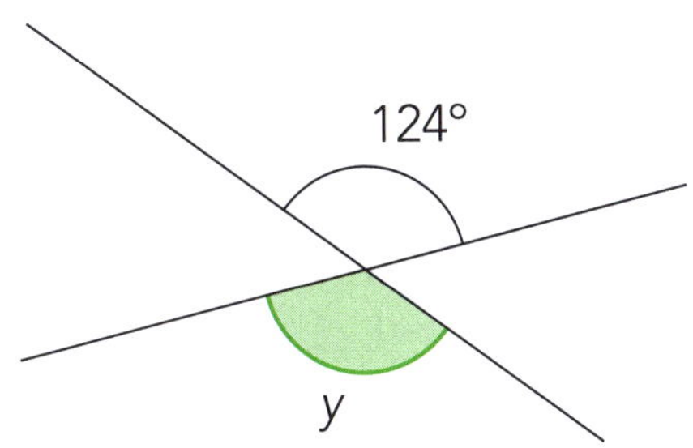

2

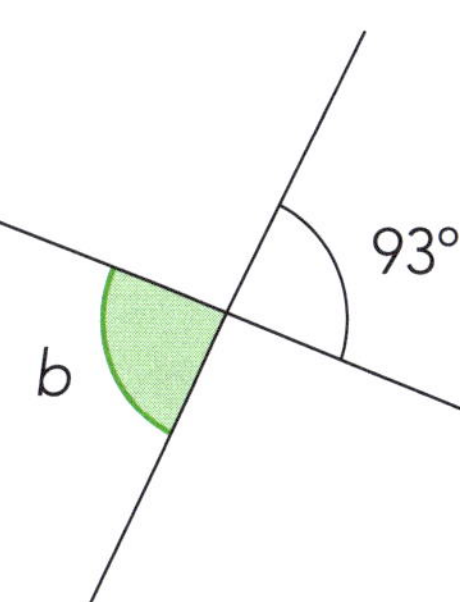

3

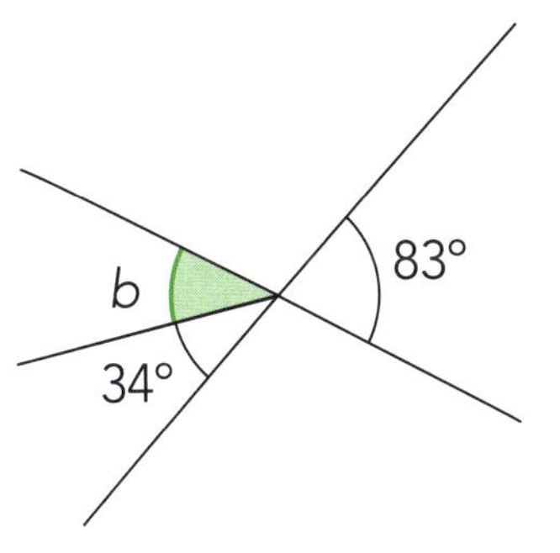

4

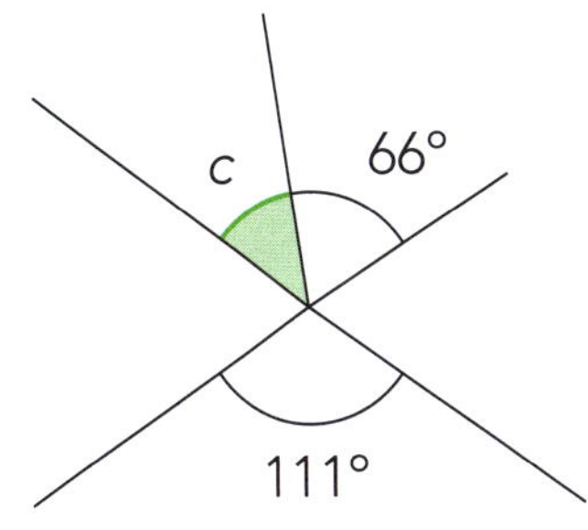

ISBN: 9780170447539 PHOTOCOPYING OF THIS PAGE IS RESTRICTED UNDER LAW.

5

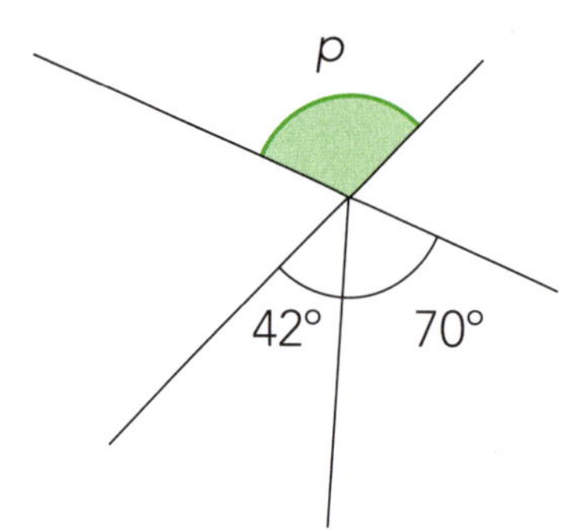

6

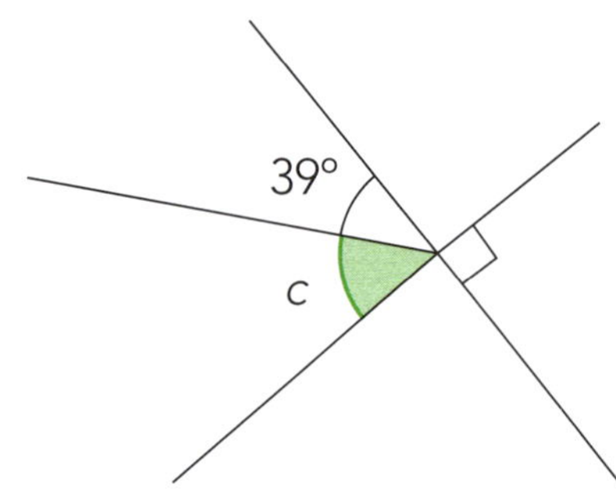

7

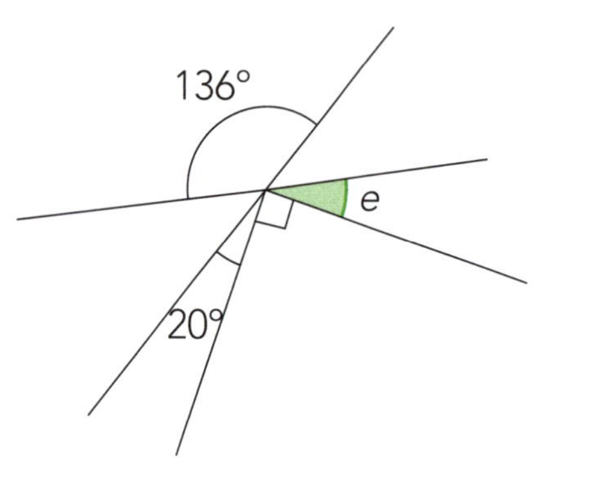

8

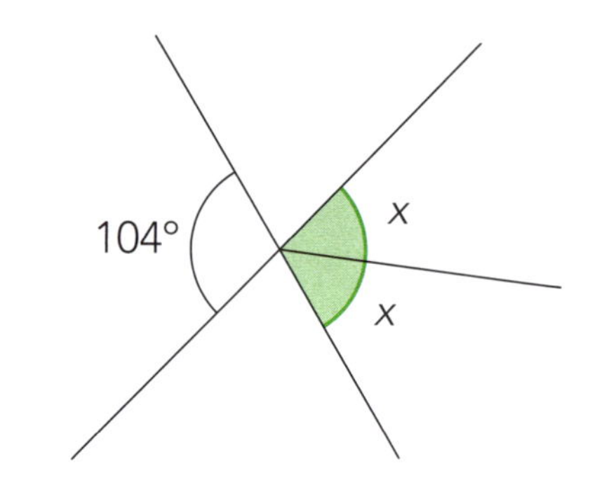

9 ∠INH = 67° and ∠MNL = 75°.

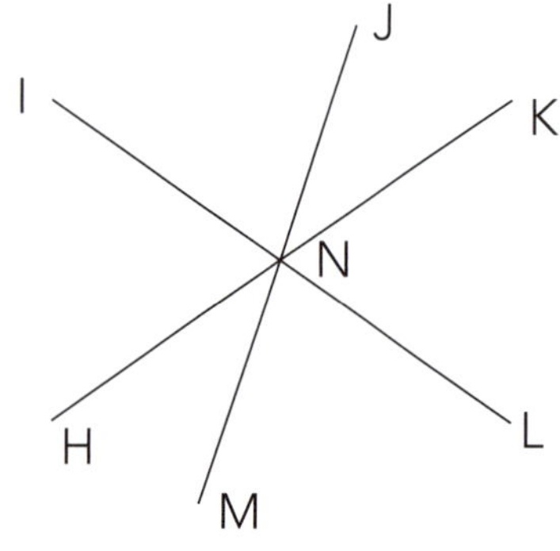

Calculate the size of ∠JNK.

10 Angles PVQ and RVS are equal.
∠UVT = 52°.

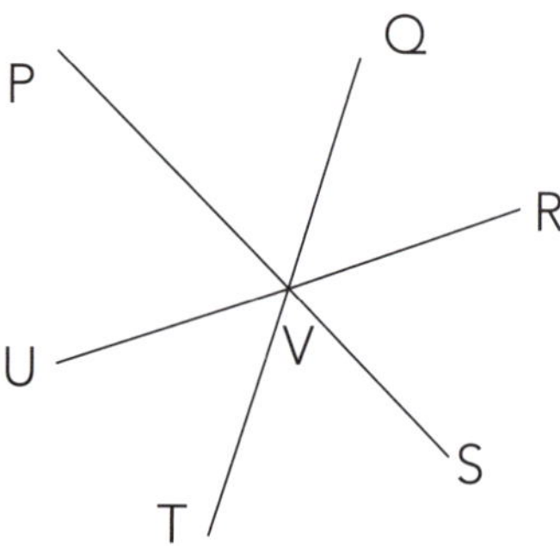

Calculate the size of ∠RVS.

PHOTOCOPYING OF THIS PAGE IS RESTRICTED UNDER LAW. ISBN: 9780170447539

Angles in a triangle

- The angles in a triangle **add to 180°**.

Examples:

1 Find the value of x.

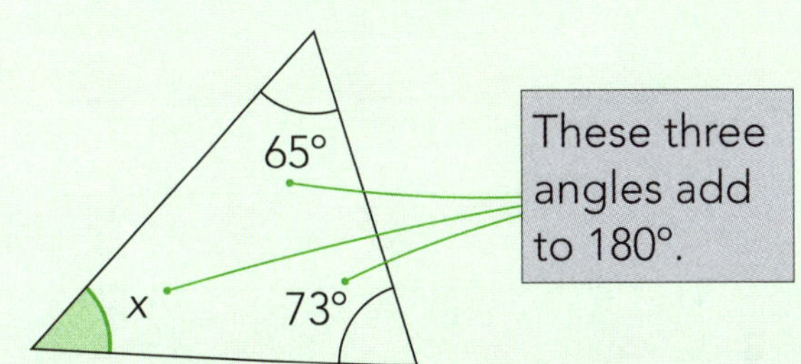

$x + 65° + 73° = 180°$
$x = 180° - 65° - 73°$
$x = 42°$

2 Find the value of z.

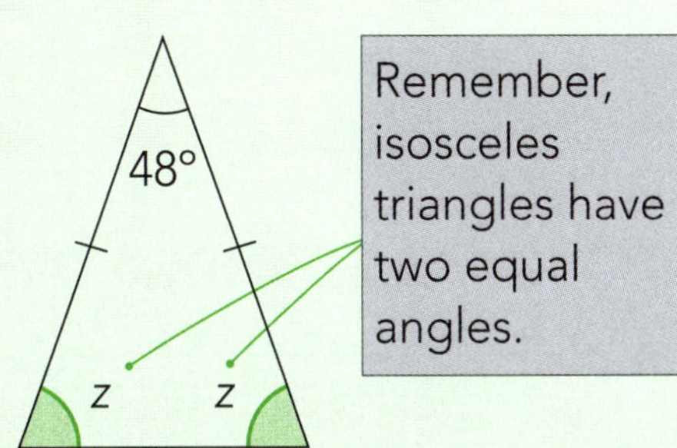

$z + z + 48° = 180°$
$2z = 180° - 48°$
$2z = 32°$
$z = 66°$

Calculate the size of the missing angles.

1

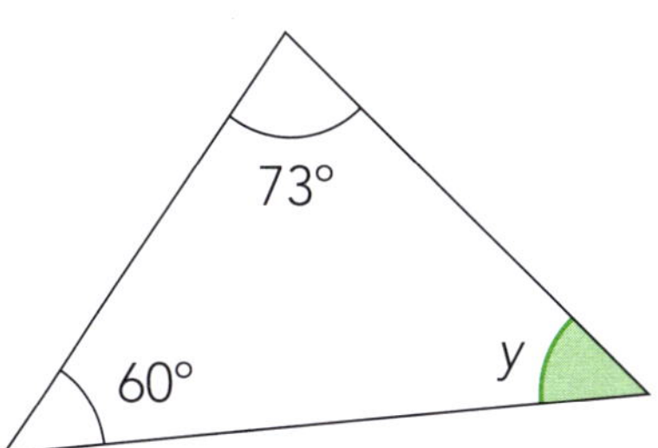

2

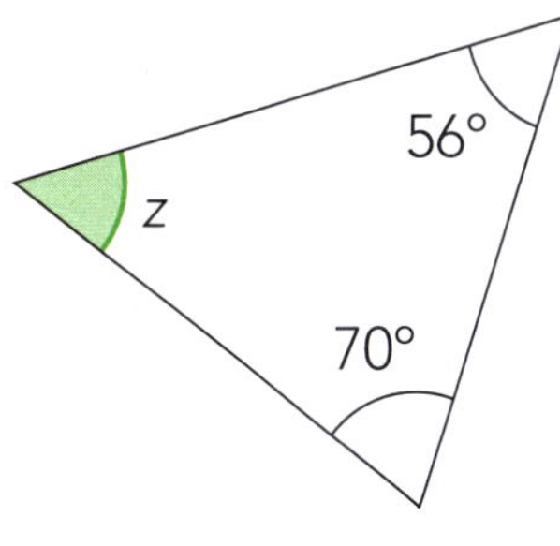

3

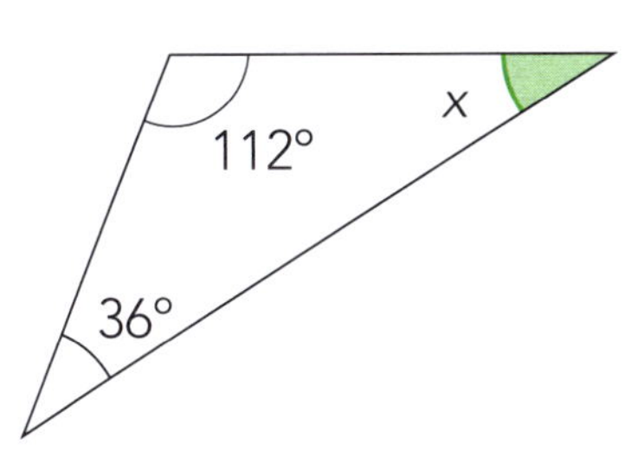

4

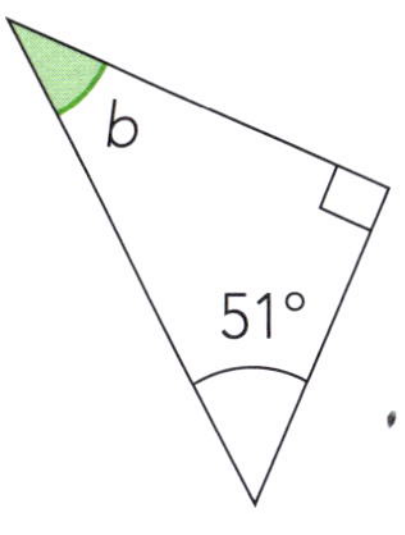

ISBN: 9780170447539
PHOTOCOPYING OF THIS PAGE IS RESTRICTED UNDER LAW.

5

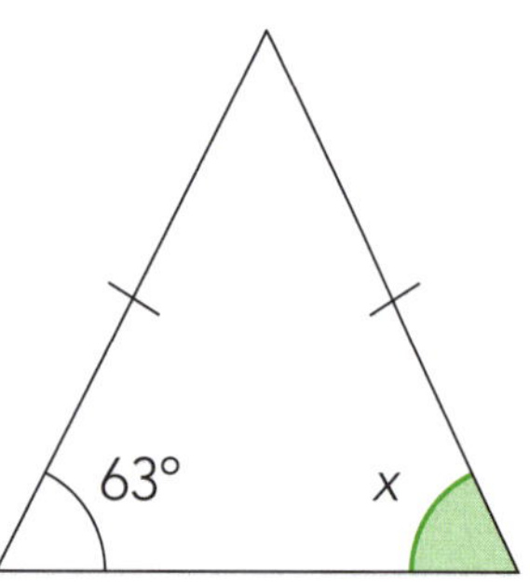

6

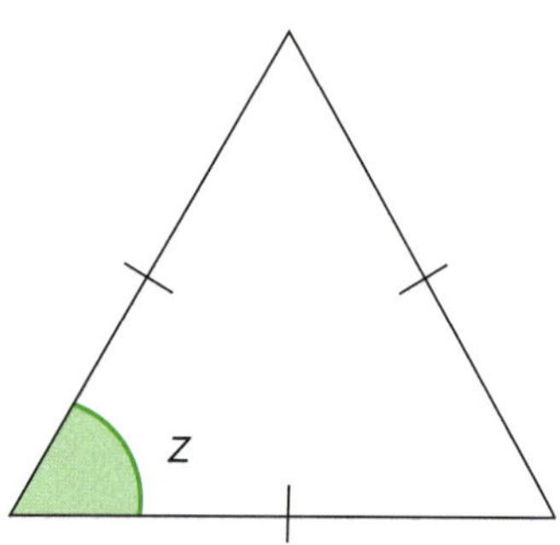

7

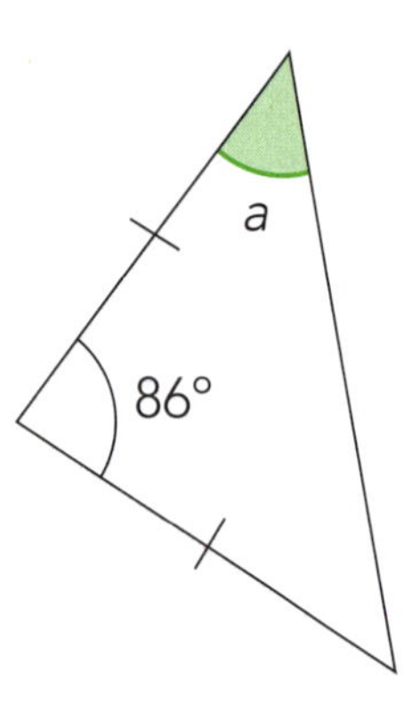

8

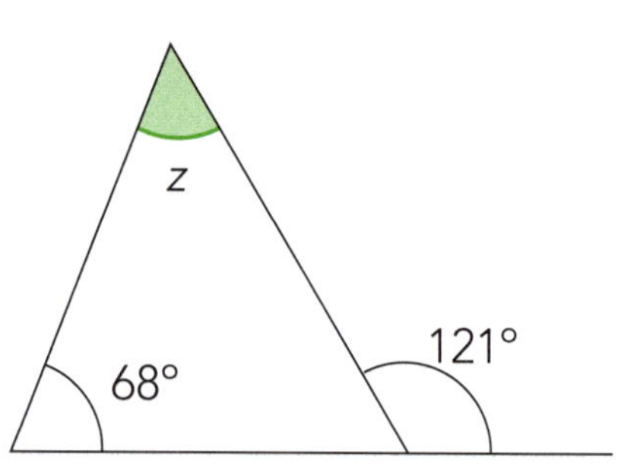

9 ∠DEF = 45° and ∠GFE = 67°.

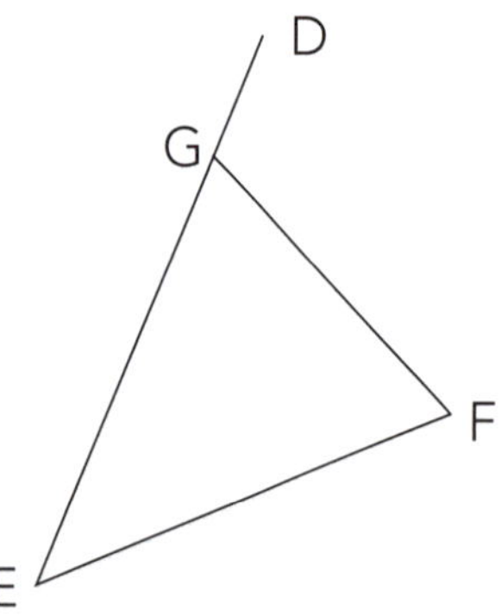

Calculate the size of ∠DGF.

10 ∠ZXY is double ∠XZY, and ∠XYZ = 51°.

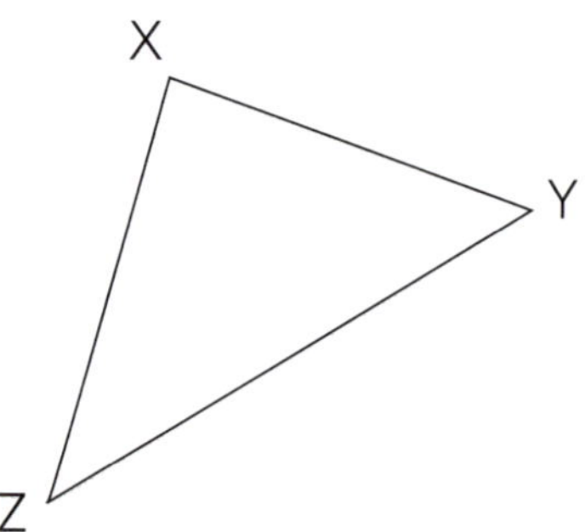

Calculate the size of ∠XZY.

PHOTOCOPYING OF THIS PAGE IS RESTRICTED UNDER LAW. ISBN: 9780170447539

Angles in a quadrilateral

- A quadrilateral is any closed shape (no gaps) with exactly **four straight sides**.
- The four angles in a quadrilateral **add to 360°**.

Examples:

1 Find the value of a.

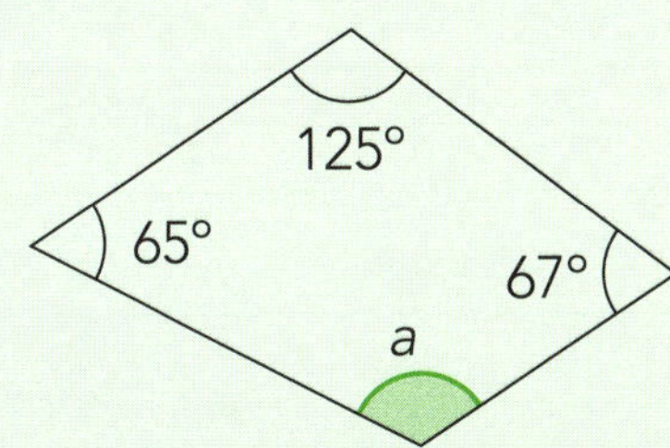

$a + 65° + 125° + 67° = 360°$
$a = 360° - 65° - 125° - 67°$
$a = 103°$

2 Find the value of x.

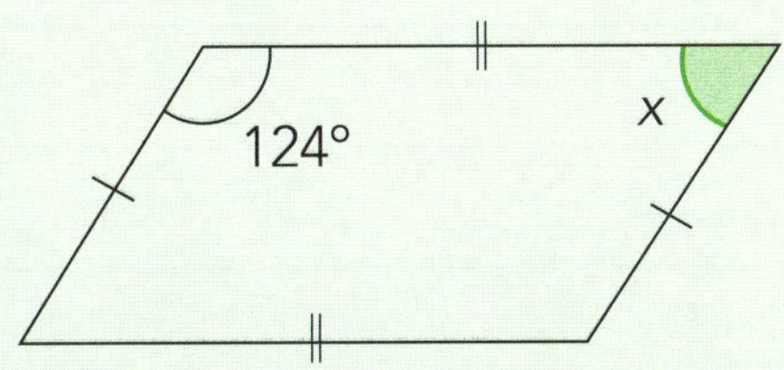

$2x + 2(124°) = 360°$
$2x = 360° - 2(124°)$
$2x = 112°$
$x = 56°$

Calculate the size of the missing angles.

1

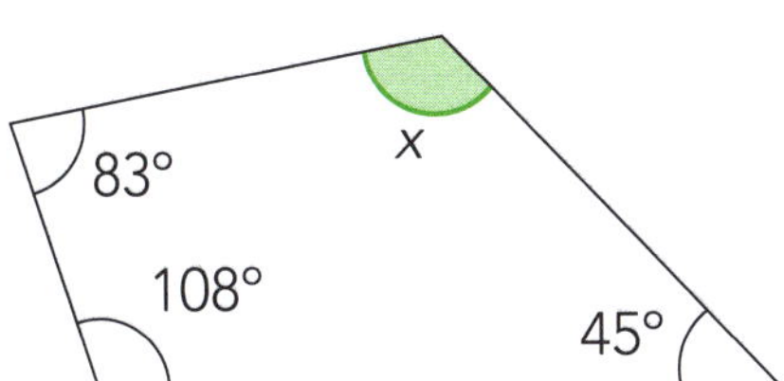

2

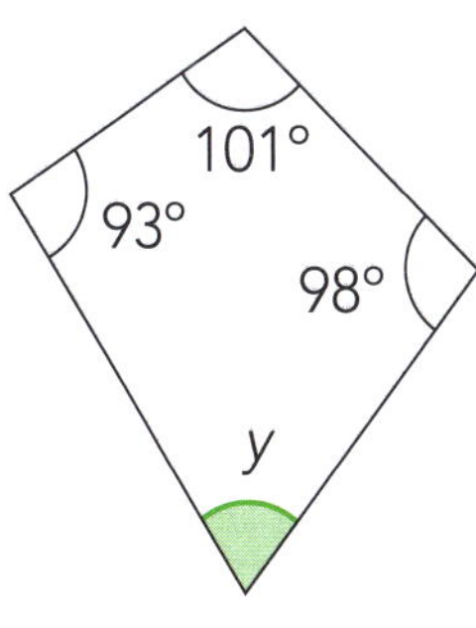

3

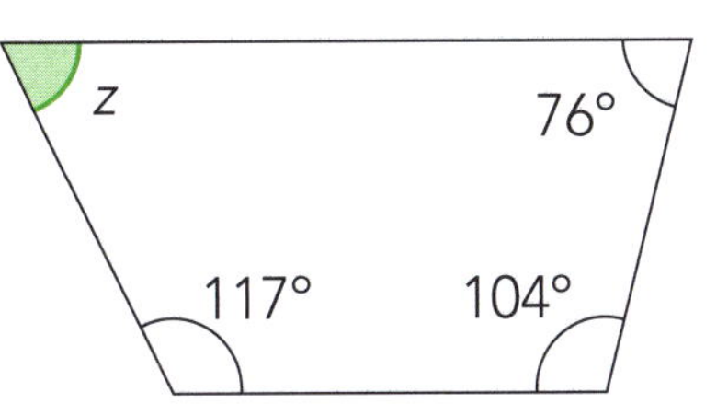

4

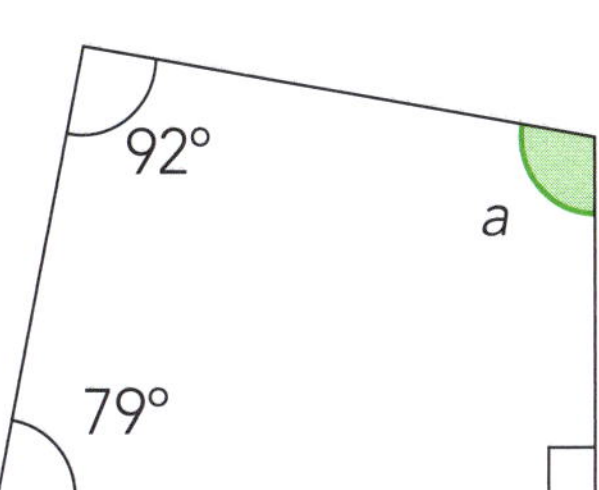

ISBN: 9780170447539 PHOTOCOPYING OF THIS PAGE IS RESTRICTED UNDER LAW.

5

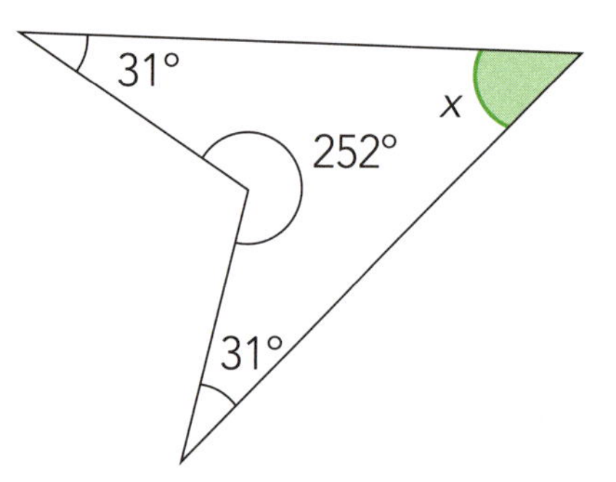

6

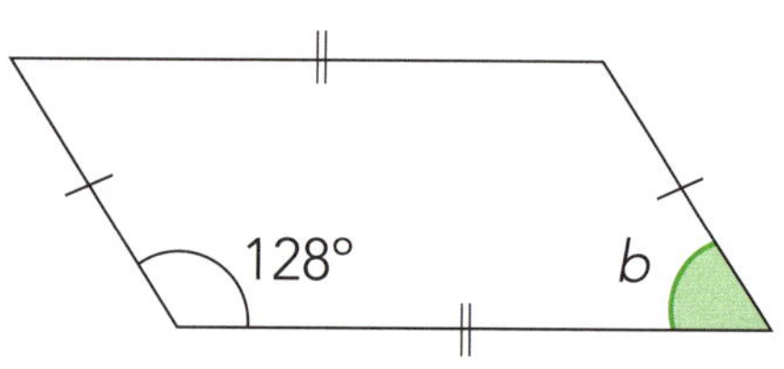

7

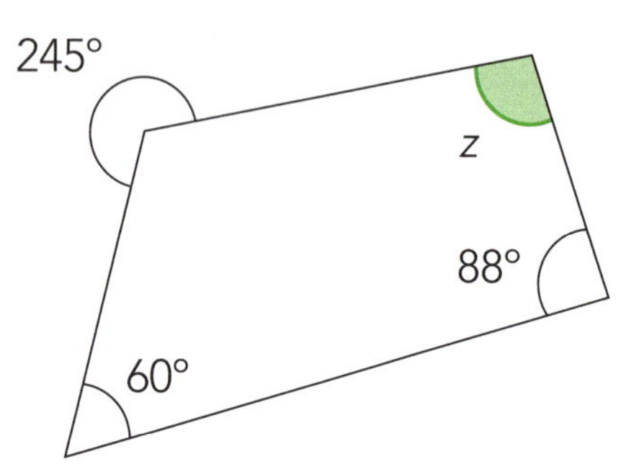

8

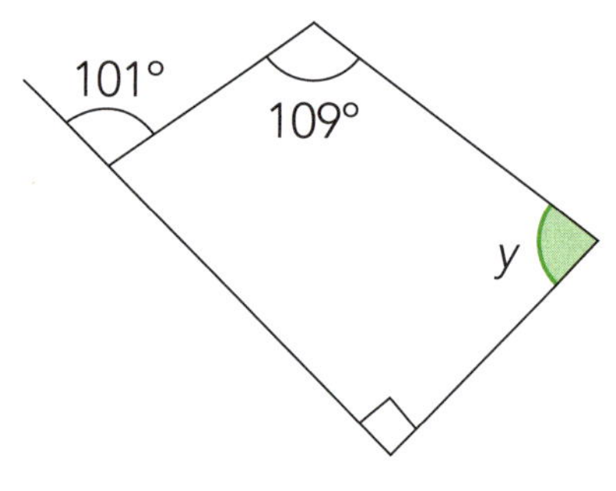

9 ∠IFG = ∠HIF: ∠GHI = 68° and ∠FGH = 102°

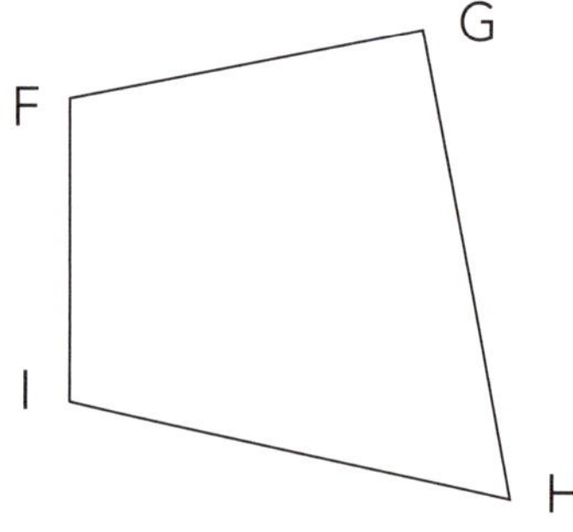

Calculate the size of ∠FIH.

10 ∠QPS is half the size of ∠QRS. ∠PQR = 72° and ∠RSP = 93°.

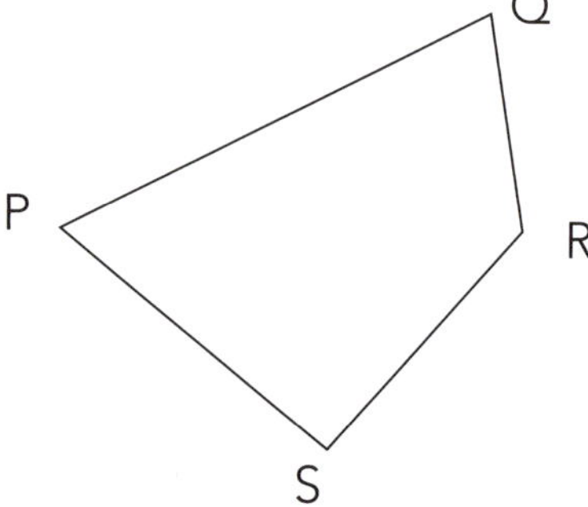

Calculate the size of ∠QPS.

PHOTOCOPYING OF THIS PAGE IS RESTRICTED UNDER LAW. ISBN: 9780170447539

Mixing it up

Calculate the size of the missing angles.

1

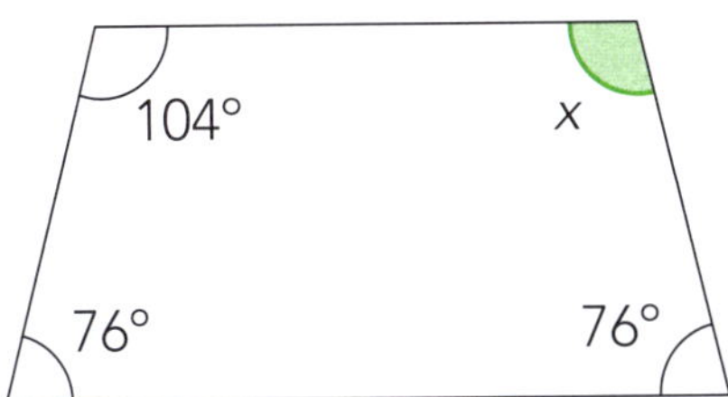

2

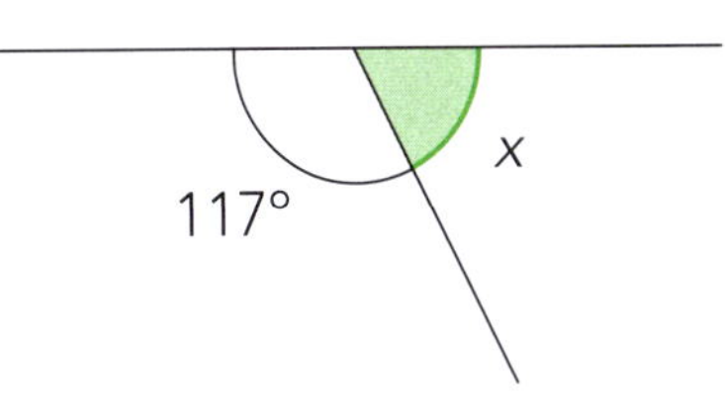

3

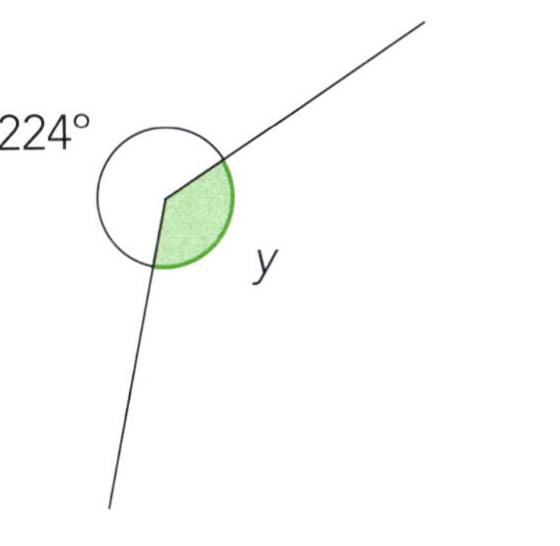

4

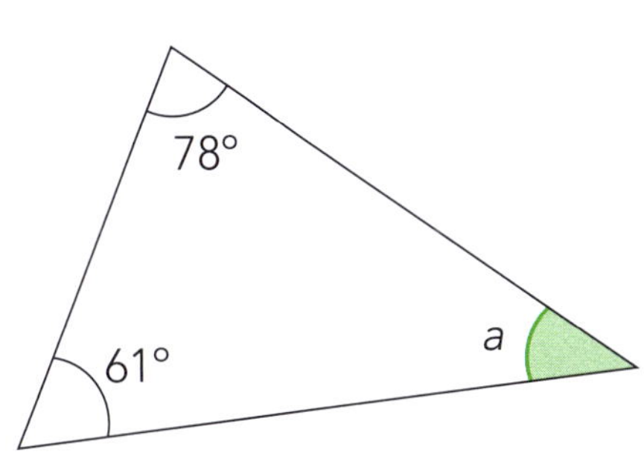

5

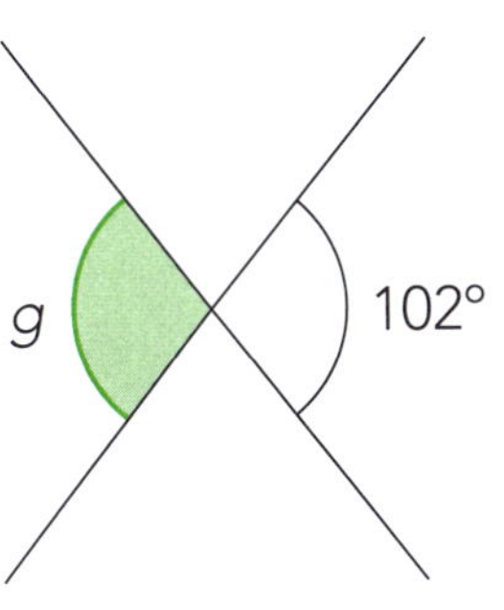

6

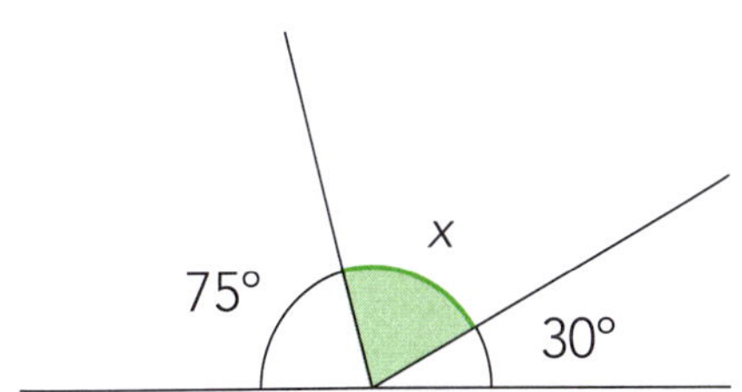

ISBN: 9780170447539 PHOTOCOPYING OF THIS PAGE IS RESTRICTED UNDER LAW.

7

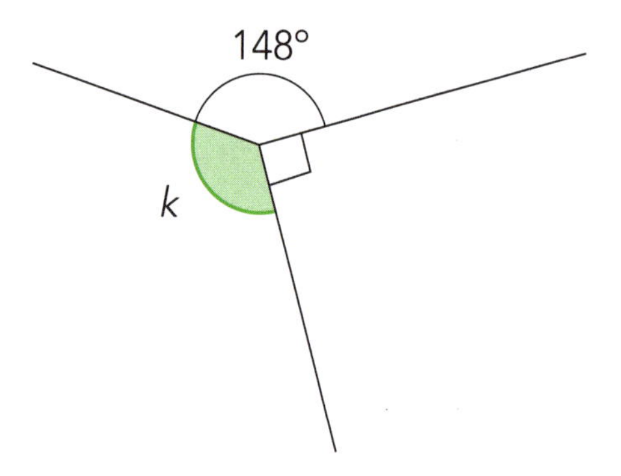

8

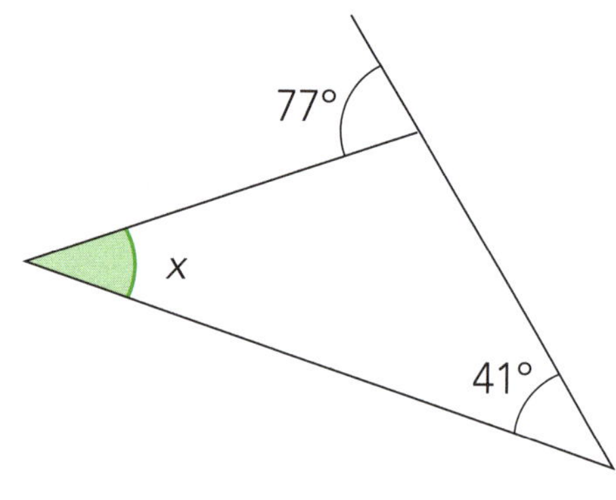

9

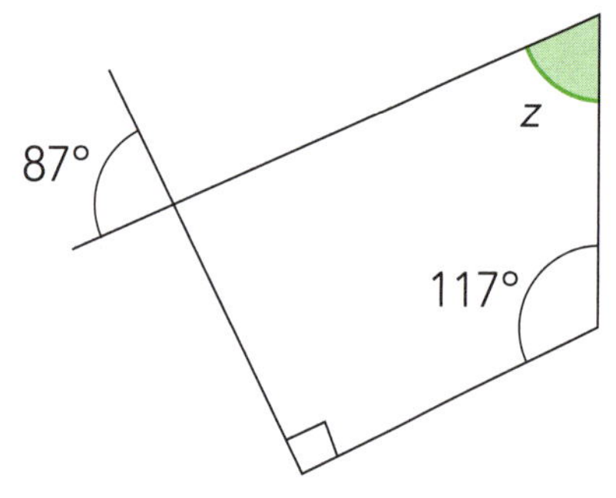

10

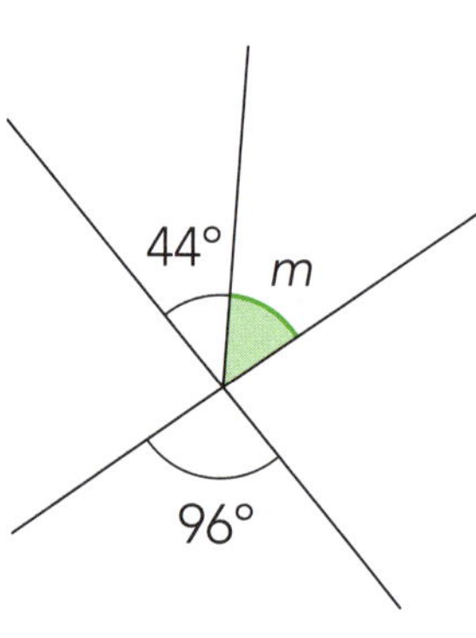

11

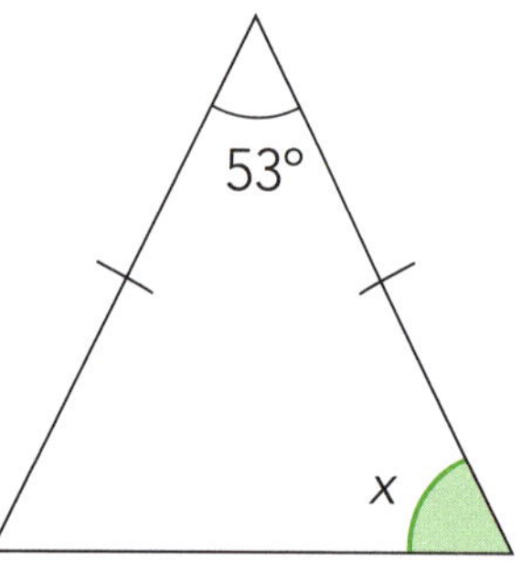

12

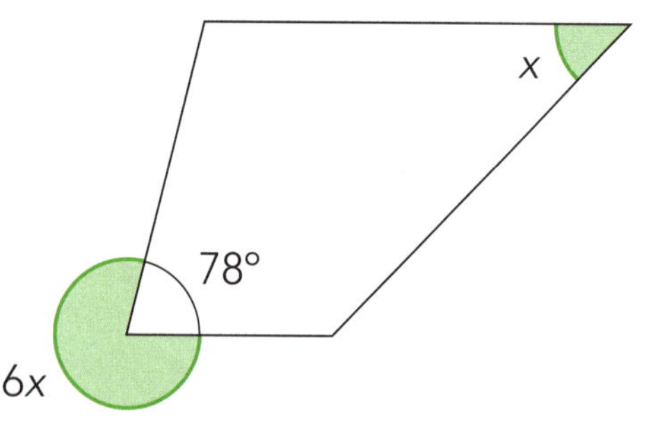

PHOTOCOPYING OF THIS PAGE IS RESTRICTED UNDER LAW. ISBN: 9780170447539

2D and 3D shapes

2D and 3D language

Dimensions

1D (one-dimensional) shapes e.g. lines • have **1** measurement: length.	**2D (two-dimensional) shapes** e.g. sheets of paper • have **2** measurements: height and width.	**3D (three-dimensional) shapes** e.g. boxes • have **3** measurements: height, width and depth.
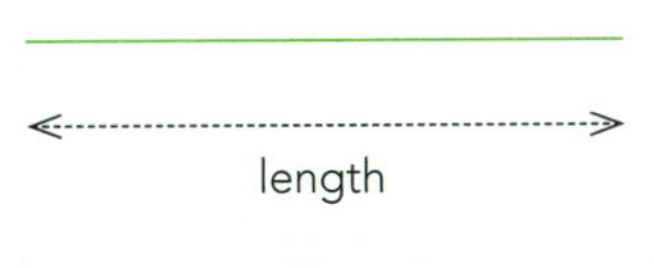	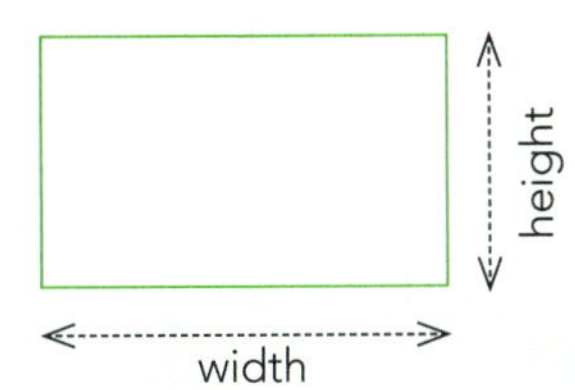	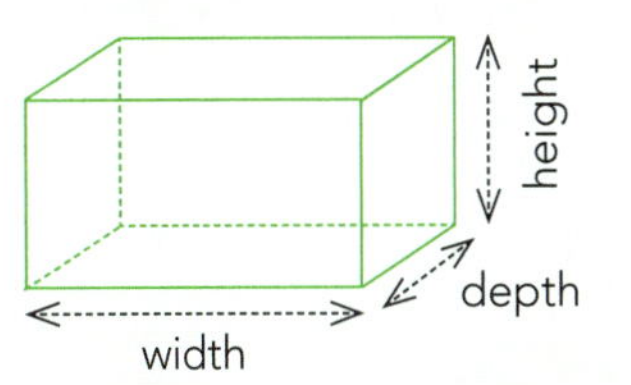

Vertices, faces, sides and edges

- We talk about **one vertex** or **several vertices**.

2D shapes have vertices, one face and sides.

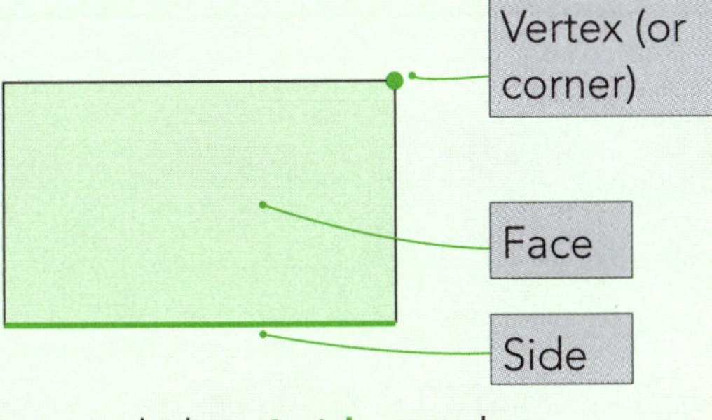

A rectangle has **4 sides** and **4 vertices**.

3D shapes have vertices, faces and edges.

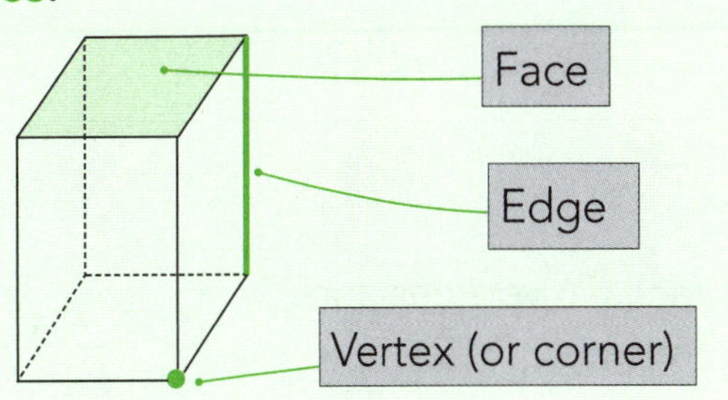

A cube has **6 faces**, **8 vertices** and **12 edges**.

Write down the numbers of vertices, edges and faces these 3D shapes have.

1

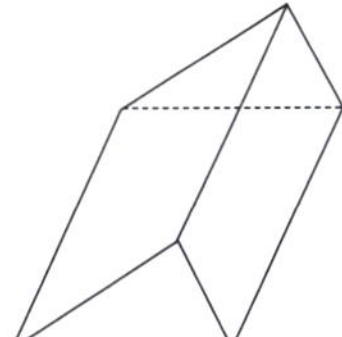

Vertices ________

Edges ________

Faces ________

2

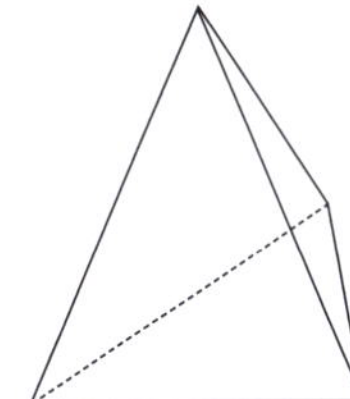

Vertices ________

Edges ________

Faces ________

3

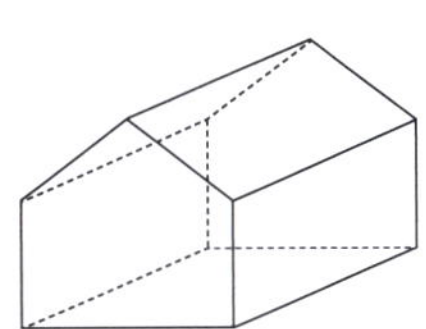

Vertices ________

Edges ________

Faces ________

4

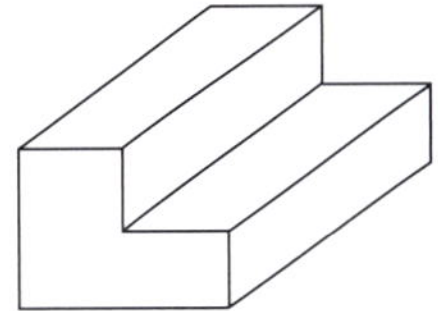

Vertices ________

Edges ________

Faces ________

ISBN: 9780170447539 PHOTOCOPYING OF THIS PAGE IS RESTRICTED UNDER LAW.

5 Connect the dots to match each shape to the correct combination of faces, vertices and edges.

6 faces, 8 vertices and 12 edges	•	•	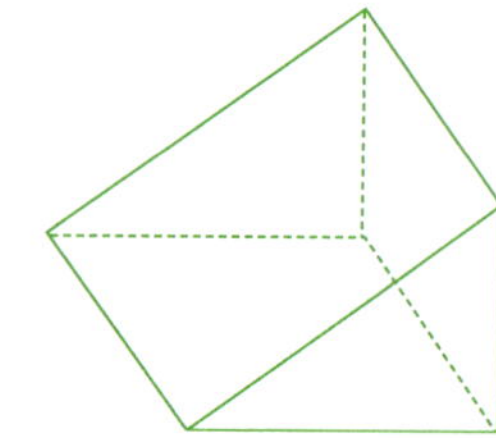
7 faces, 7 vertices and 12 edges	•	•	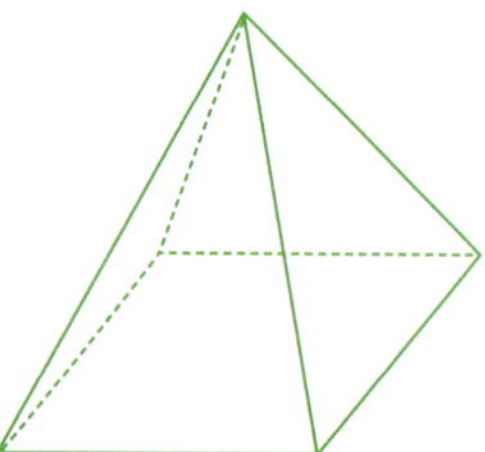
8 faces, 12 vertices and 18 edges	•	•	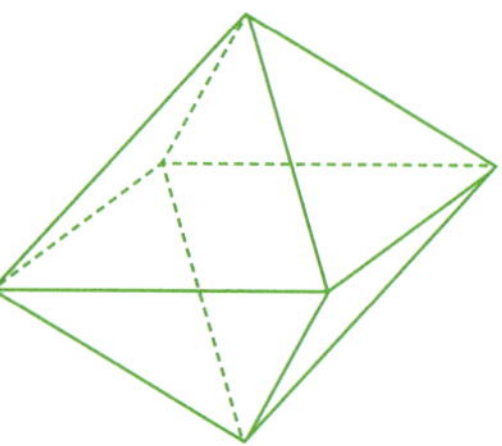
8 faces, 6 vertices and 12 edges	•	•	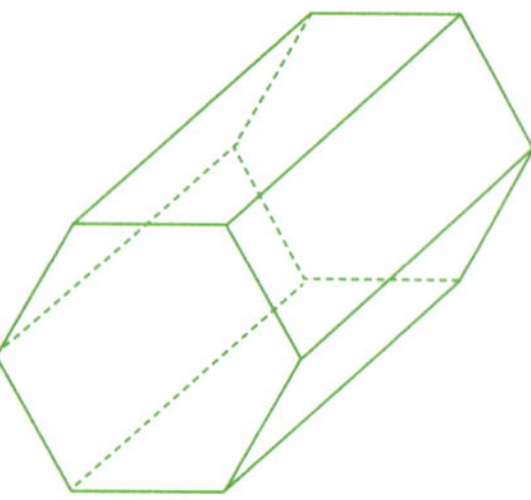
5 faces, 6 vertices and 9 edges	•	•	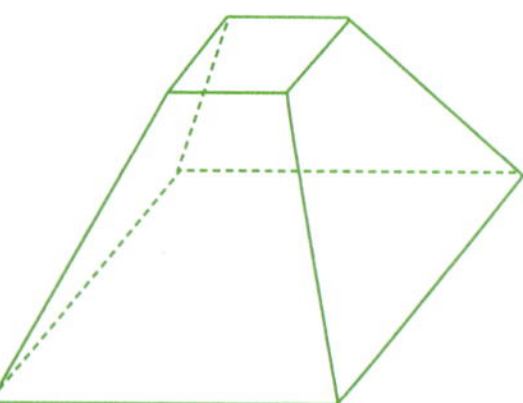
5 faces, 5 vertices and 8 edges	•	•	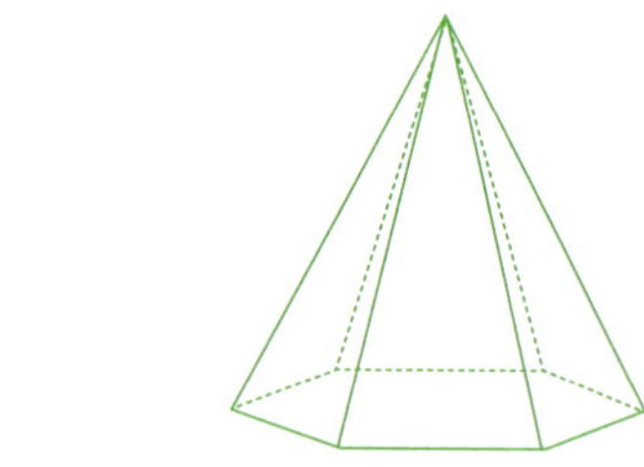

PHOTOCOPYING OF THIS PAGE IS RESTRICTED UNDER LAW. ISBN: 9780170447539

Prisms

- A prism is any three-dimensional shape with **two identical ends** and **flat sides**.
- The identical ends must be parallel.

Examples:

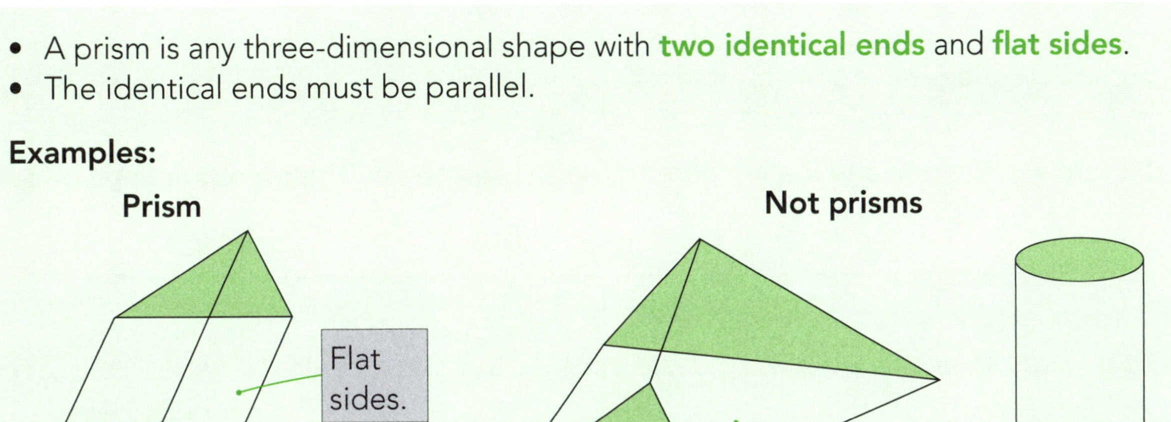

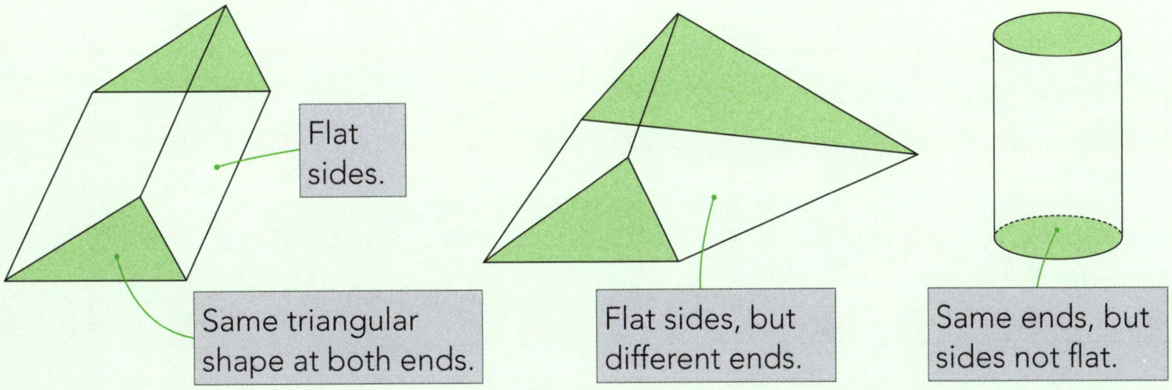

Note: Although a cylinder is not a prism, it follows all mathematical rules that apply to prisms.

Indicate whether these shapes are prisms (✓) or not (×). If they are not, give the reason.

1 ☐ ______________________

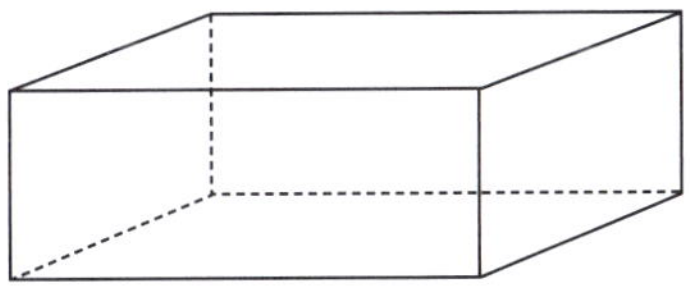

2 ☐ ______________________

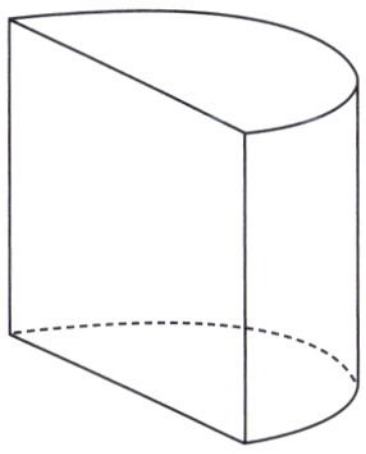

3 ☐ ______________________

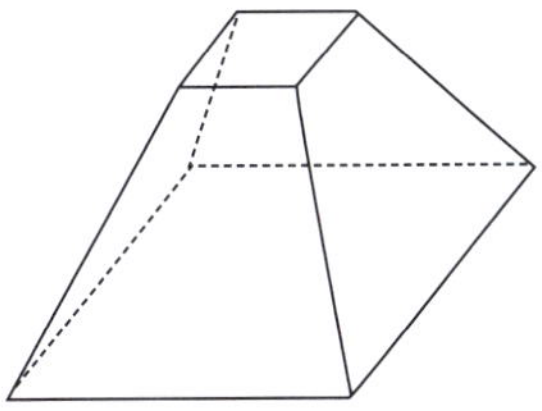

4 ☐ ______________________

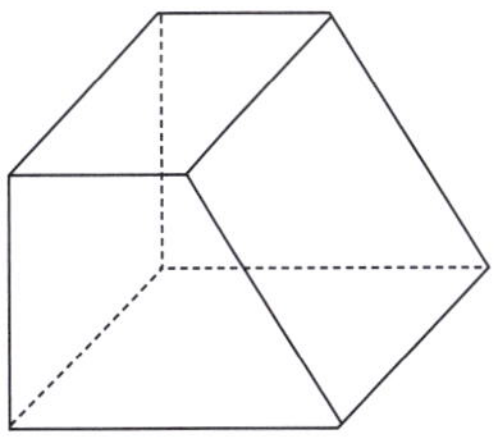

5 ☐ ______________________

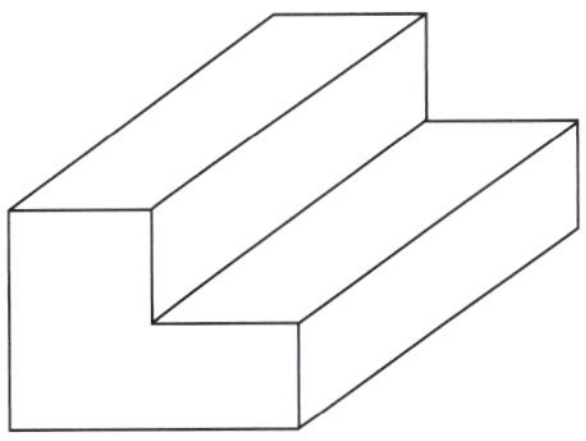

6 ☐ ______________________

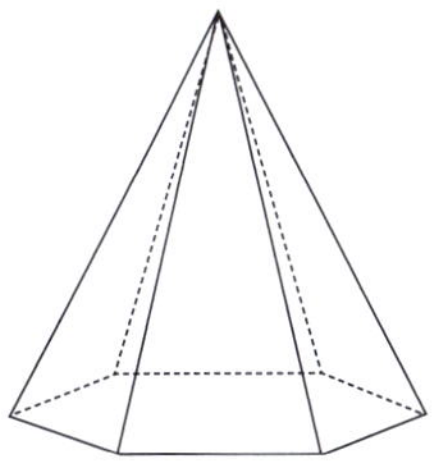

ISBN: 9780170447539
PHOTOCOPYING OF THIS PAGE IS RESTRICTED UNDER LAW.

Naming 3D shapes

- Some 3D shapes have specific names.

Use the terms in the box and match them to the shapes below. The terms are used once only.

Cylinder	Cube	Hexagonal prism	Hemisphere
Triangular prism	Sphere	Cuboid	Triangular-based pyramid
Square-based pyramid	Cone	Pentagonal prism	Octahedron

1 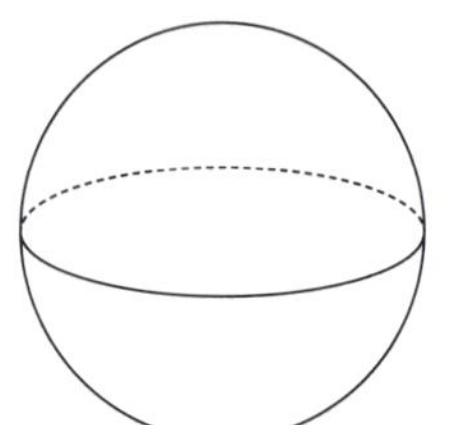

____

2 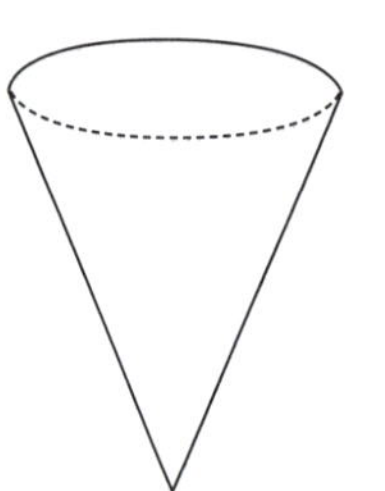

____

3 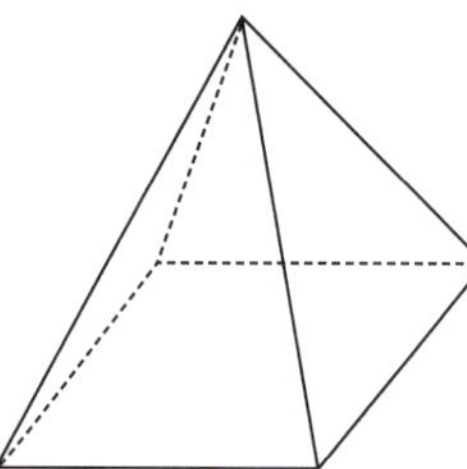

____

4 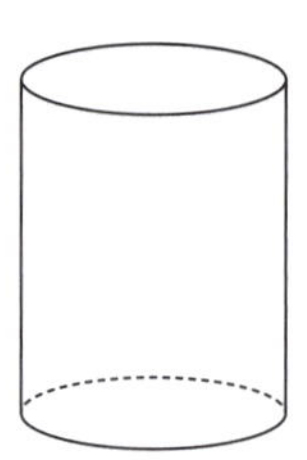

____

5 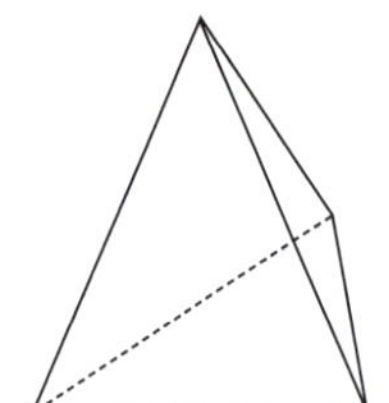

____

6 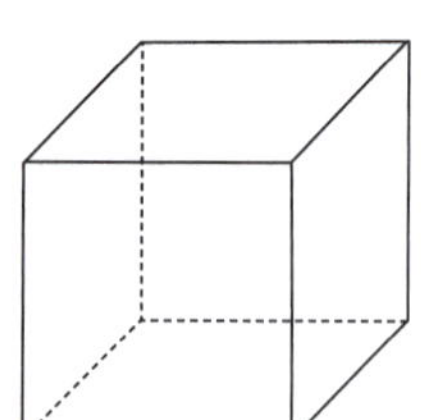

____

7 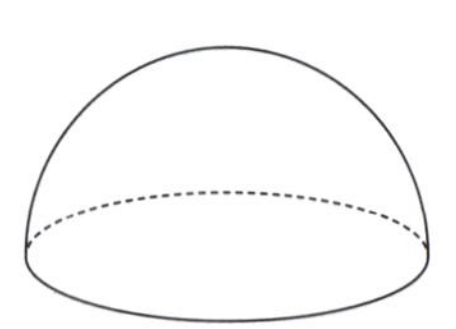

____

8 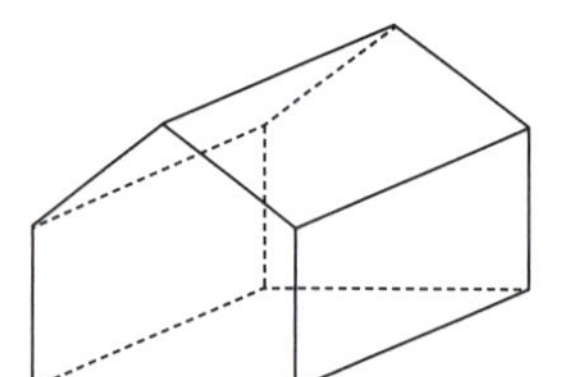

____

9 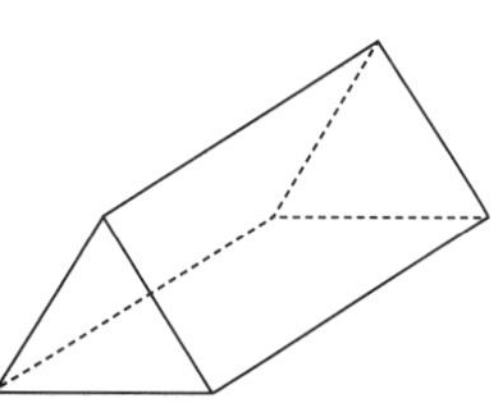

____

10 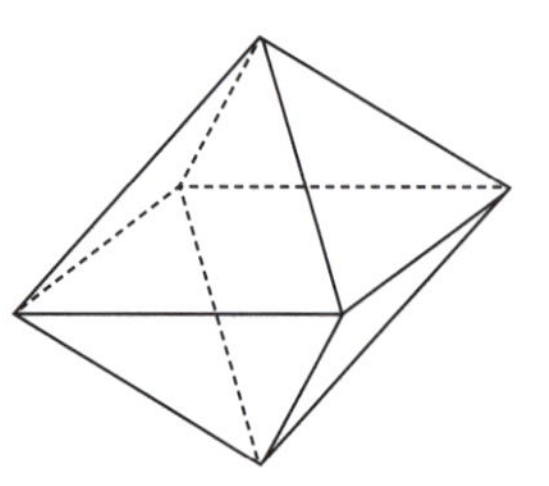

____

11 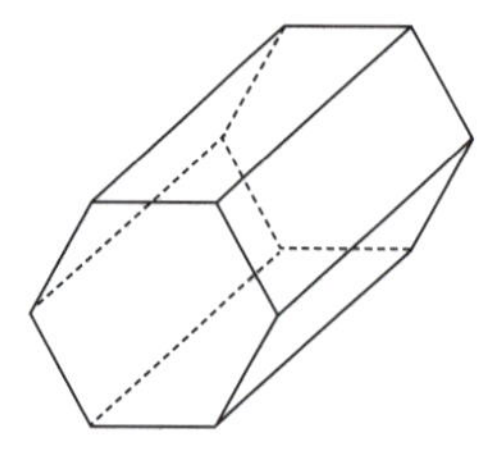

____

12 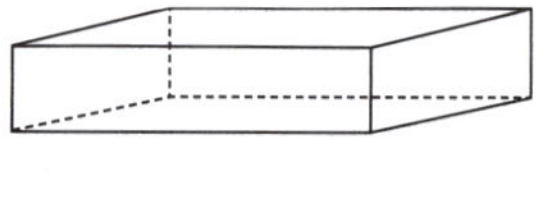

____

PHOTOCOPYING OF THIS PAGE IS RESTRICTED UNDER LAW.
ISBN: 9780170447539

Nets

- Nets are the two-dimensional version of three-dimensional shapes.
- When nets are cut out and folded correctly, they form a solid.

Example:
A closed cube is made up of **6** squares, which could be unfolded to look like the net on the far right.

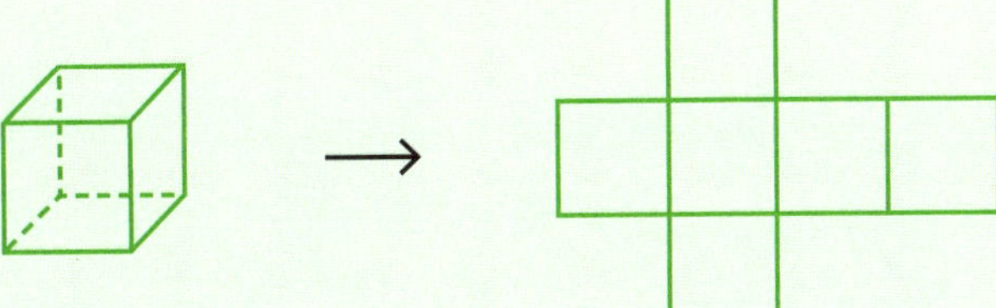

1 Highlight or shade the nets that could form a closed cube. You should find 11.

2 Match each net to the solid it would make. The nets are not drawn to scale.

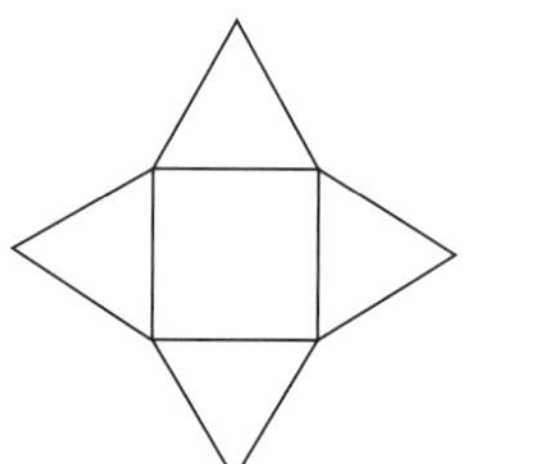
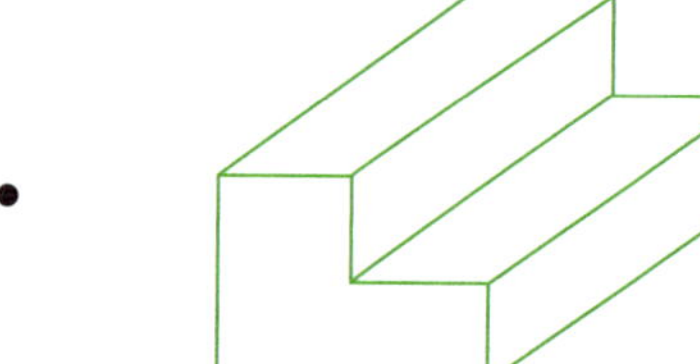
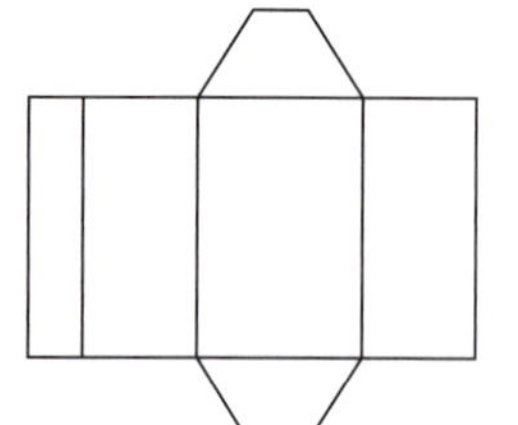

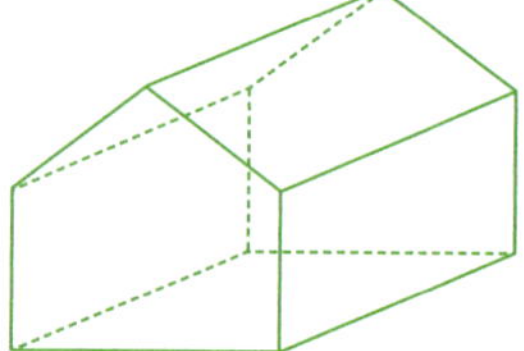
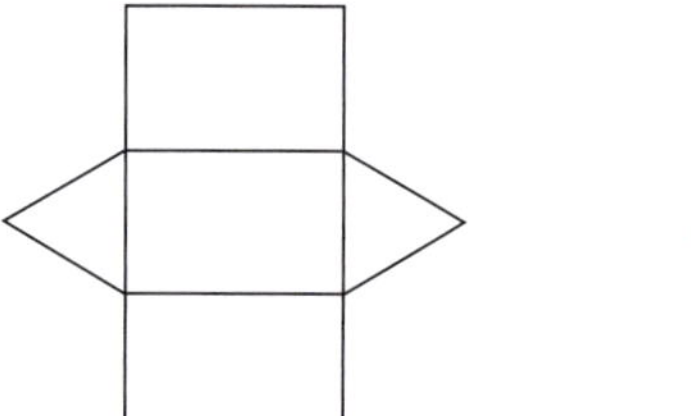

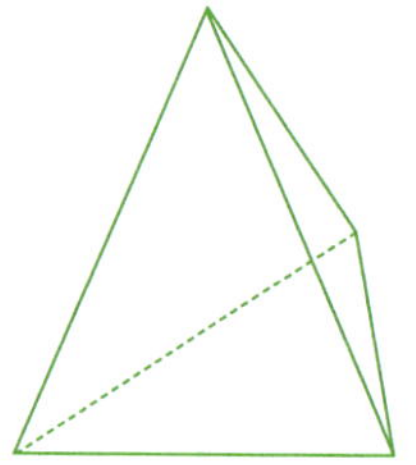
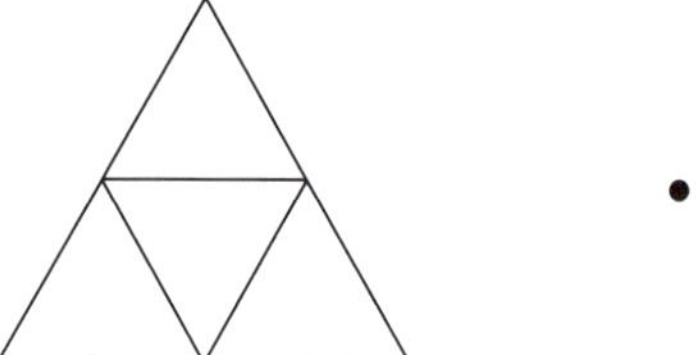

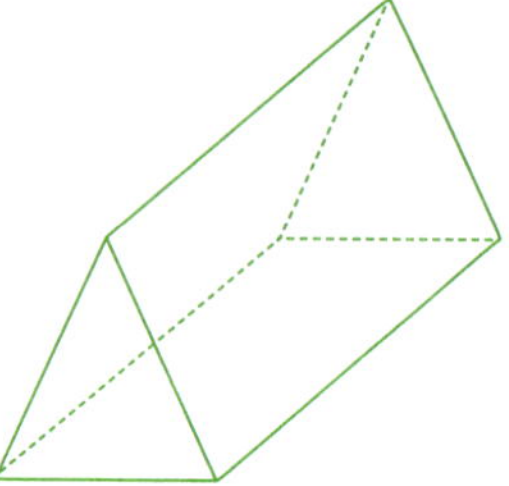
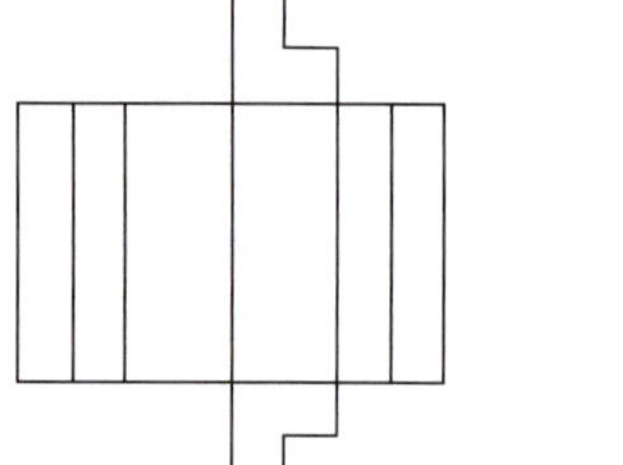

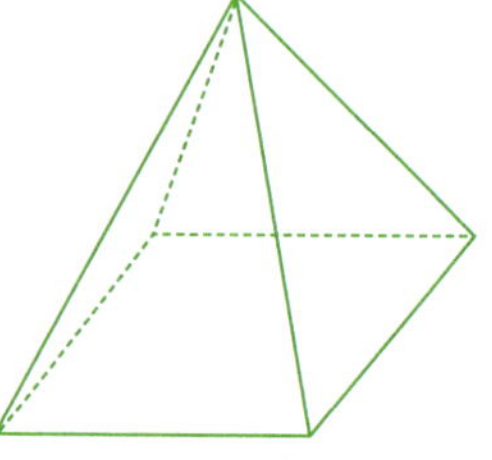
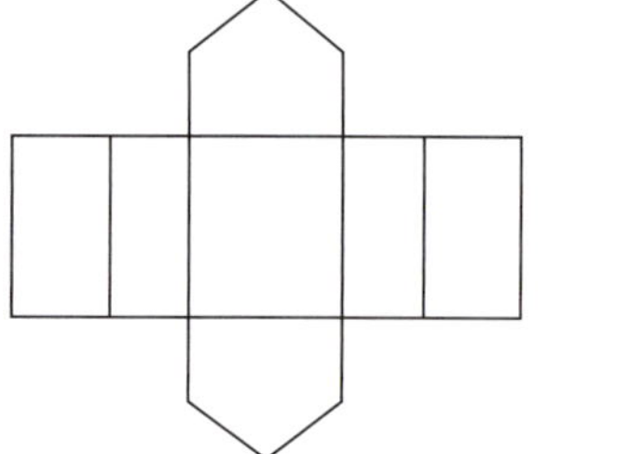

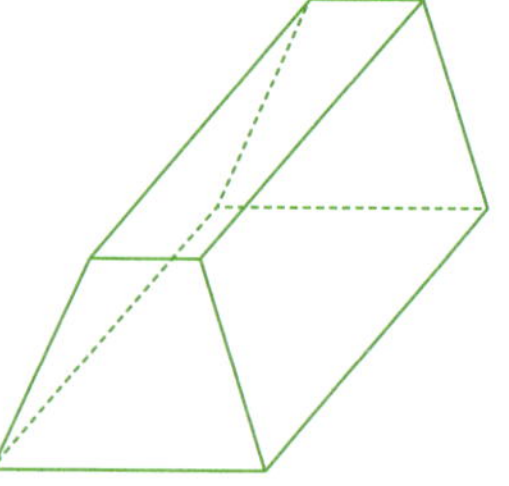

PHOTOCOPYING OF THIS PAGE IS RESTRICTED UNDER LAW.
ISBN: 9780170447539

Isometrics

Copying isometric shapes

- The dots on isometric paper make it easy to draw 3D shapes.

One cube would look like this:

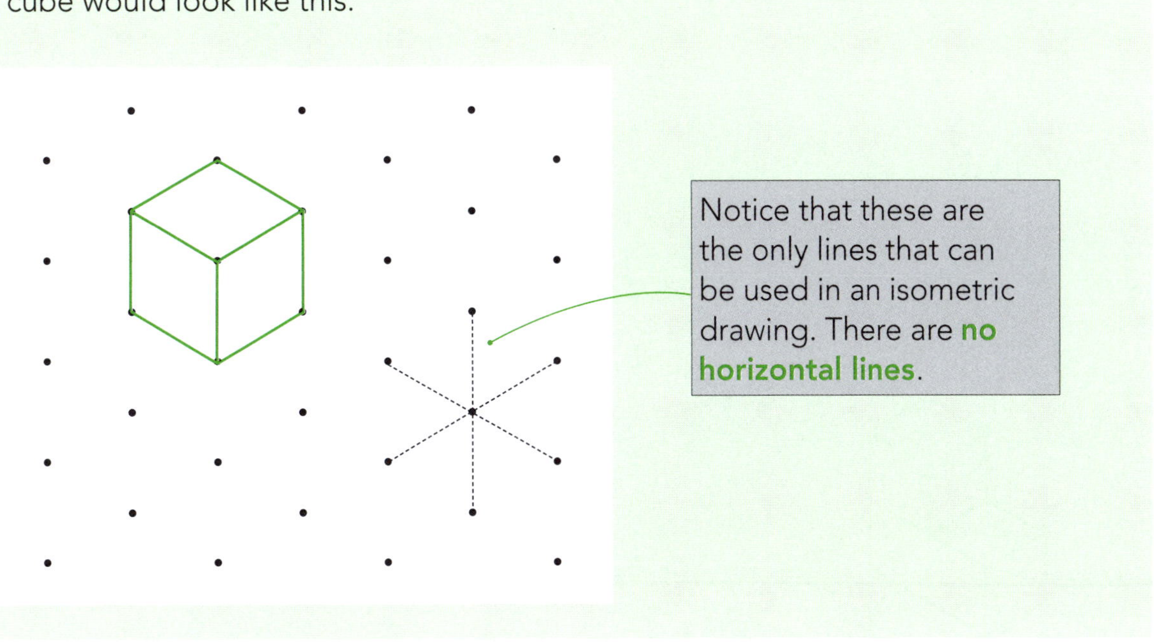

Copy these shapes, showing the junctions between each block. The first one has been started for you. Use a ruler.

1

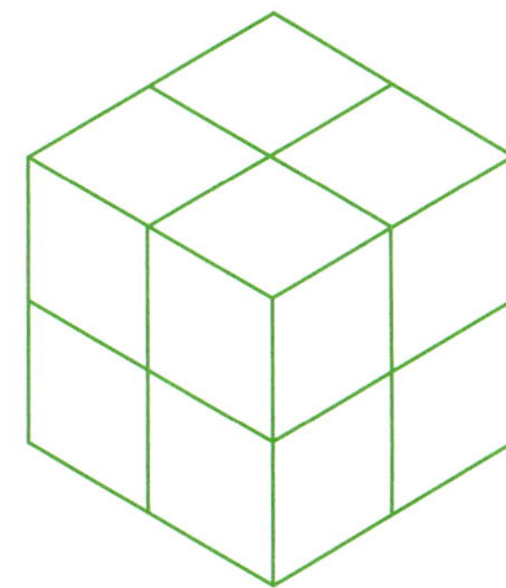

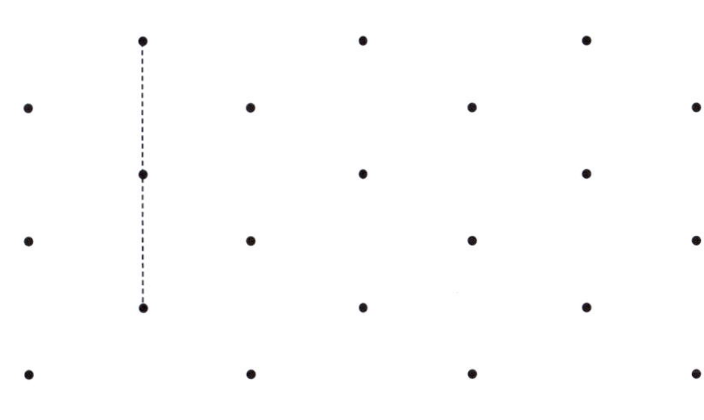

2

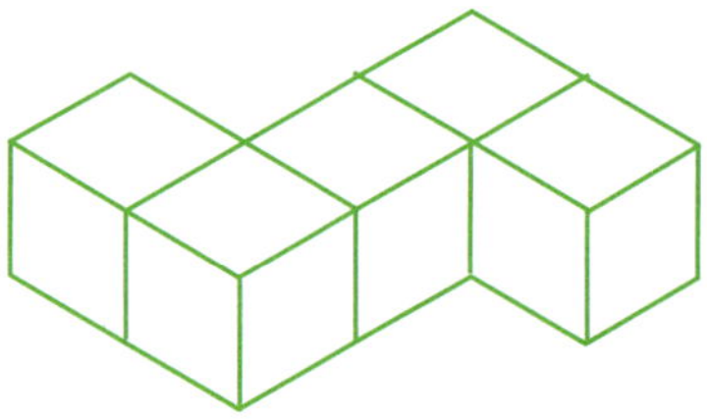

3

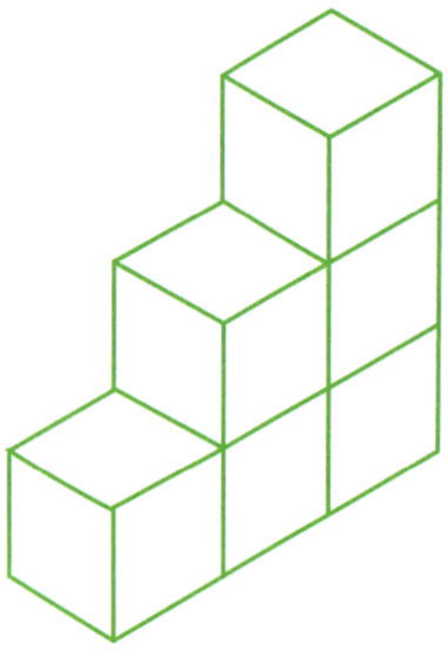

4

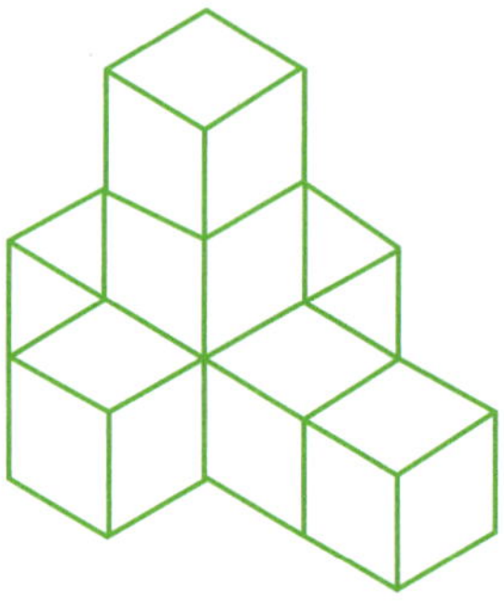

PHOTOCOPYING OF THIS PAGE IS RESTRICTED UNDER LAW. ISBN: 9780170447539

Draw the outlines of these shapes **without** showing the junctions between blocks. The first one has been started for you.

5

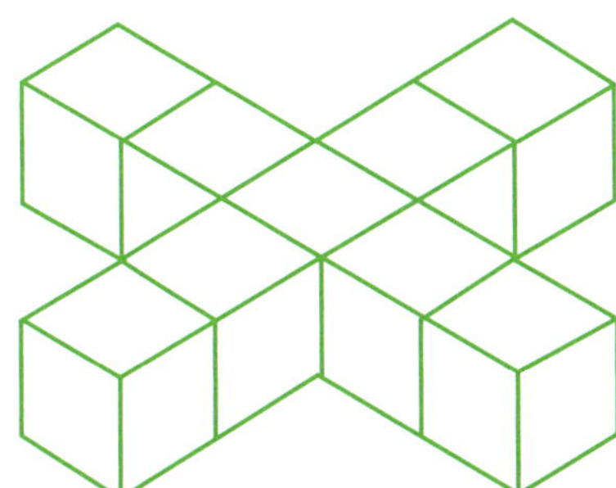

6

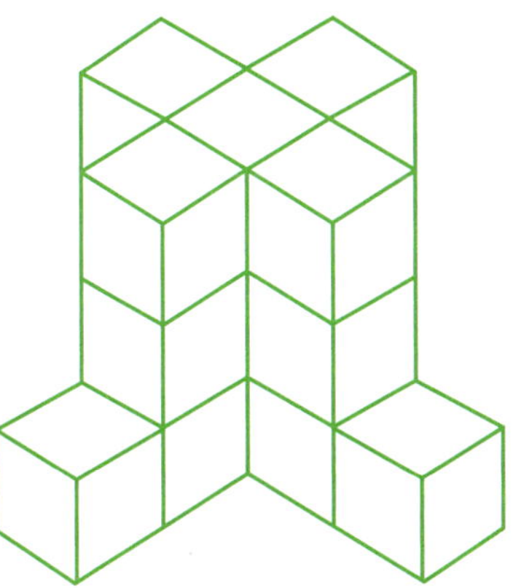

7

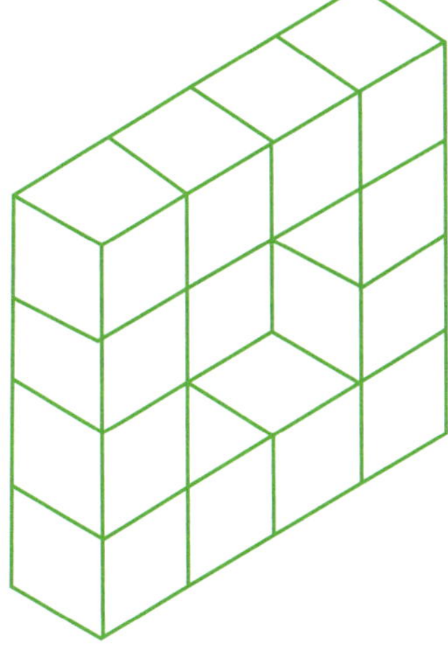

Drawing isometric shapes from numbers in each column

- Another way of showing the numbers of blocks in some shapes is to draw it from the top, and write in the number of blocks in each column.

Example:

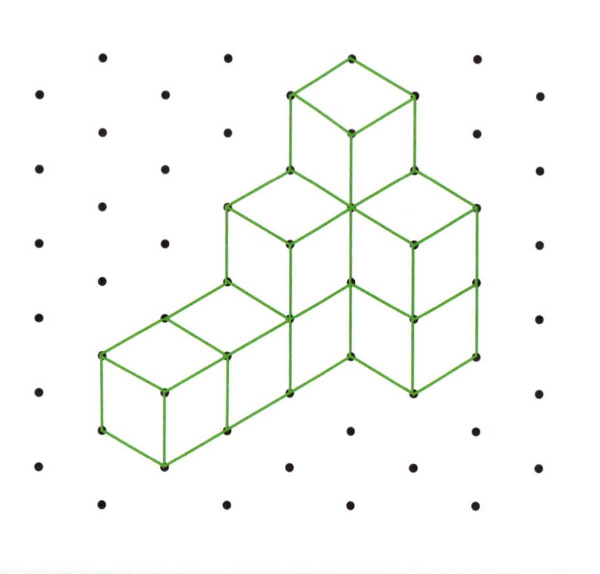

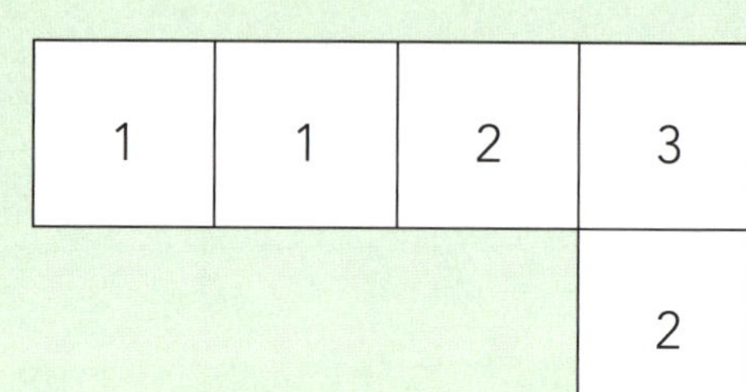

Write down the number of blocks in each column of these shapes. Unless otherwise shown, assume the bases are at least one block deep.

1

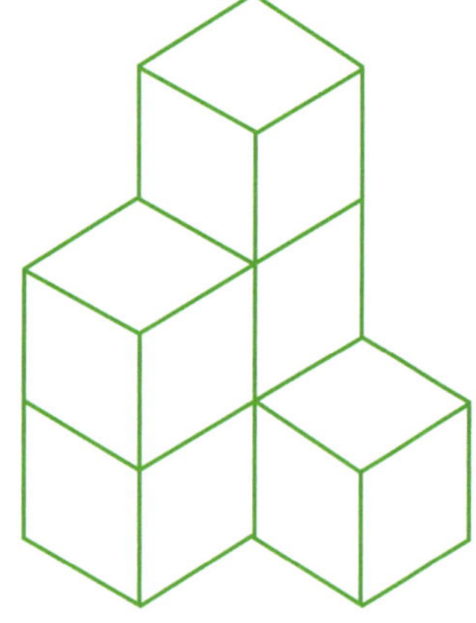

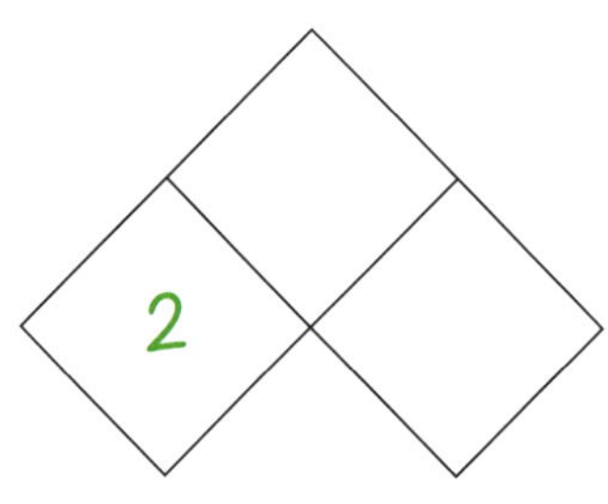

PHOTOCOPYING OF THIS PAGE IS RESTRICTED UNDER LAW.
ISBN: 9780170447539

2

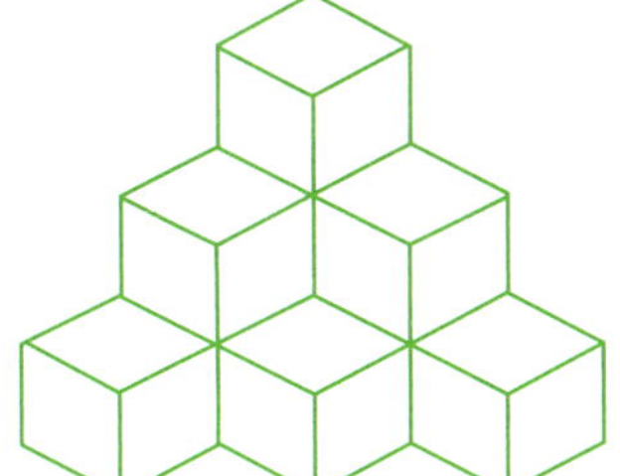

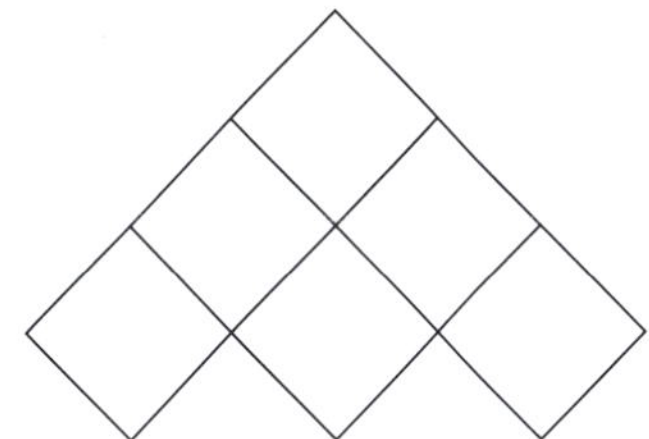

3

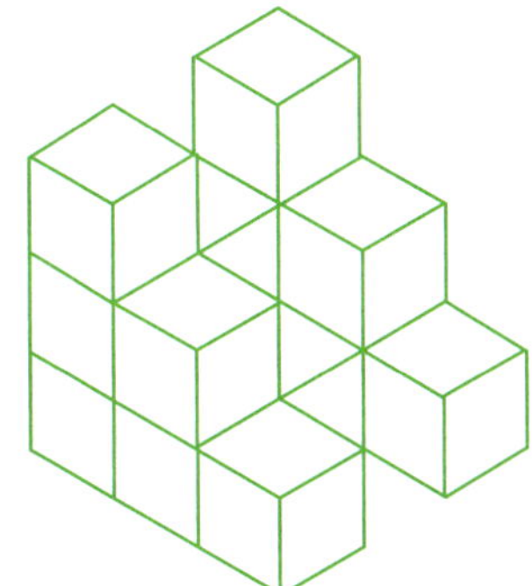

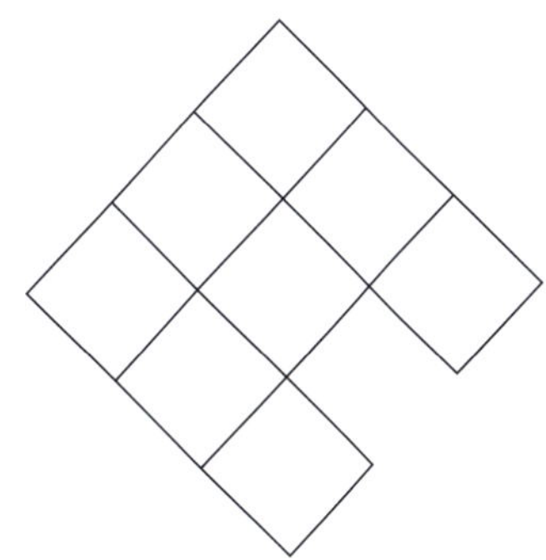

4

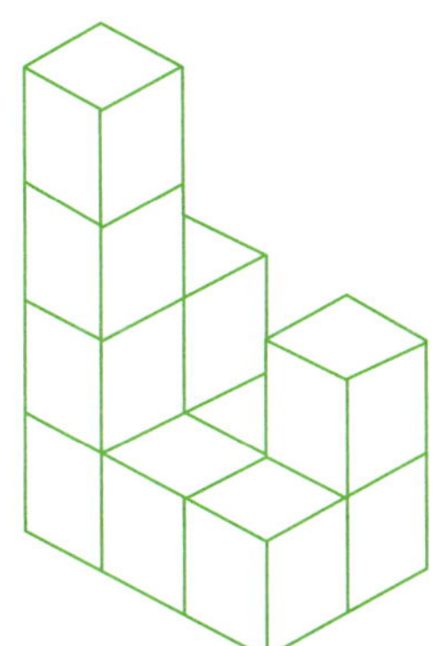

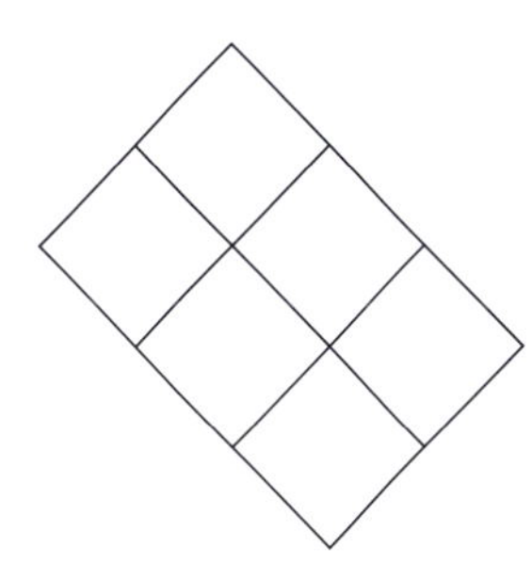

5

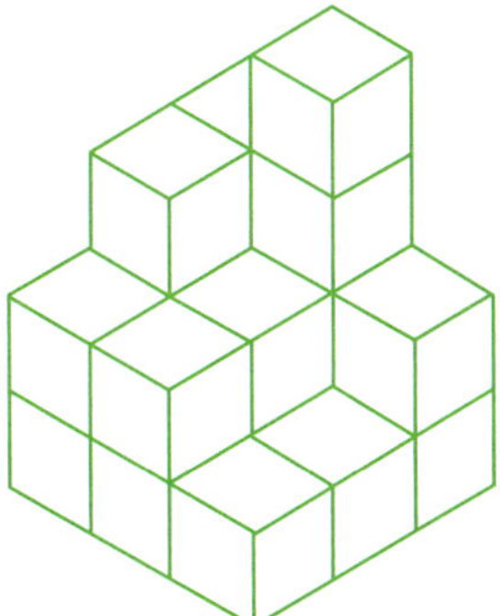

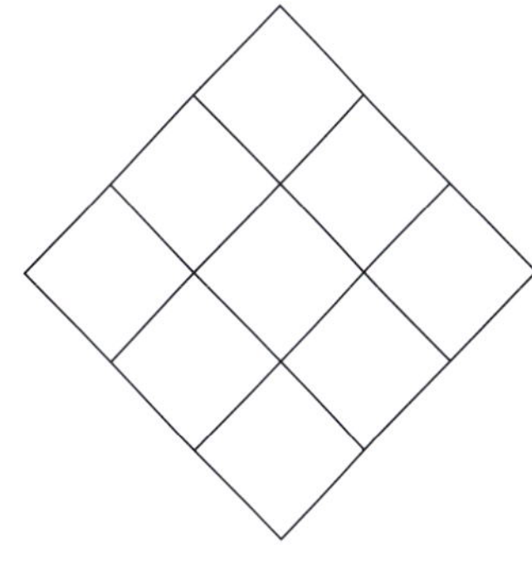

6

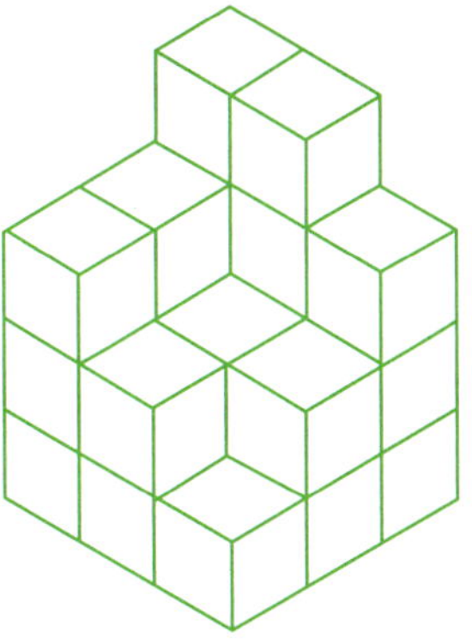

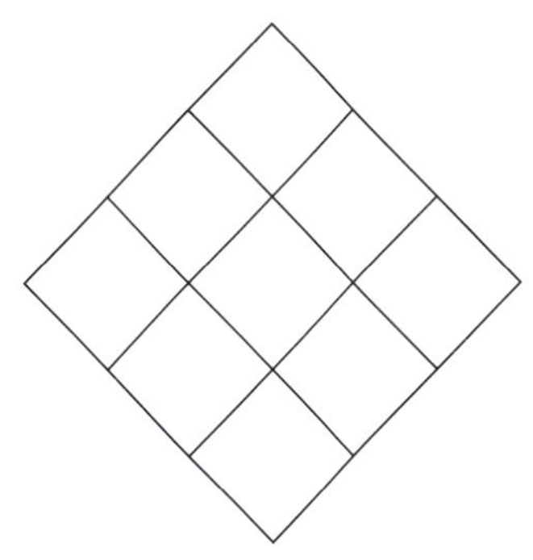

ISBN: 9780170447539 PHOTOCOPYING OF THIS PAGE IS RESTRICTED UNDER LAW.

Draw these structures on the isometric grids. Hint: Building them with blocks first may help.

7

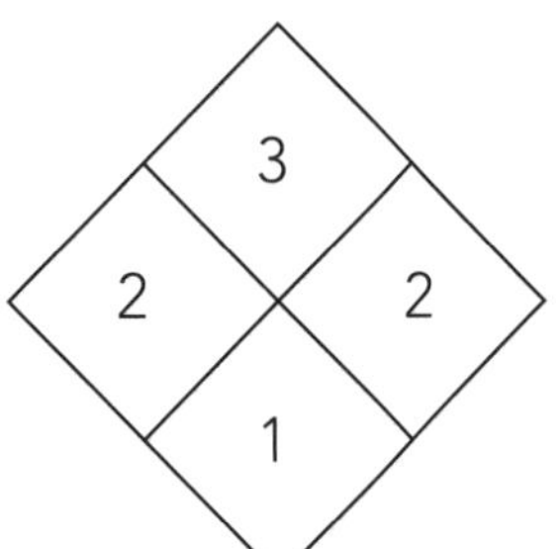

8

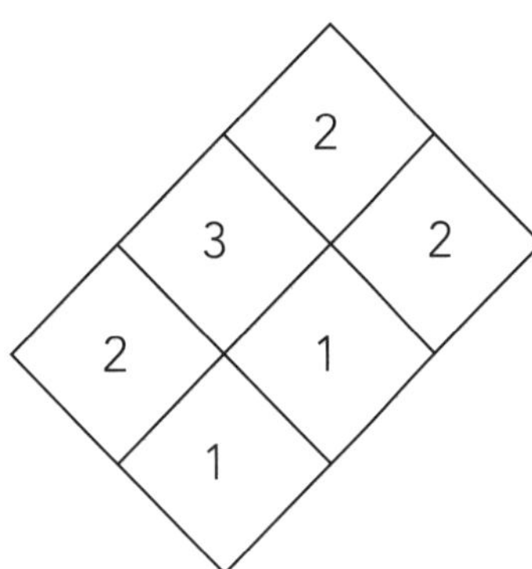

9

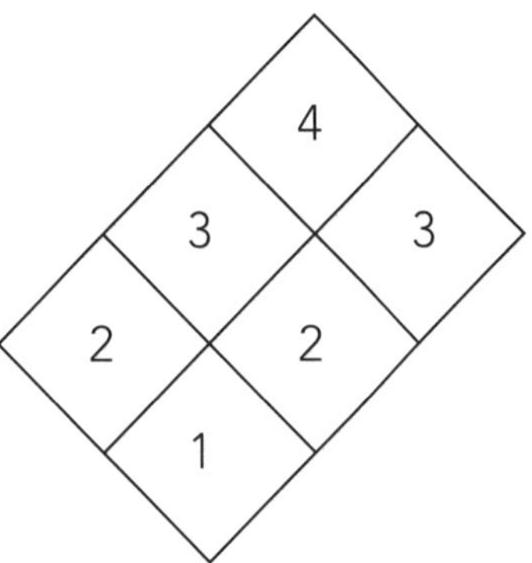

PHOTOCOPYING OF THIS PAGE IS RESTRICTED UNDER LAW. ISBN: 9780170447539

10

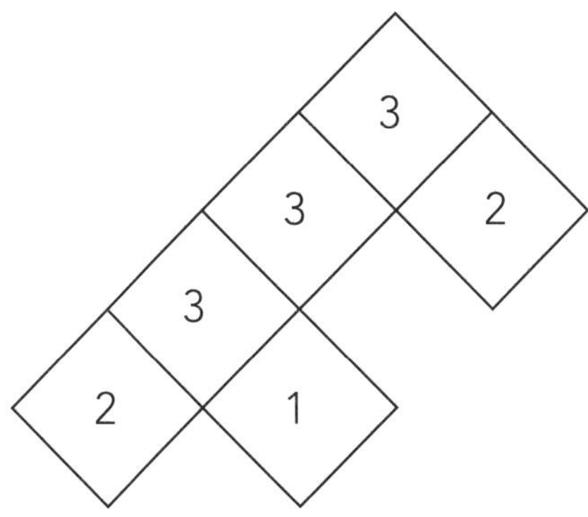

11

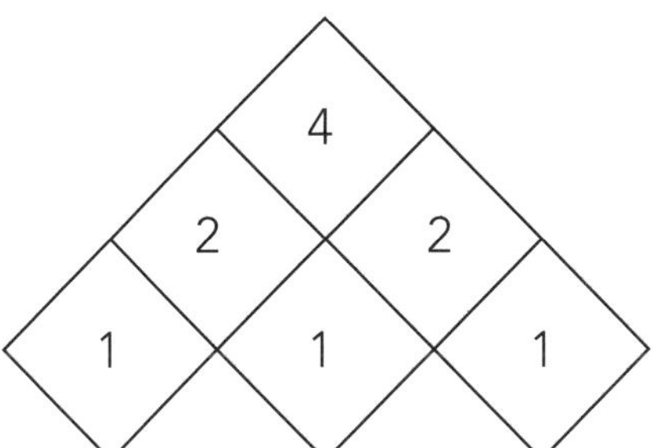

12

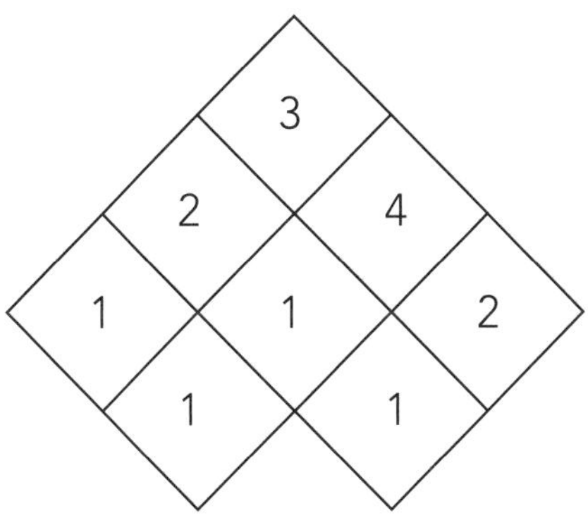

ISBN: 9780170447539 PHOTOCOPYING OF THIS PAGE IS RESTRICTED UNDER LAW.

Different views of isometric diagrams

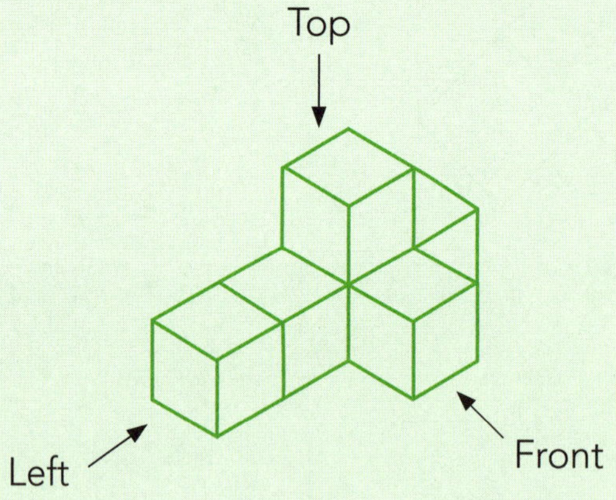

Top

Left

Front

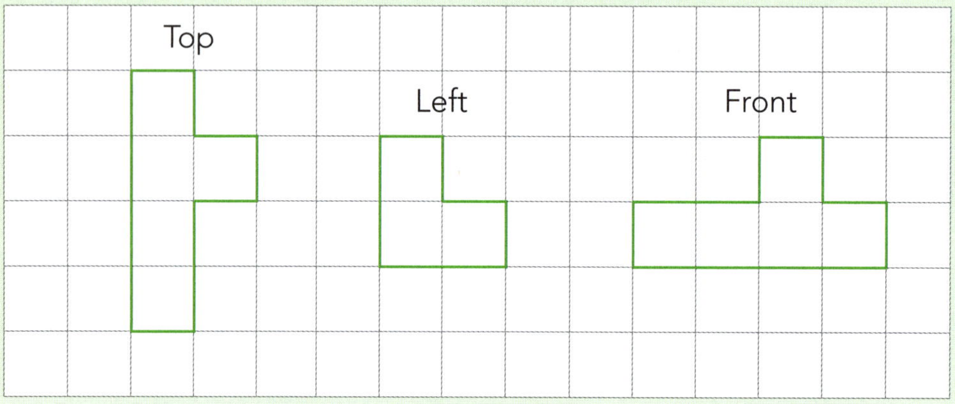

Top

Left

Front

Match these shapes with their 2D views. There are no blocks hidden in behind.

A

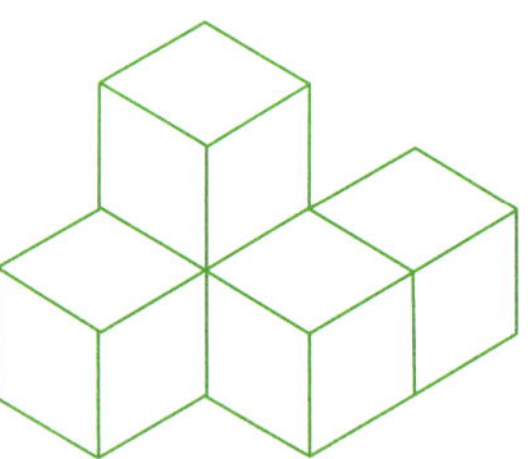

B

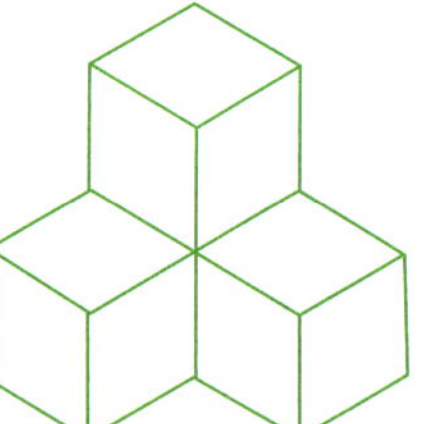

C

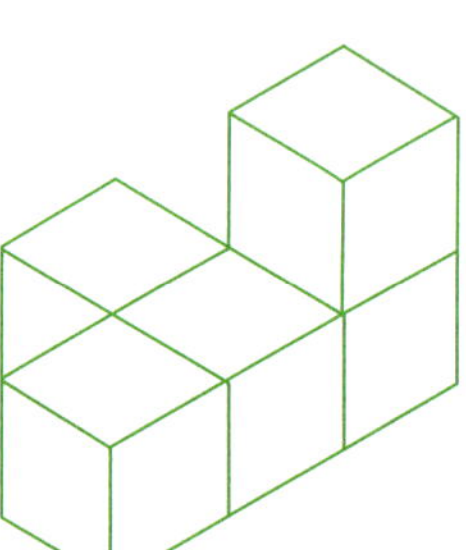

D

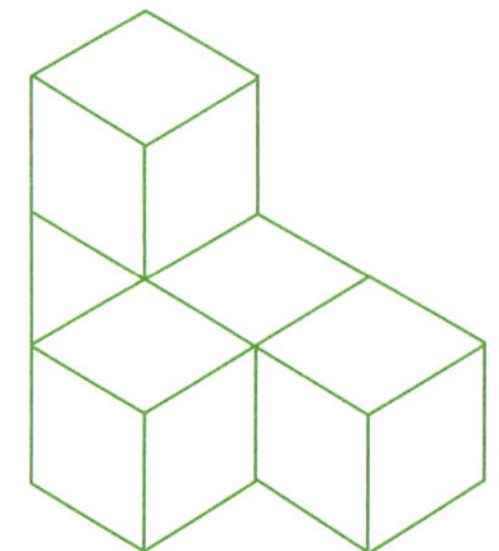

E

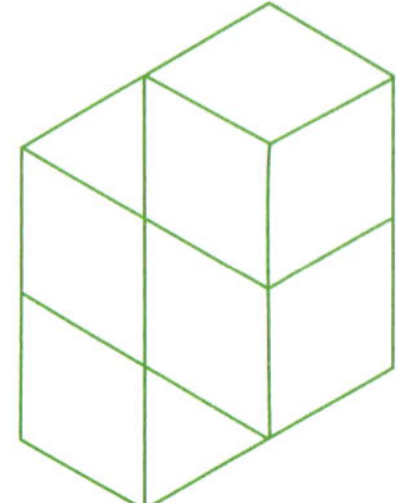

F

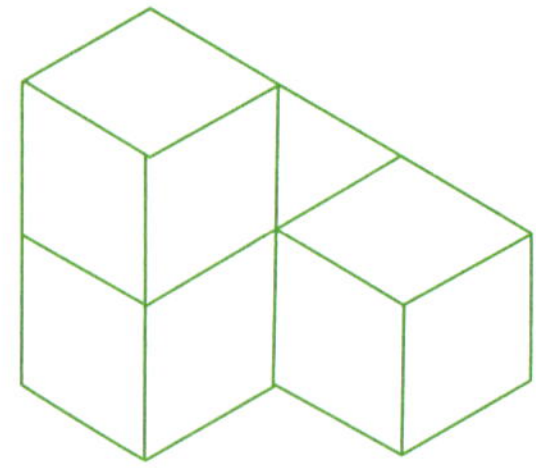

PHOTOCOPYING OF THIS PAGE IS RESTRICTED UNDER LAW.
ISBN: 9780170447539

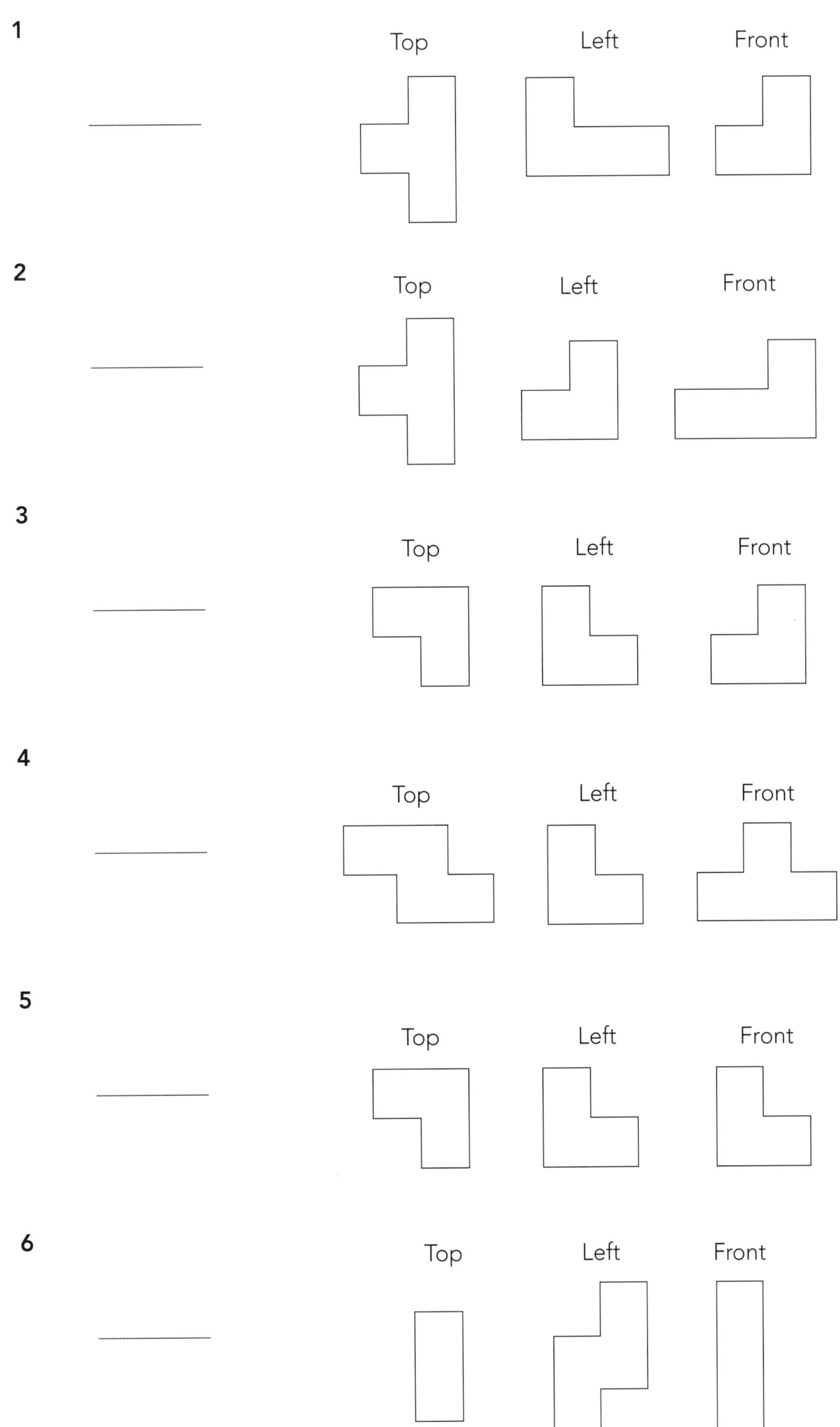

ISBN: 9780170447539 PHOTOCOPYING OF THIS PAGE IS RESTRICTED UNDER LAW.

Draw the top, left and front views of these shapes.

Top Left Front

7

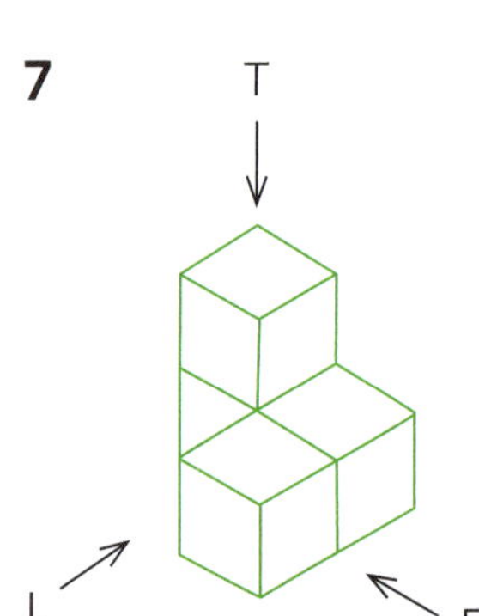

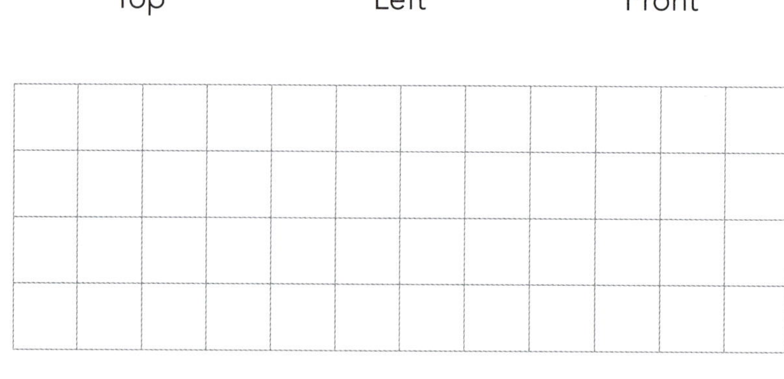

8

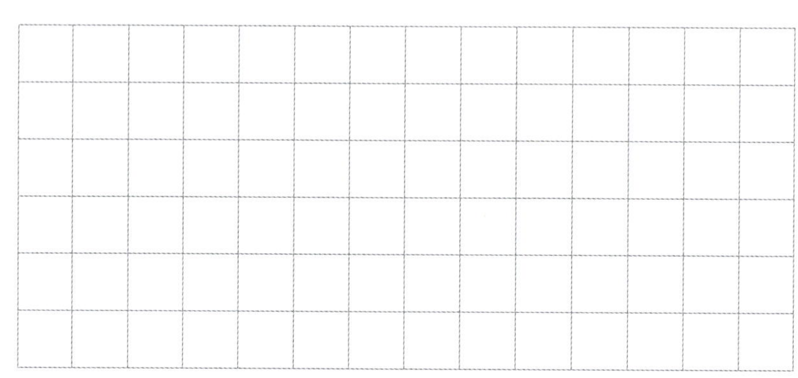

9

10

PHOTOCOPYING OF THIS PAGE IS RESTRICTED UNDER LAW. ISBN: 9780170447539

Challenge 2

This is a different type of isometric paper. There are 12 ways of drawing this figure on isometric paper. Three are done for you. See how many you can draw.

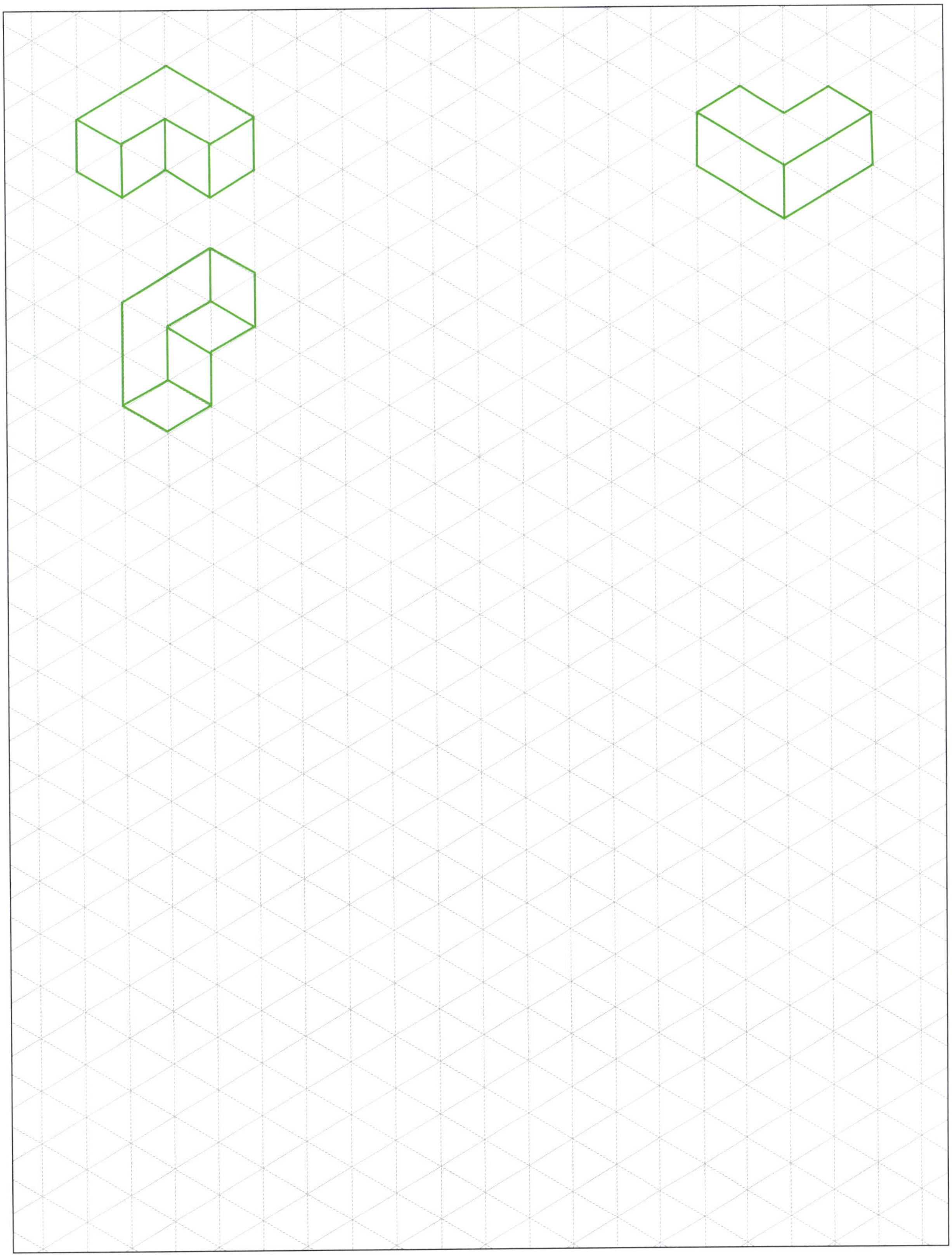

Position and orientation

Directions and bearings

- Bearings are used in navigation to define **direction** in a **horizontal** plane.
- Directions can be given in terms of north, south, east and west.
- North is always given as the starting point.

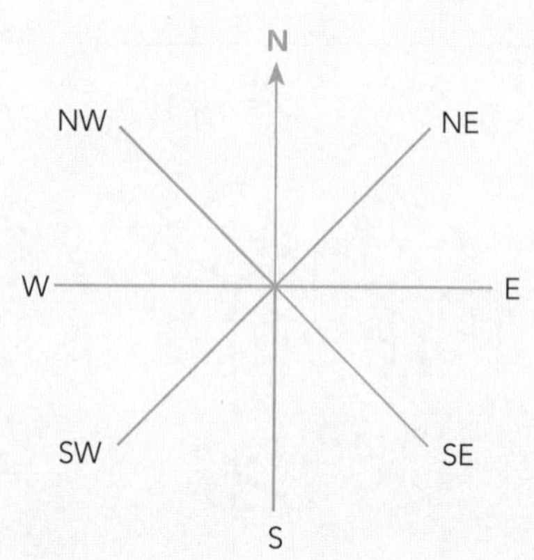

- Bearings are measured in **degrees** in a **clockwise direction from north (000° or 360°)**.
- All bearings must have **three digits**.

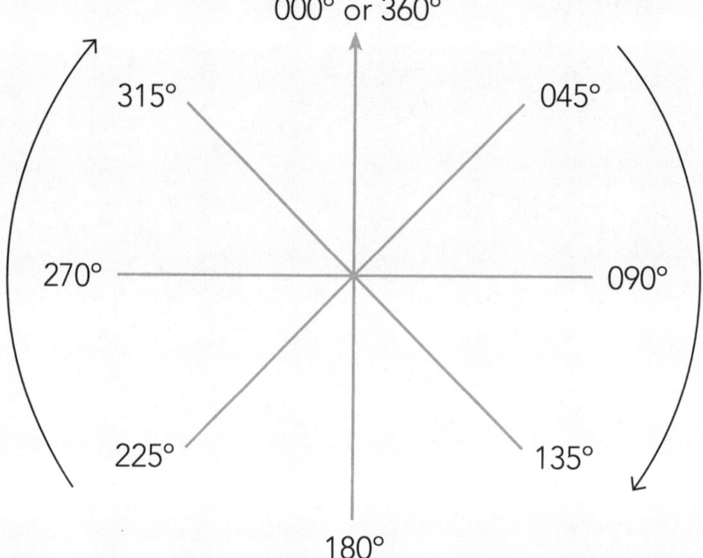

Examples:

1

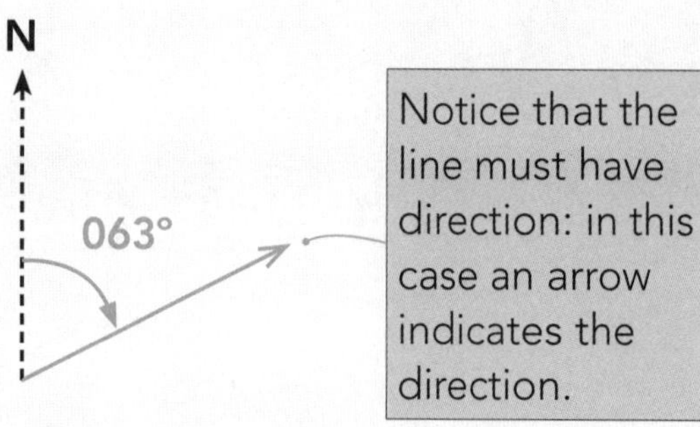

2

PHOTOCOPYING OF THIS PAGE IS RESTRICTED UNDER LAW. ISBN: 9780170447539

Match the bearings and the compass directions in the lists to each of the diagrams. They are either in the direction of the arrow or from A to B.

045°	225°	315°	135°	180°	090°	000°	270°
W	NE	S	E	NW	SE	SW	N

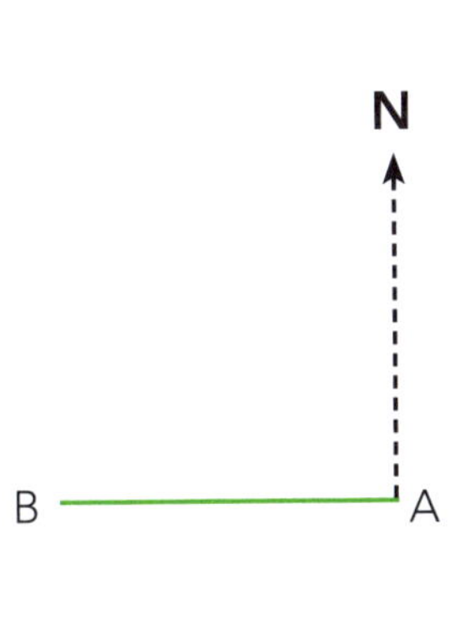

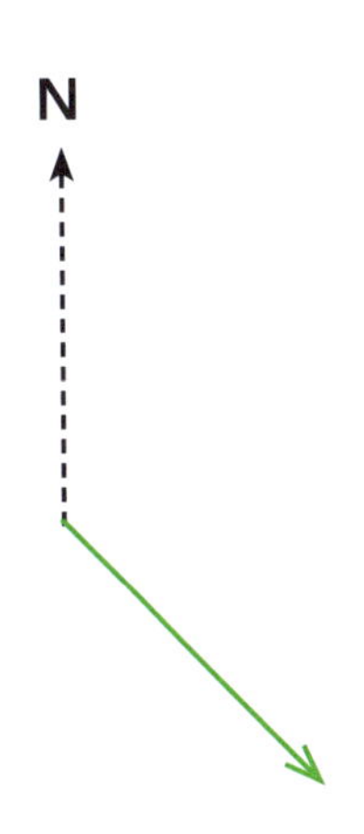

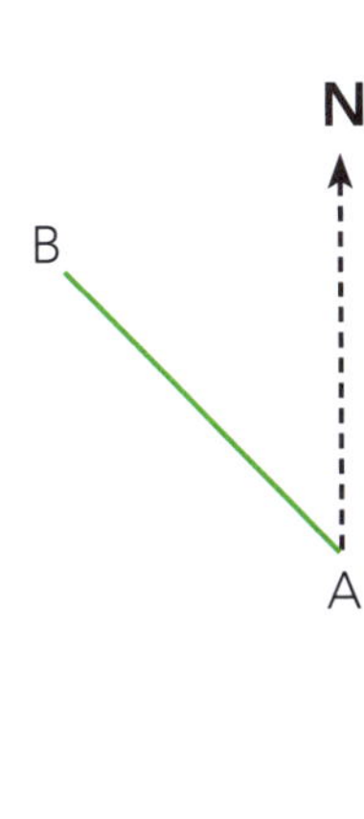

1 270° W

2 ______ ______

3 ______ ______

4 ______ ______

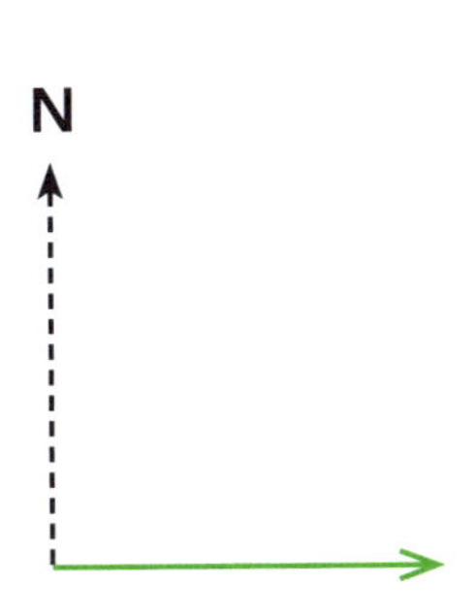

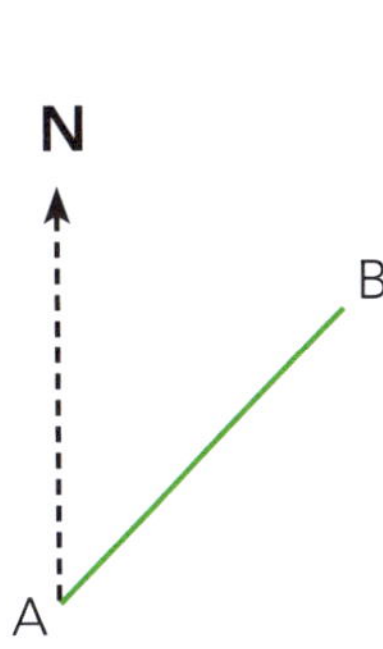

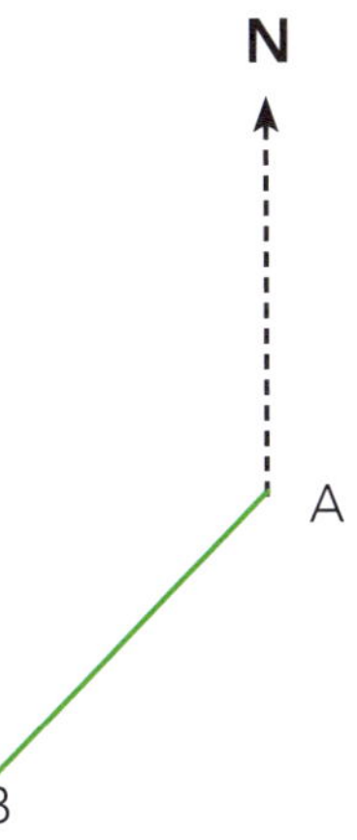

5 ______ ______

6 ______ ______

7 ______ ______

8 ______ ______

ISBN: 9780170447539 PHOTOCOPYING OF THIS PAGE IS RESTRICTED UNDER LAW.

9 Scott walks anticlockwise around this path, starting at point A. Write the bearing and direction he will need to walk for each stretch of path. Select your answers from the lists below.

225°	045°	270°	180°	360°	135°	090°	315°
S	NE	W	SE	N	SW	E	NW

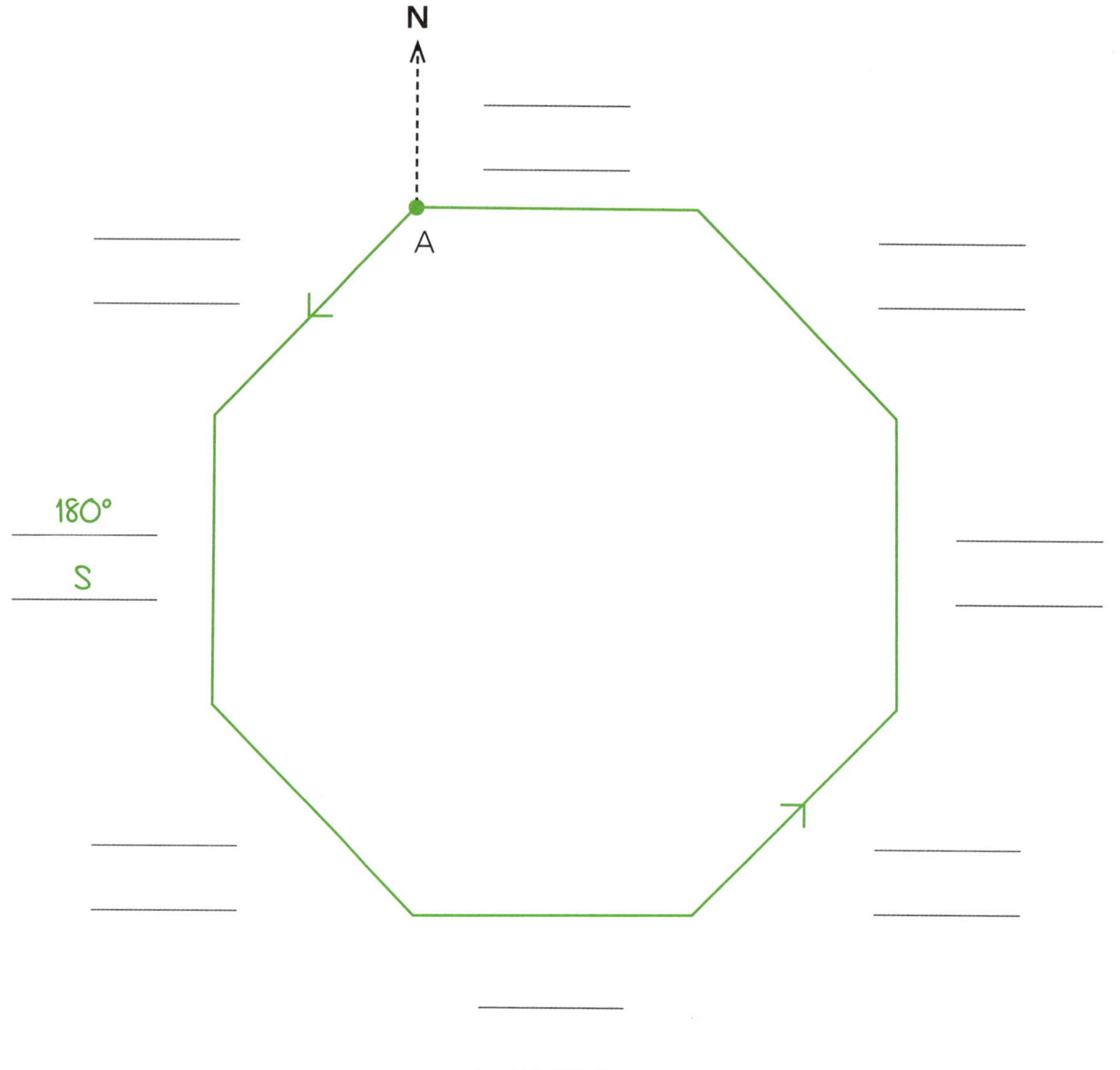

10 Give the bearing and direction if a person made the following changes to their course.

		Bearing	Direction
a	From a bearing of 045°, make a 90° right turn.	________	________
b	From a bearing of 180°, make a 135° right turn.	________	________
c	From a bearing of 225°, make a 135° right turn.	________	________

PHOTOCOPYING OF THIS PAGE IS RESTRICTED UNDER LAW. ISBN: 9780170447539

Location: grid references

- Grid references are used to identify **locations** on a map.
- We will consider **4**-point and **6**-point references.
- As with coordinates, **horizontal values** are always given **before vertical values**.

4-point grid references

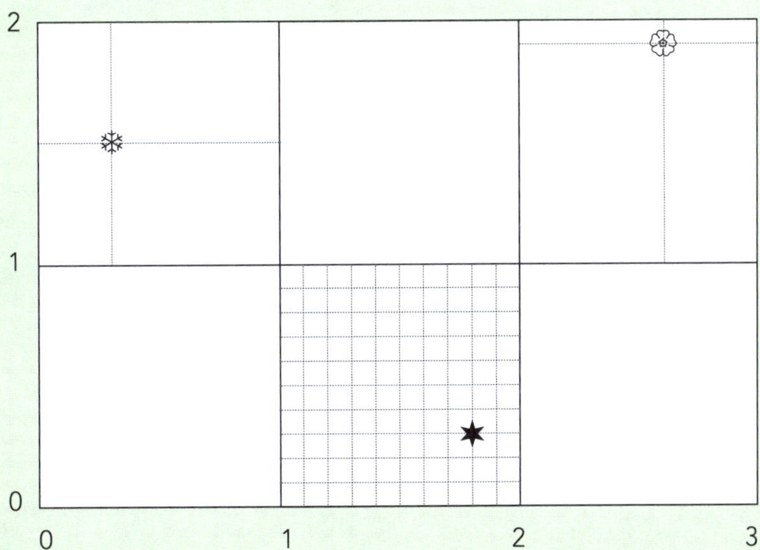

Example: The star (✶)

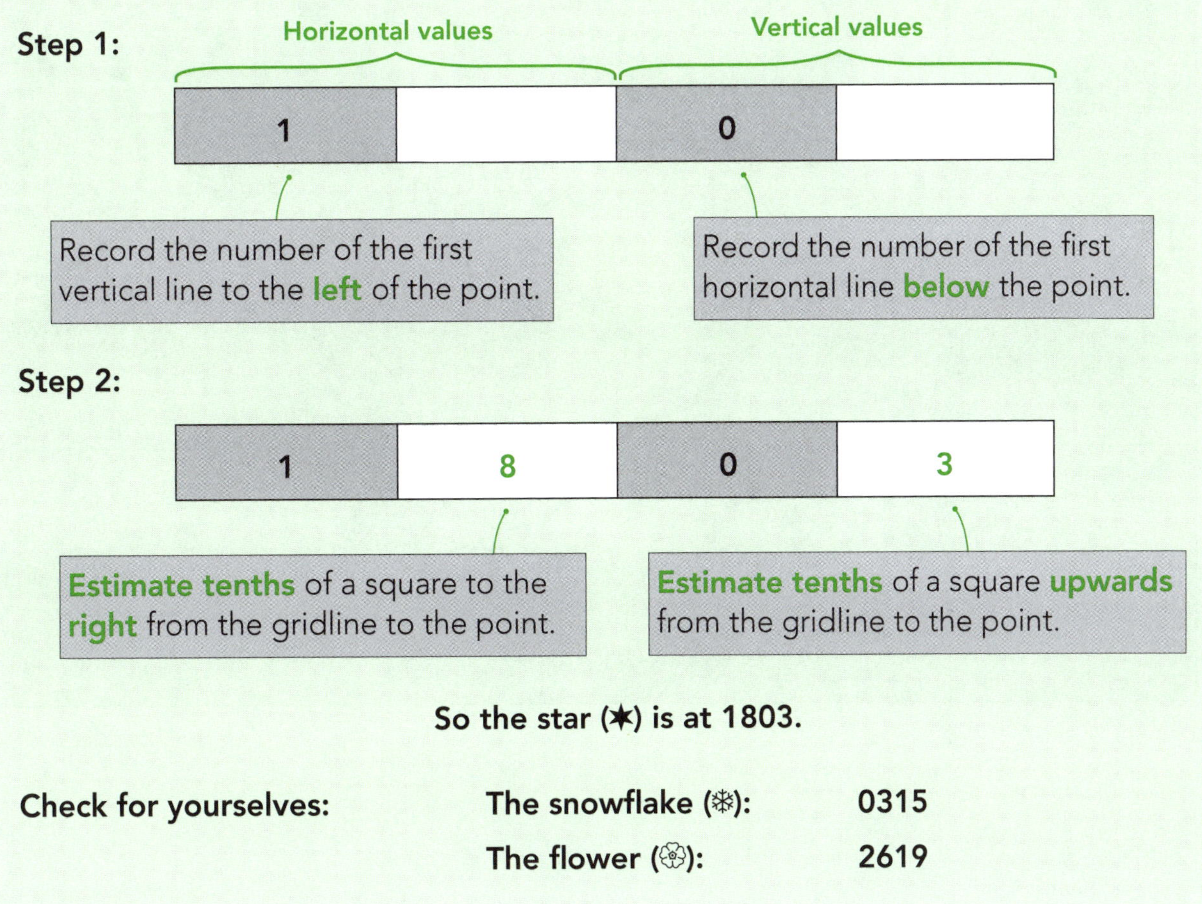

So the star (✶) is at 1803.

Check for yourselves:

The snowflake (❄):	**0315**
The flower (✿):	**2619**

ISBN: 9780170447539 PHOTOCOPYING OF THIS PAGE IS RESTRICTED UNDER LAW.

This map shows part of Auckland Zoo. Use the key to help you estimate the grid references for the **centres** of the symbols described.

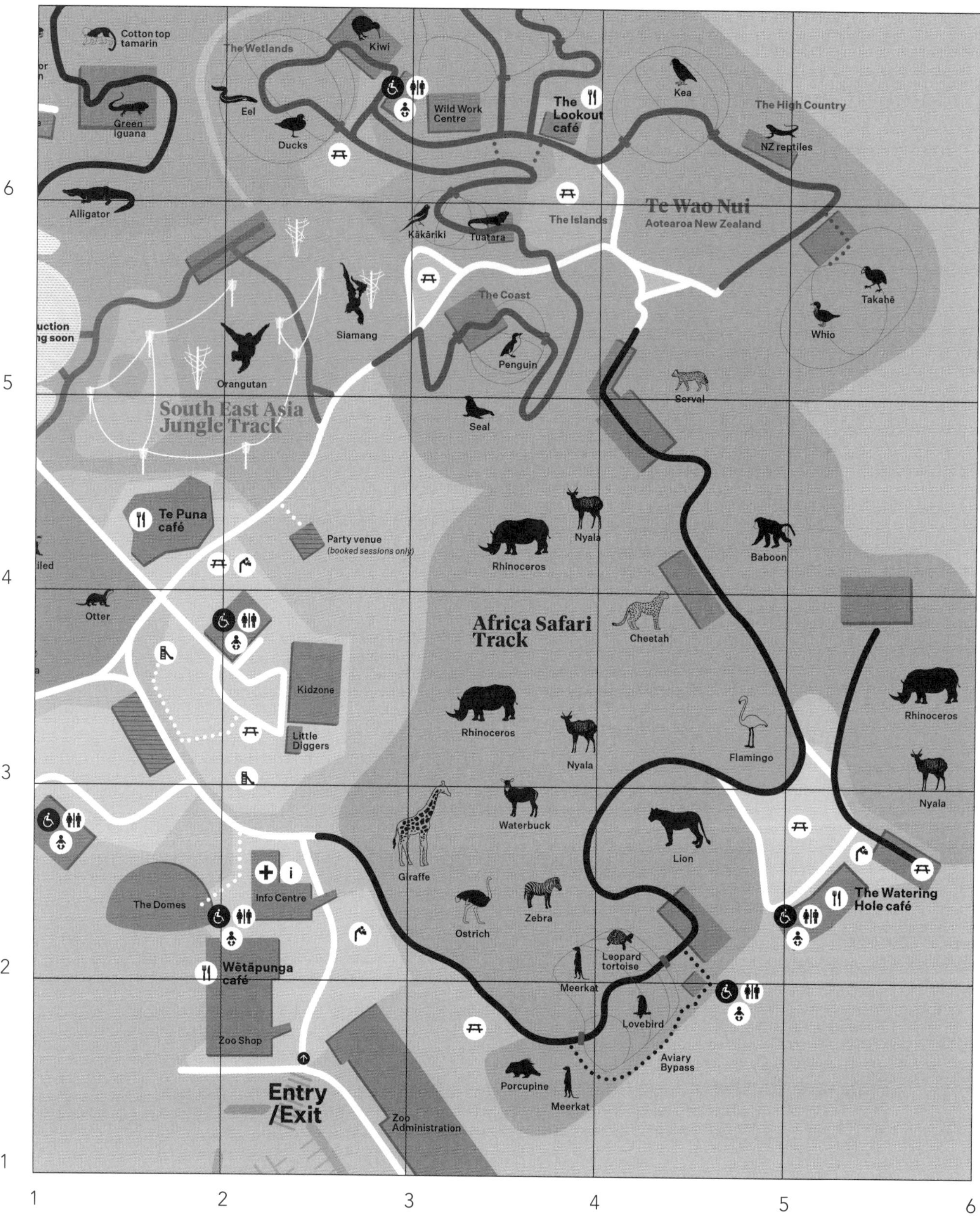

PHOTOCOPYING OF THIS PAGE IS RESTRICTED UNDER LAW. ISBN: 9780170447539

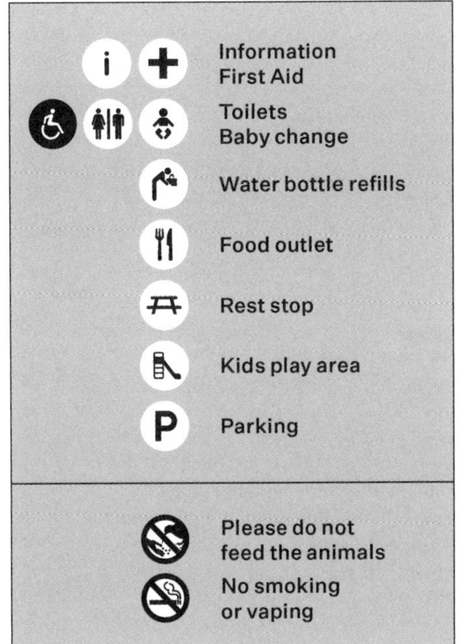

What would you find at the following grid references?

1 2416 ____________________

2 3643 ____________________

3 1361 ____________________

4 5324 ____________________

5 3156 ____________________

6 4239 ____________________

Write grid references for the centres of the animals or the symbols.

7 The whio. __________

8 The party venue. __________

9 The green iguana. __________

10 First aid. __________

11 The baboon. __________

12 The Lookout cafe. __________

6-point grid references

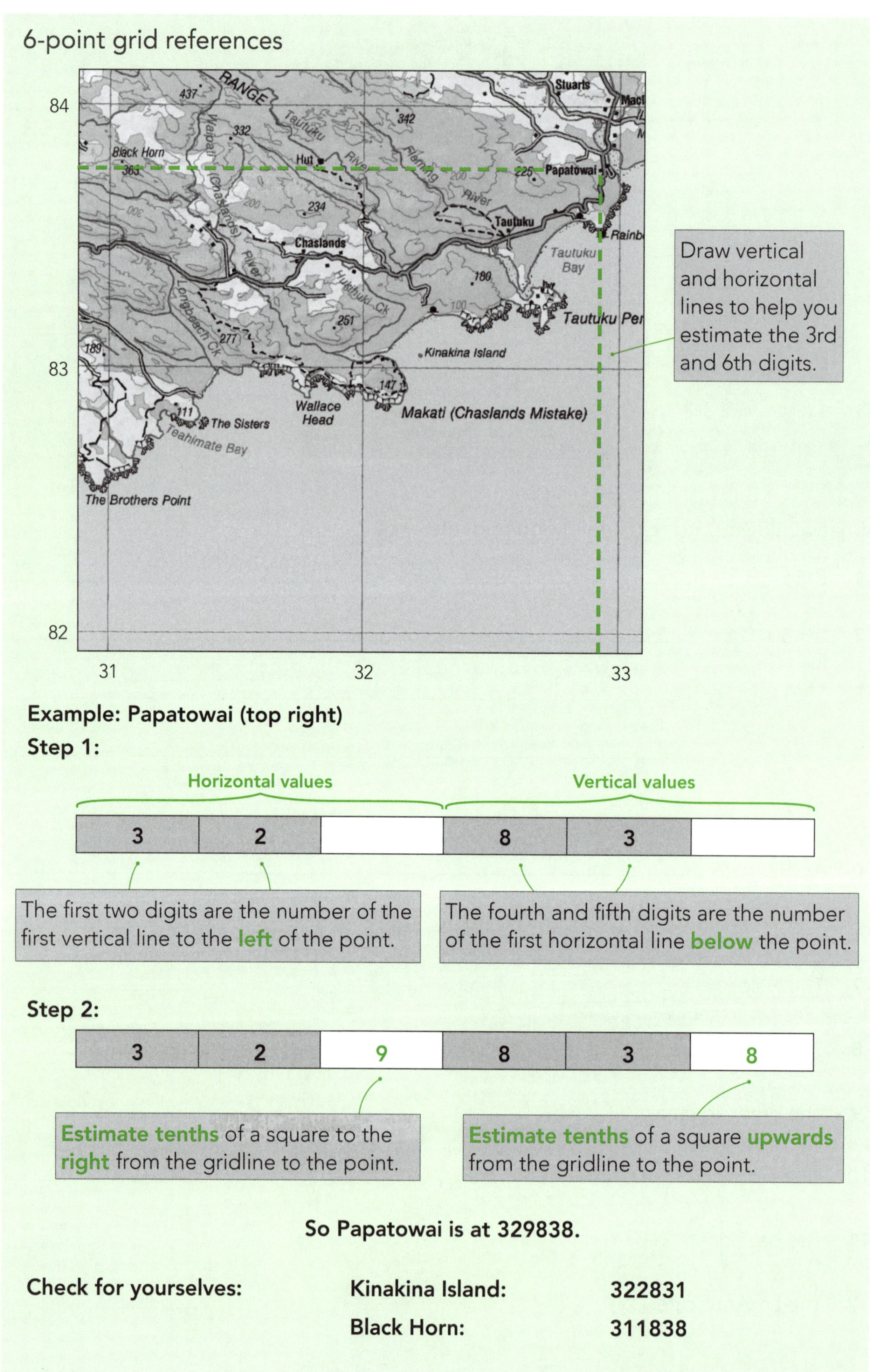

Example: Papatowai (top right)

Step 1:

Horizontal values			Vertical values		
3	2		8	3	

The first two digits are the number of the first vertical line to the **left** of the point.

The fourth and fifth digits are the number of the first horizontal line **below** the point.

Step 2:

3	2	9	8	3	8

Estimate tenths of a square to the **right** from the gridline to the point.

Estimate tenths of a square **upwards** from the gridline to the point.

So Papatowai is at 329838.

Check for yourselves:

Kinakina Island:	**322831**
Black Horn:	**311838**

PHOTOCOPYING OF THIS PAGE IS RESTRICTED UNDER LAW. ISBN: 9780170447539

What would you find at the following grid references?

16 310825 ______________ **17** 318838 ______________

18 327841 ______________ **19** 314828 ______________

20 317834 ______________ **21** 322828 ______________

Write grid references for the following places.

22 The mouth of the Fleming River ______________

23 Tautuku ______________

24 Wallace Head ______________

25 Black Horn ______________

If the distance between the gridlines is 5 km, estimate, to the nearest kilometre, the direct distance between the following points.

26 The Brothers Point and Makati ______________

27 The Brothers Point and Tautuku ______________

28 Chaslands and Tautuku ______________

29 Chaslands and the Hut ______________

From the list below, select the best estimate of direction for a straight line between the following points.

W	NE	SW	N	SE	NW	S	E

30 From Chaslands to Wallace Head ______________

31 From The Sisters to Chaslands ______________

32 Papatowai to the Hut ______________

33 The Sisters to The Brothers Point ______________

ISBN: 9780170447539 PHOTOCOPYING OF THIS PAGE IS RESTRICTED UNDER LAW.

Paths and directions

- Specifying a path requires both **direction** and **distance**.
- You will need a **ruler** in order to measure the distances.
- Angles used in these paths are selections from the following:

000°	045°	090°	135°	180°	225°	270°	315°

Example:
Scale: 1 cm = 100 m

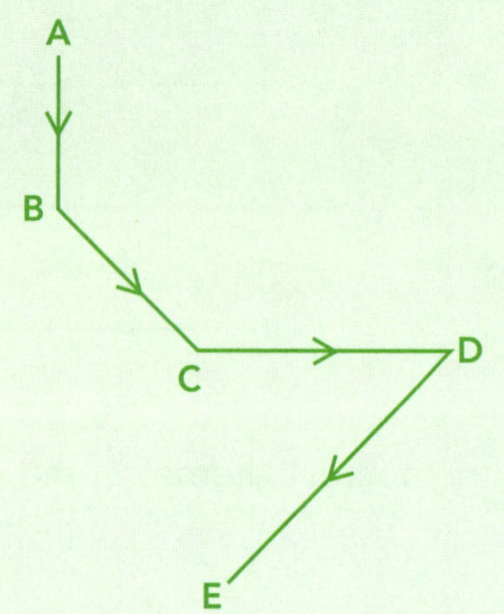

From A, go 150 m at a bearing of 180° to B.

From B, go 200 m at a bearing of 135° to C.

From C, go 260 m at a bearing of 090° to D.

From D, go 320 m at a bearing of 225° to E.

Write the paths for each of these routes using the bearings listed above and distances.
Scale: 1 cm = 100 m.

1

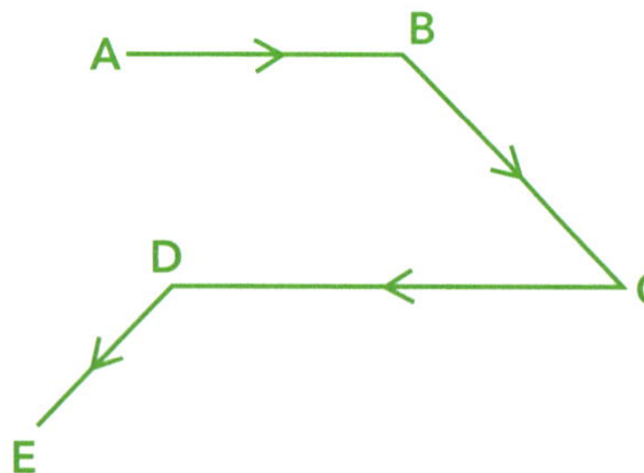

From A, go ______ m at a bearing of ______° to B.

From B, go ______ m at a bearing of ______° to C.

From C, go ______ m at a bearing of ______° to D.

From D, go ______ m at a bearing of ______° to E.

2

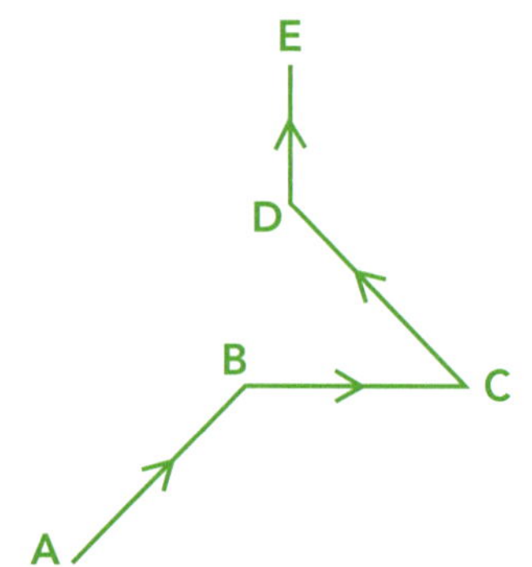

From A, go ______ m at a bearing of ______° to B.

From B, go ______ m at a bearing of ______° to C.

From C, go ______ m at a bearing of ______° to D.

From D, go ______ m at a bearing of ______° to E.

PHOTOCOPYING OF THIS PAGE IS RESTRICTED UNDER LAW.
ISBN: 9780170447539

3

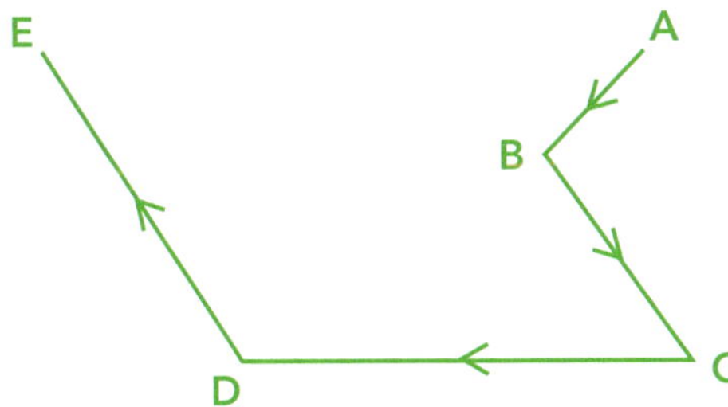

From A, go ______ m at a bearing of ______° to B.

From B, go ______ m at a bearing of ______° to C.

From C, go ______ m at a bearing of ______° to D.

From D, go ______ m at a bearing of ______° to E.

4

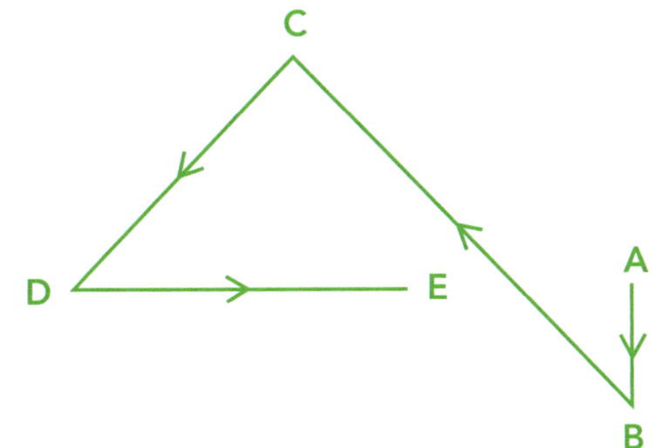

From A, go ______ m at a bearing of ______° to B.

From B, go ______ m at a bearing of ______° to C.

From C, go ______ m at a bearing of ______° to D.

From D, go ______ m at a bearing of ______° to E.

5

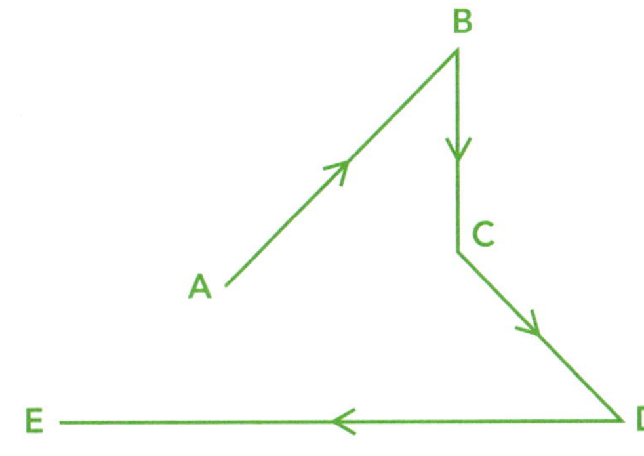

From A, go ______ m at a bearing of ______° to B.

From B, go ______ m at a bearing of ______° to C.

From C, go ______ m at a bearing of ______° to D.

From D, go ______ m at a bearing of ______° to E.

6

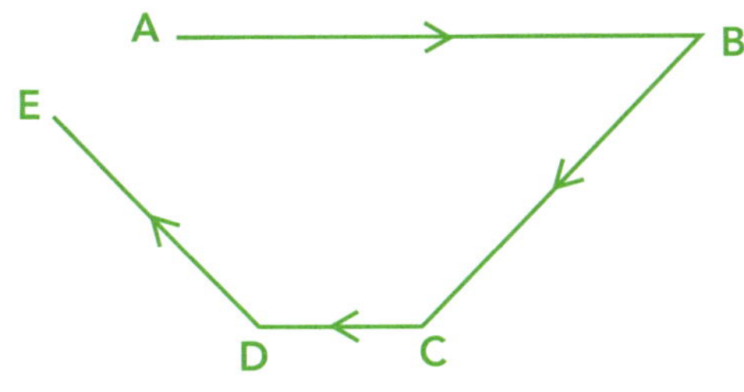

From A, go ______ m at a bearing of ______° to B.

From B, go ______ m at a bearing of ______° to C.

From C, go ______ m at a bearing of ______° to D.

From D, go ______ m at a bearing of ______° to E.

 PHOTOCOPYING OF THIS PAGE IS RESTRICTED UNDER LAW.

This map shows part of central Christchurch.

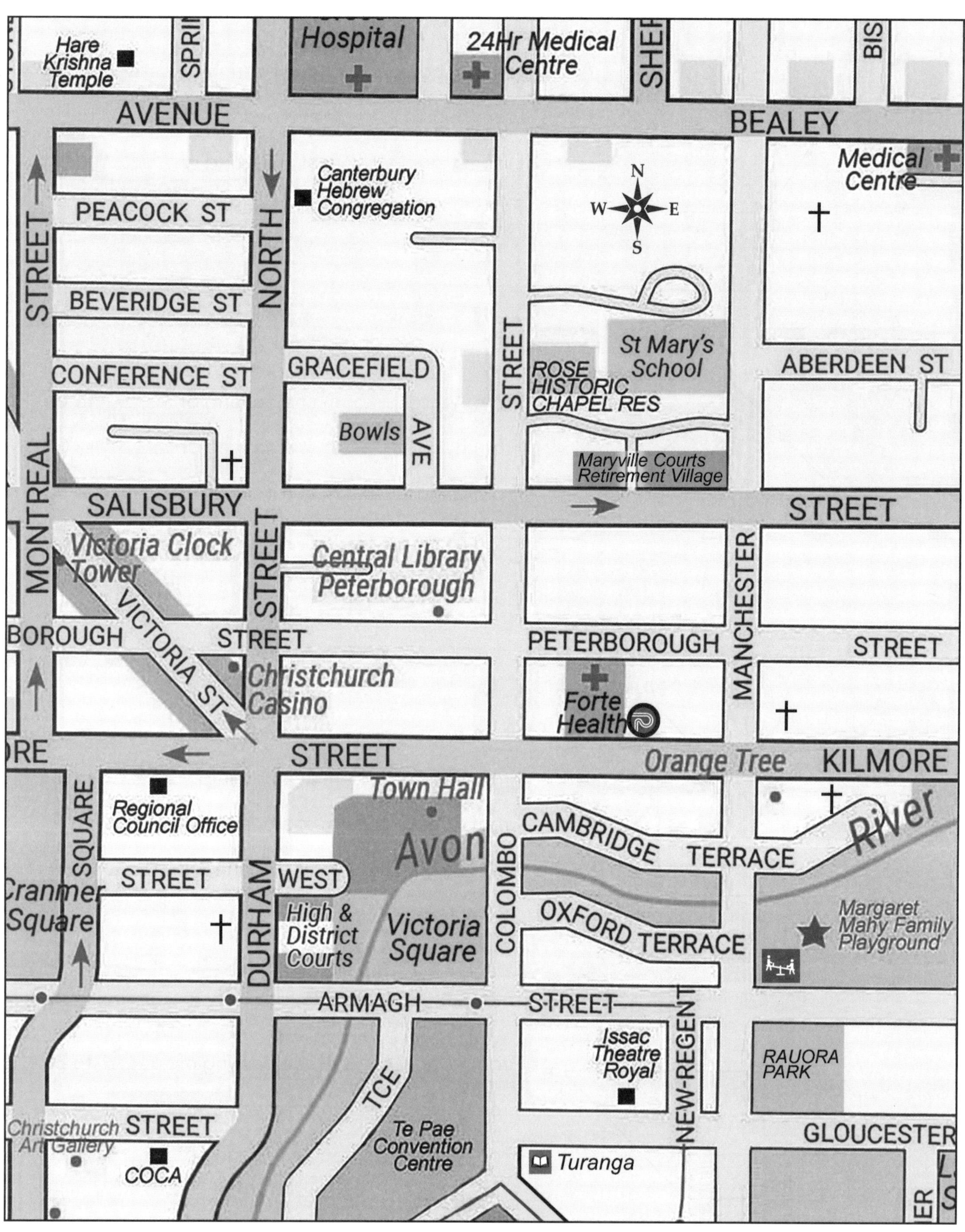

PHOTOCOPYING OF THIS PAGE IS RESTRICTED UNDER LAW. ISBN: 9780170447539

Key:

	Post Office	†	Church
✚	Hospital		Library
	Playground		

Scale: 1 cm = 50 m

Examples:

1 The width of St Mary's School (near the top and between Colombo and Manchester Streets) is 2.4 cm on the map = 2.4 x 50 m = 120 m on the ground.

2 Colombo Street between Kilmore Street and Bealey Avenue is 11.6 cm on the map = 11.6 x 50 m = 580 m on the ground.

3 180 m on the ground = $\frac{180}{50}$ = 3.6 cm on the map.

Follow these walking routes and answer the questions.

7 From the Christchurch Town Hall, you walk on a bearing of 270° along Kilmore Street for about 175 m, then walk on a bearing of 315° and continue in that direction for 275 m. What would you see on your left? ________________

8 From the library (Turanga — centre bottom of the map), you walk on a bearing of 090° about 180 m, then about 100 m on a bearing of 000° and then about 75 m on a bearing of 090°. What would you see on the north side of the road? ________________

9 From the Regional Council Office in Kilmore Street, you walk 75 m on a bearing of 090°, about 300 m on a bearing of 315° and then 400 m on a bearing of 000°. Turn right and walk about 80 m on a bearing of 090°. What would you see on the north side of the road? ________________

Use directions and approximate distances to describe the following walking routes.

10 From the Orange Tree on Manchester Street to the Canterbury Hebrew Congregation on Durham Street North via Bealey Avenue.

____

____

11 From the southeast corner of Victoria Square to the COCA art gallery on Gloucester Street (bottom left).

____

____

ISBN: 9780170447539 PHOTOCOPYING OF THIS PAGE IS RESTRICTED UNDER LAW.

Transformation geometry

- A transformation (e.g. translation, reflection, rotation, enlargement) is the changing or moving of a figure by following certain rules.
- The transformed figure is called the **image**.
- A transformation may change the position, size, shape or orientation of the object.

Translation	Reflection
The figure is **shifted**.	The figure is **reflected in a mirror** line.
Rotation	**Enlargement**
The figure **rotates around a point**.	The figure **gets bigger or smaller**.

PHOTOCOPYING OF THIS PAGE IS RESTRICTED UNDER LAW. ISBN: 9780170447539

Translation

- When translated, the figure is **shifted**.

The **direction** and **distance** are often described using **vectors**:

$\begin{pmatrix} a \\ b \end{pmatrix}$

a is the **left** or **right** movement

b is the **up** or **down** movement

↕ranslation

An easy way to remember this.

$\begin{pmatrix} a \\ b \end{pmatrix}$

***a* is positive** means move **right** →
***a* is negative** means move **left** ←

***b* is positive** means move **up** ↑
***b* is negative** means move **down** ↓

Examples:

1 $\begin{pmatrix} 4 \\ 3 \end{pmatrix}$

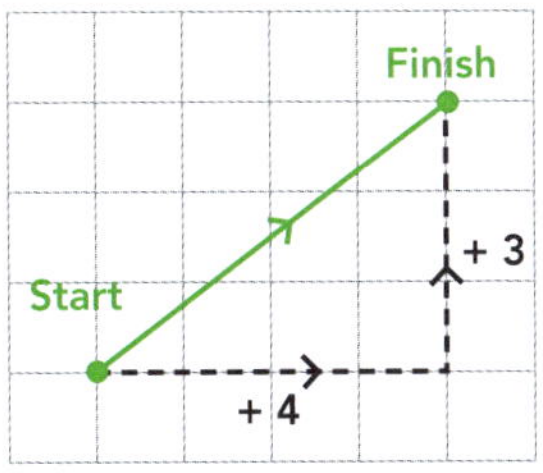

Start, + 4, + 3, Finish

or

Start, + 3, + 4, Finish

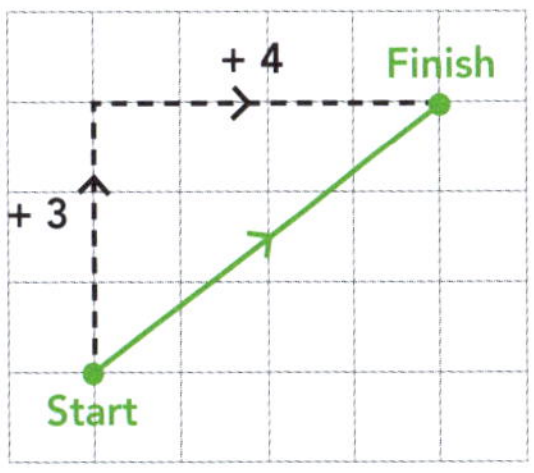

Notice that it doesn't matter whether you go across 4 squares first or up 3 squares first.

2 $\begin{pmatrix} -3 \\ -2 \end{pmatrix}$

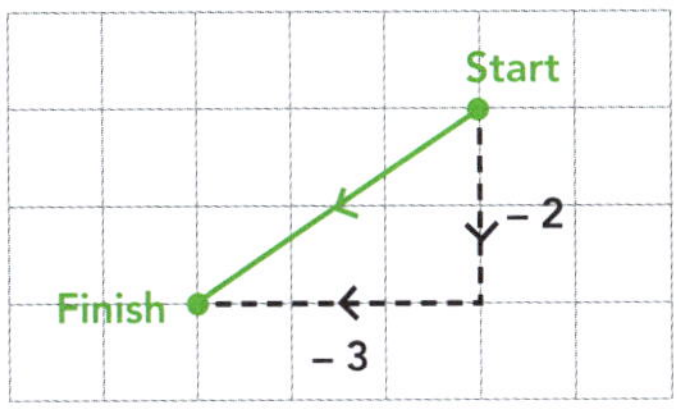

Start, − 2, − 3, Finish

or

Start, − 3, − 2, Finish

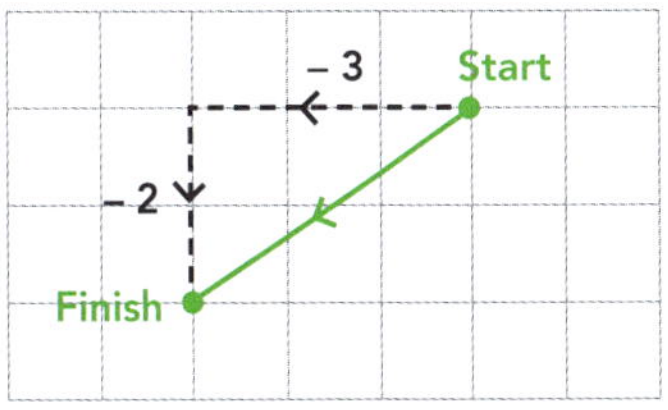

ISBN: 9780170447539 PHOTOCOPYING OF THIS PAGE IS RESTRICTED UNDER LAW.

Match these vectors to one of the descriptions below.

$\begin{pmatrix}-4\\2\end{pmatrix}$	$\begin{pmatrix}3\\1\end{pmatrix}$	$\begin{pmatrix}-2\\5\end{pmatrix}$	$\begin{pmatrix}4\\-2\end{pmatrix}$	$\begin{pmatrix}-1\\-5\end{pmatrix}$	$\begin{pmatrix}1\\-5\end{pmatrix}$	$\begin{pmatrix}-3\\1\end{pmatrix}$	$\begin{pmatrix}2\\5\end{pmatrix}$

1 Right two and up five $\begin{pmatrix} \\ \end{pmatrix}$

2 Right three and up one $\begin{pmatrix} \\ \end{pmatrix}$

3 Left four and up two $\begin{pmatrix} \\ \end{pmatrix}$

4 Left one and down five $\begin{pmatrix} \\ \end{pmatrix}$

5 Right four and down two $\begin{pmatrix} \\ \end{pmatrix}$

6 Left two and up five $\begin{pmatrix} \\ \end{pmatrix}$

7 Left three and up one $\begin{pmatrix} \\ \end{pmatrix}$

8 Right one and down five $\begin{pmatrix} \\ \end{pmatrix}$

Describe in words what these vectors mean.

9

$\begin{pmatrix}2\\3\end{pmatrix}$ __________ two and

__________ three

10

$\begin{pmatrix}4\\-1\end{pmatrix}$ __________ four and

__________ one

11

$\begin{pmatrix}-3\\5\end{pmatrix}$ __________ three and

__________ five

12

$\begin{pmatrix}-1\\-6\end{pmatrix}$ __________ one and

__________ six

13

$\begin{pmatrix}-2\\4\end{pmatrix}$ ______________________________

____

14

$\begin{pmatrix}6\\-3\end{pmatrix}$ ______________________________

____

PHOTOCOPYING OF THIS PAGE IS RESTRICTED UNDER LAW. ISBN: 9780170447539

15 Match these vectors to those on the grid.

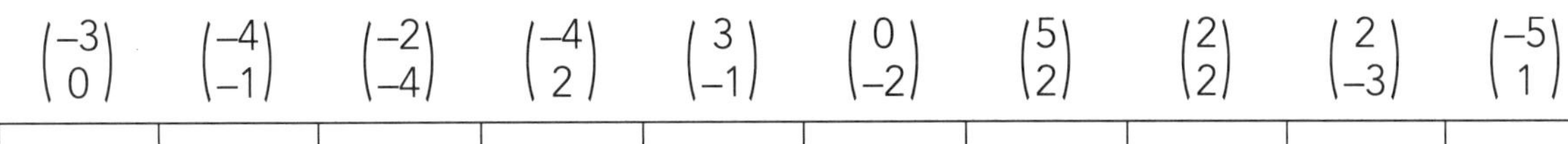

$\begin{pmatrix}-3\\0\end{pmatrix}$	$\begin{pmatrix}-4\\-1\end{pmatrix}$	$\begin{pmatrix}-2\\-4\end{pmatrix}$	$\begin{pmatrix}-4\\2\end{pmatrix}$	$\begin{pmatrix}3\\-1\end{pmatrix}$	$\begin{pmatrix}0\\-2\end{pmatrix}$	$\begin{pmatrix}5\\2\end{pmatrix}$	$\begin{pmatrix}2\\2\end{pmatrix}$	$\begin{pmatrix}2\\-3\end{pmatrix}$	$\begin{pmatrix}-5\\1\end{pmatrix}$

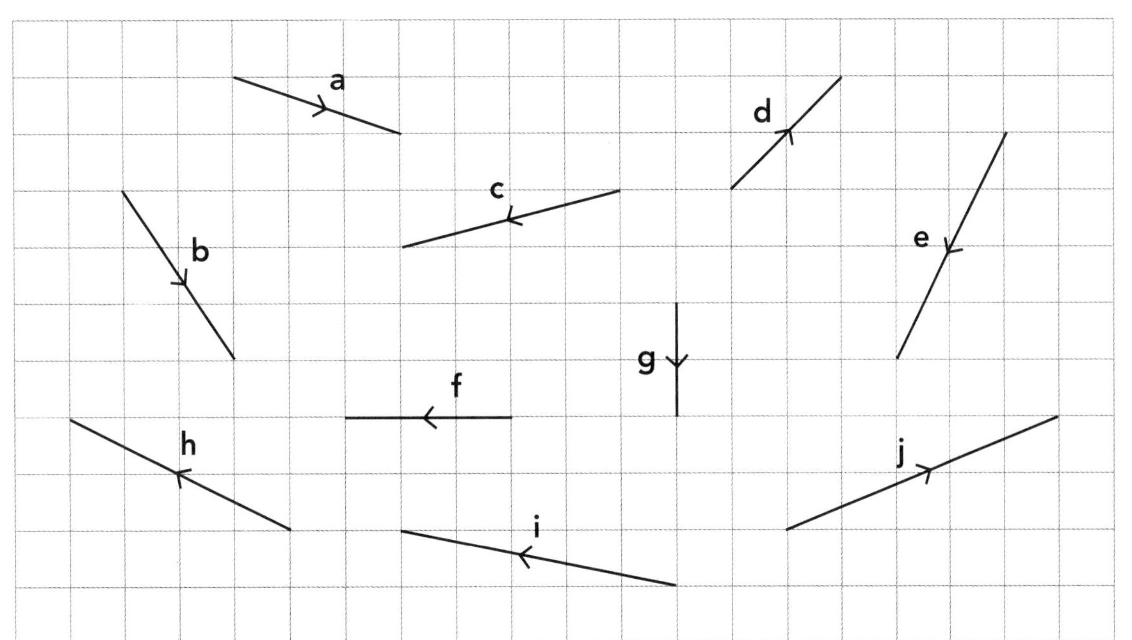

16 Write vectors for each of the those on the grid.

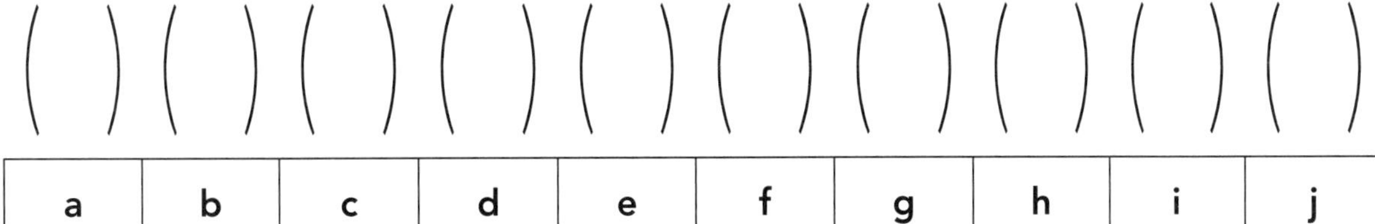

$\begin{pmatrix}\ \\ \ \end{pmatrix}$	$\begin{pmatrix}\ \\ \ \end{pmatrix}$	$\begin{pmatrix}\ \\ \ \end{pmatrix}$	$\begin{pmatrix}\ \\ \ \end{pmatrix}$	$\begin{pmatrix}\ \\ \ \end{pmatrix}$	$\begin{pmatrix}\ \\ \ \end{pmatrix}$	$\begin{pmatrix}\ \\ \ \end{pmatrix}$	$\begin{pmatrix}\ \\ \ \end{pmatrix}$	$\begin{pmatrix}\ \\ \ \end{pmatrix}$	$\begin{pmatrix}\ \\ \ \end{pmatrix}$
a	b	c	d	e	f	g	h	i	j

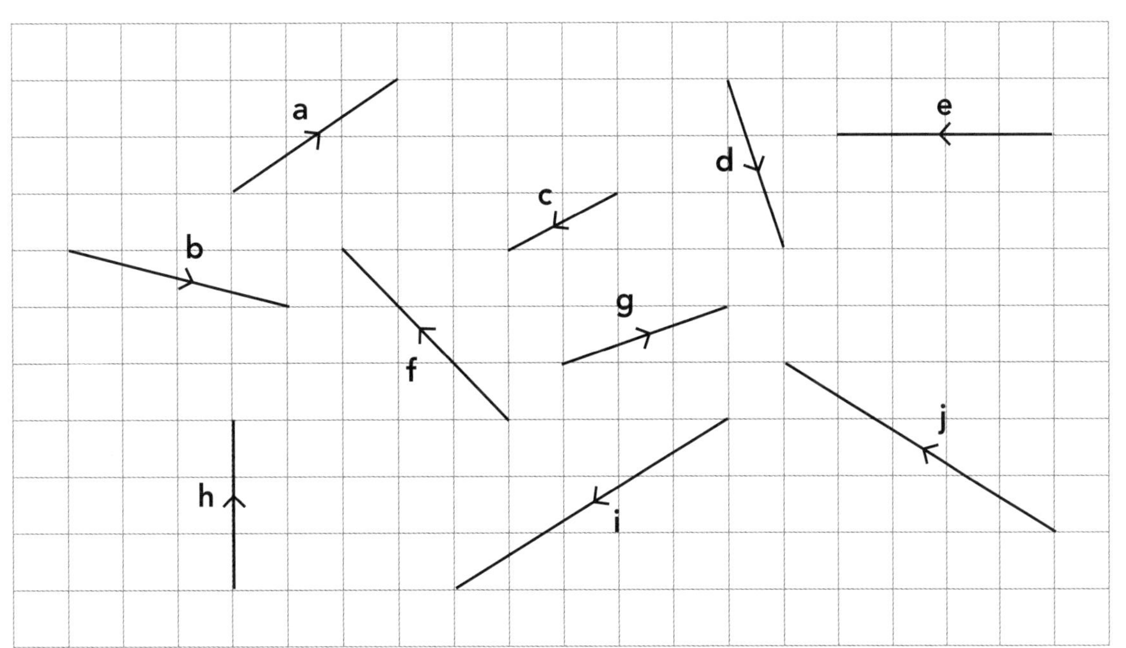

ISBN: 9780170447539 PHOTOCOPYING OF THIS PAGE IS RESTRICTED UNDER LAW.

Write the vector for the translation of each figure. The green shape is the original.

17

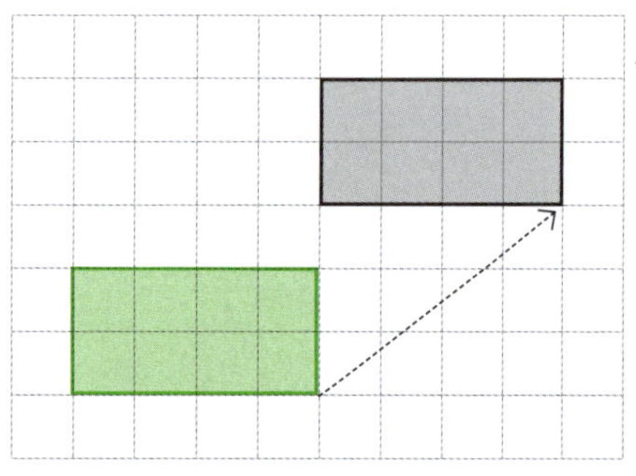

( )

18

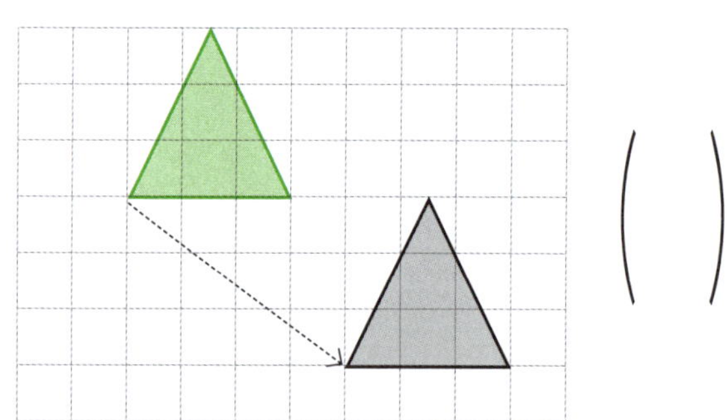

( )

19

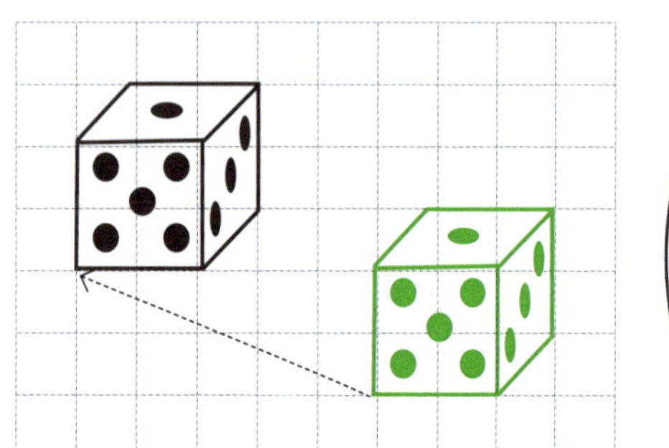

( )

20

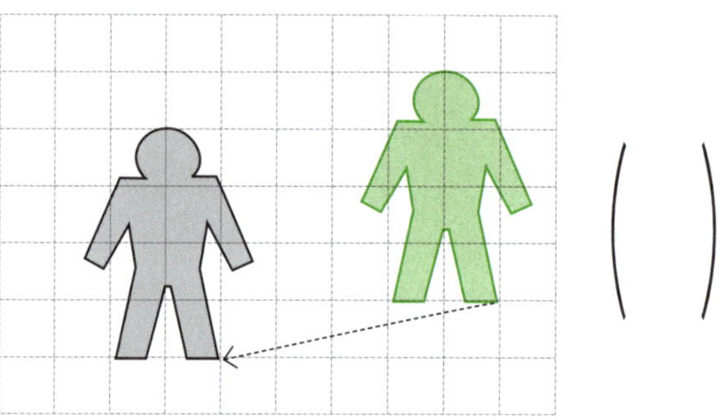

( )

21

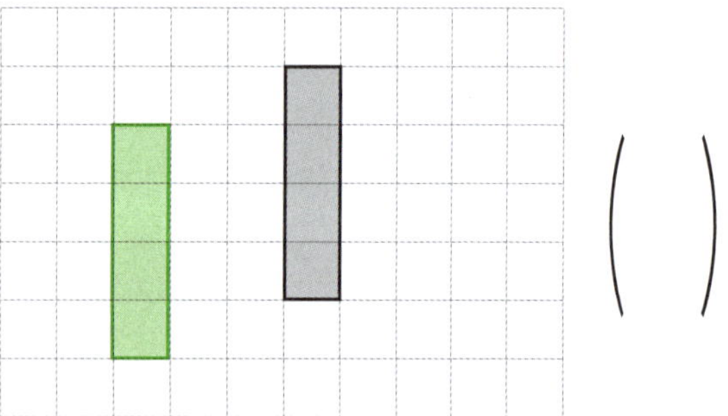

( )

22

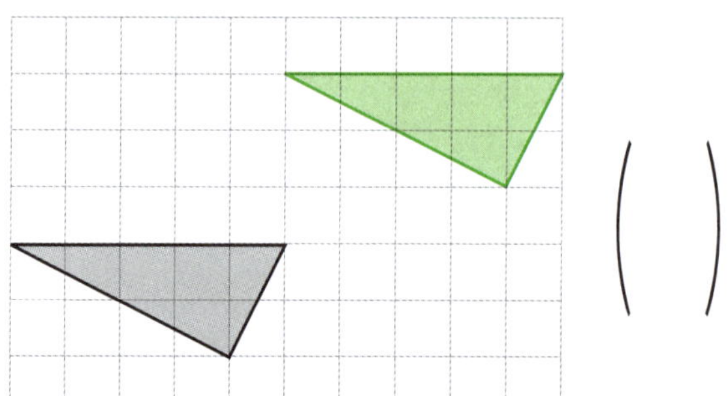

( )

23

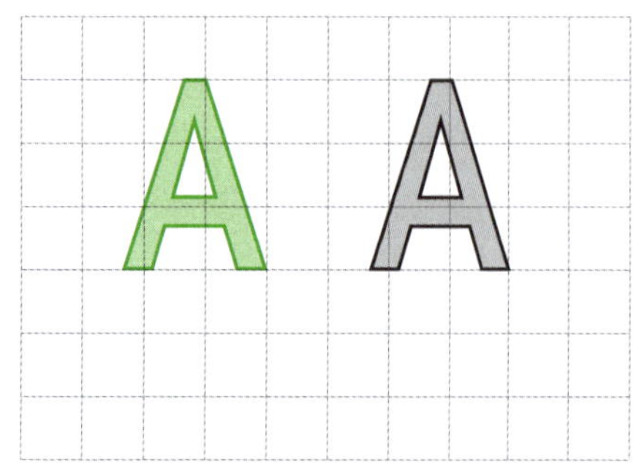

( )

24

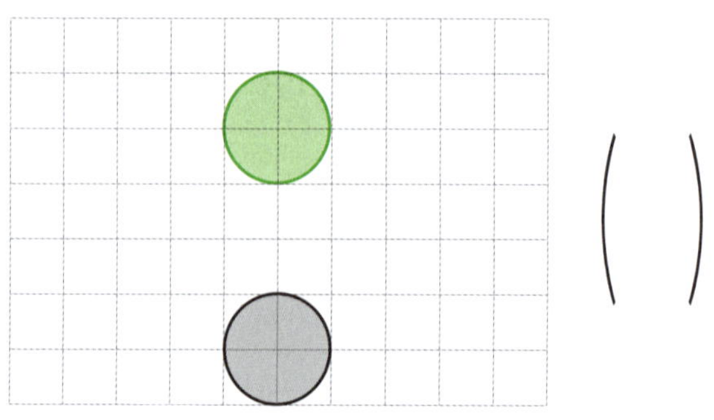

( )

PHOTOCOPYING OF THIS PAGE IS RESTRICTED UNDER LAW. ISBN: 9780170447539

Reflection

- The figure is **reflected in a mirror** line.

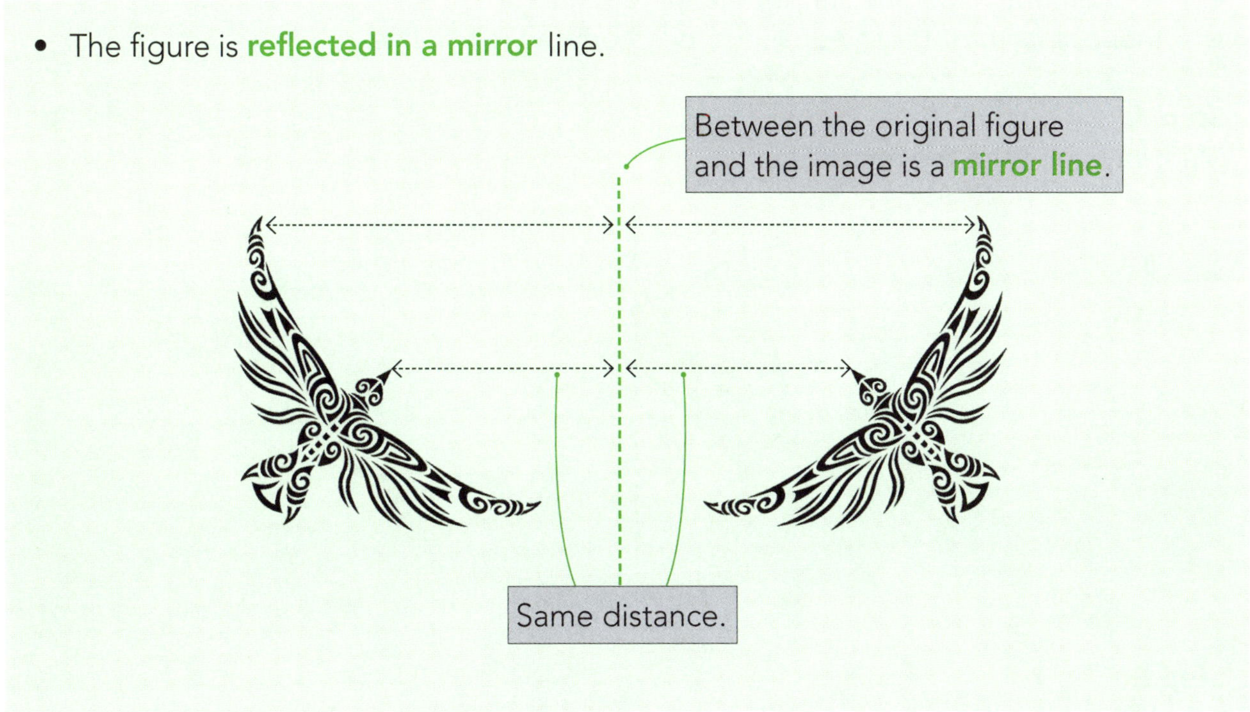

Draw mirror lines for the following reflections.

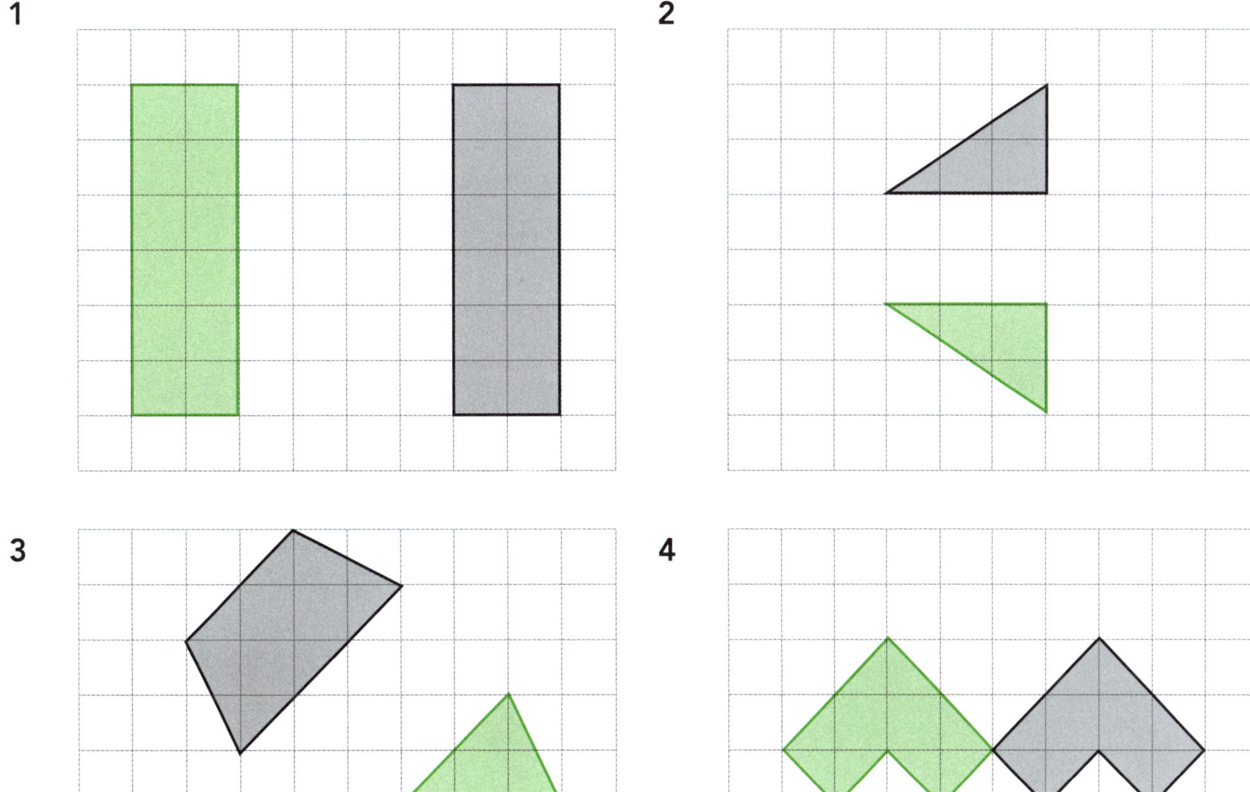

ISBN: 9780170447539 PHOTOCOPYING OF THIS PAGE IS RESTRICTED UNDER LAW.

Drawing reflections

- Points on the mirror line stay on the mirror line.
- Other points must be an equal distance from the mirror line.

Step 1
Mark any points on the mirror line.

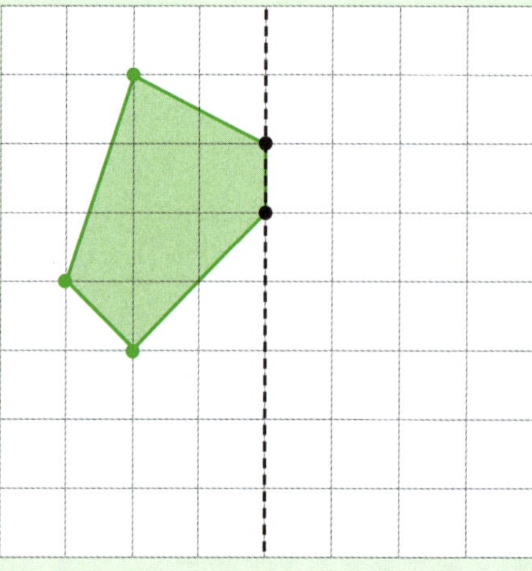

Step 2
Using lines at right angles to the mirror line, mark points that are the same distance from it, but on the opposite side.

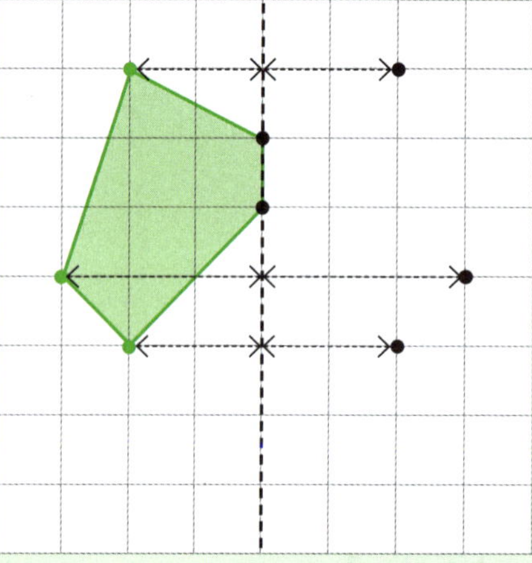

Step 3
Connect the points.

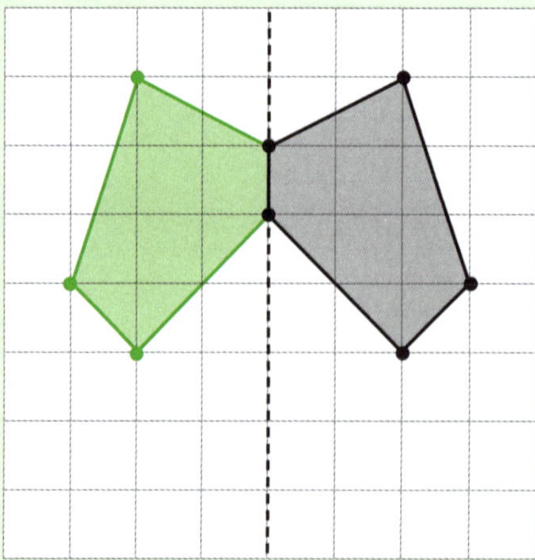

PHOTOCOPYING OF THIS PAGE IS RESTRICTED UNDER LAW.
ISBN: 9780170447539

Draw reflections of the following figures.

1

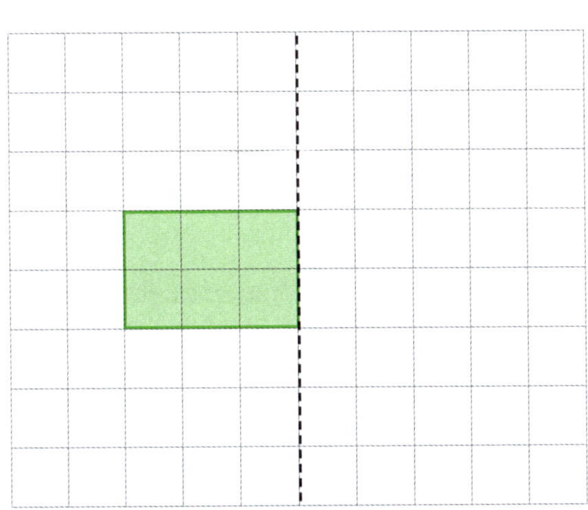

2

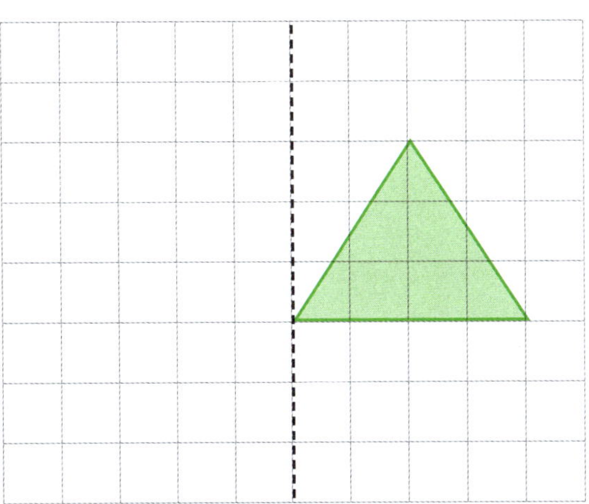

3

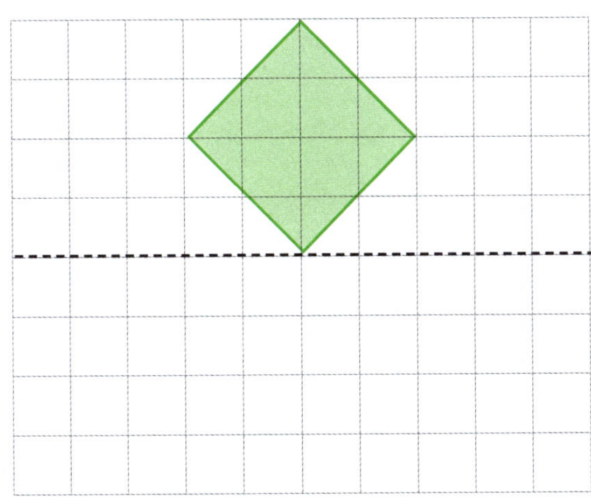

4

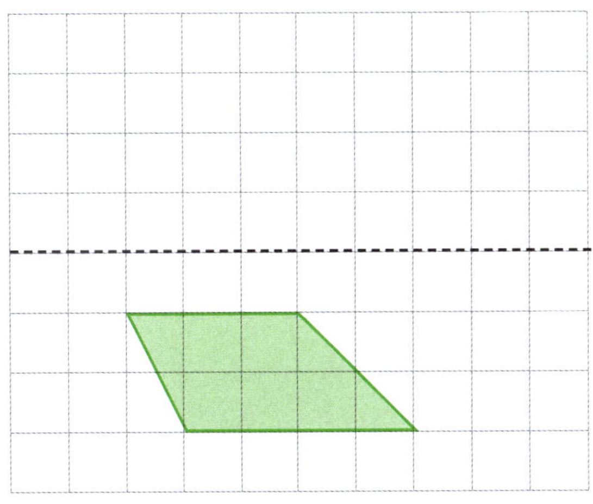

5

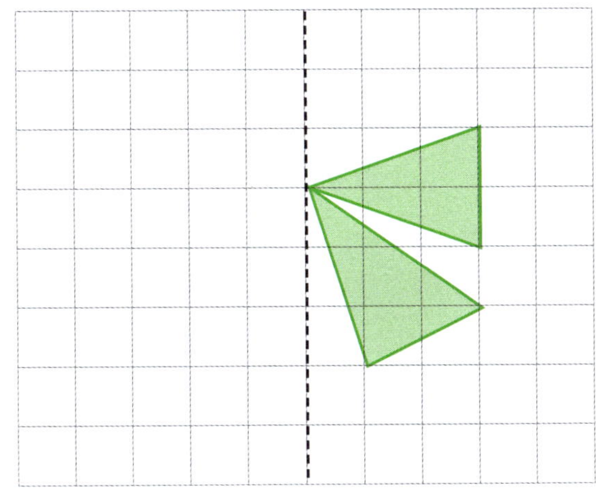

6 The first point has been found for you.

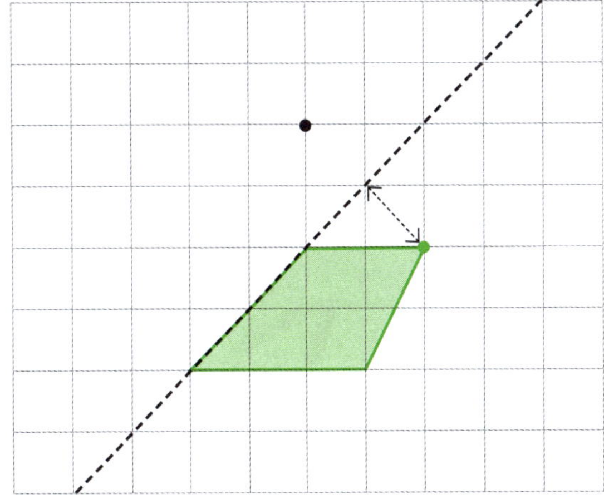

ISBN: 9780170447539 PHOTOCOPYING OF THIS PAGE IS RESTRICTED UNDER LAW.

Line symmetry

- Some figures form reflections of themselves in a mirror line.
- They are said to have **line symmetry**.
- **Each mirror line** that can be drawn through a figure is known as **a line of symmetry**.
- The **order** of line symmetry is the **number of lines of symmetry** in a figure.

This figure has **one** line of symmetry.

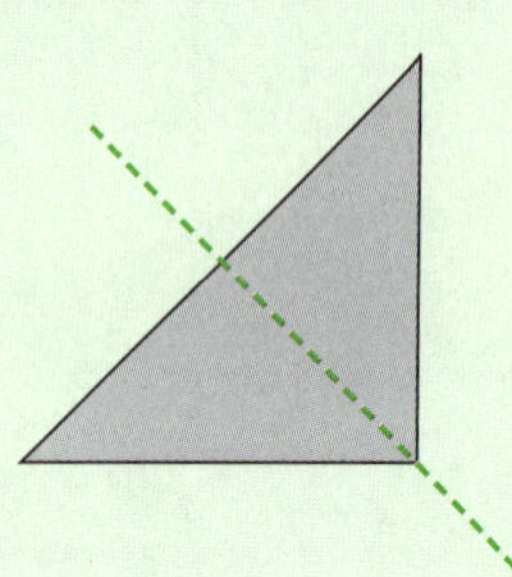

Order of line symmetry = 1

This figure has **four** lines of symmetry.

Order of line symmetry = 4

Draw all the lines of symmetry on these figures and write the order of line symmetry for each.

1

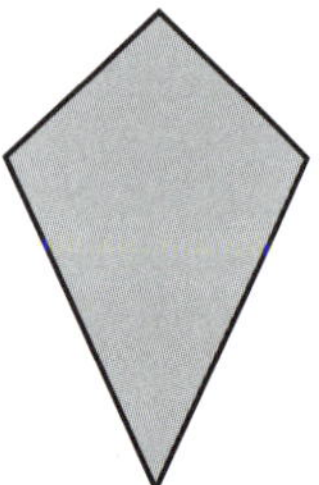

Order of line symmetry = ________

2

Order of line symmetry = ________

3

Order of line symmetry = ________

4

Order of line symmetry = ________

PHOTOCOPYING OF THIS PAGE IS RESTRICTED UNDER LAW.
ISBN: 9780170447539

5

Order of line symmetry = ________

6

Order of line symmetry = ________

7

Order of line symmetry = ________

8

Order of line symmetry = ________

9

Order of line symmetry = ________

10

Order of line symmetry = ________

11

Order of line symmetry = ________

12

Order of line symmetry = ________

ISBN: 9780170447539 PHOTOCOPYING OF THIS PAGE IS RESTRICTED UNDER LAW.

Rotation

- The figure **rotates around a point**.
- The **point** is known as the **centre of rotation**.
- Rotations, unless specified otherwise, are always measured in a **clockwise direction**.

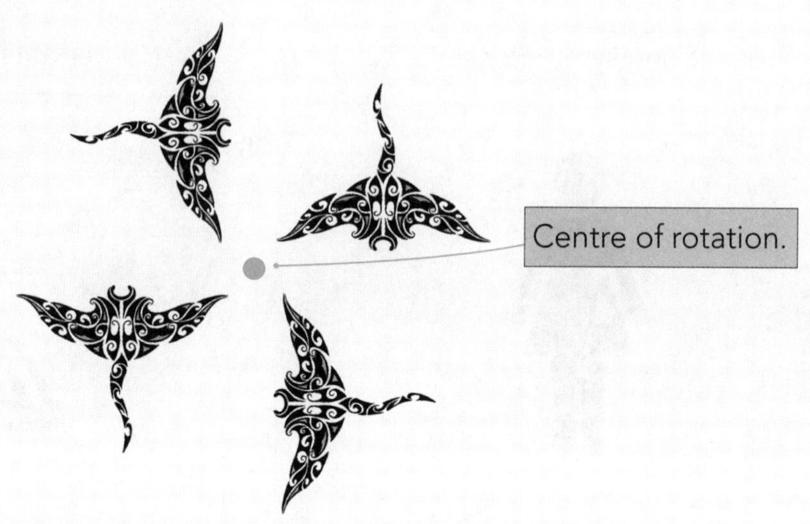

We will use only these angles:

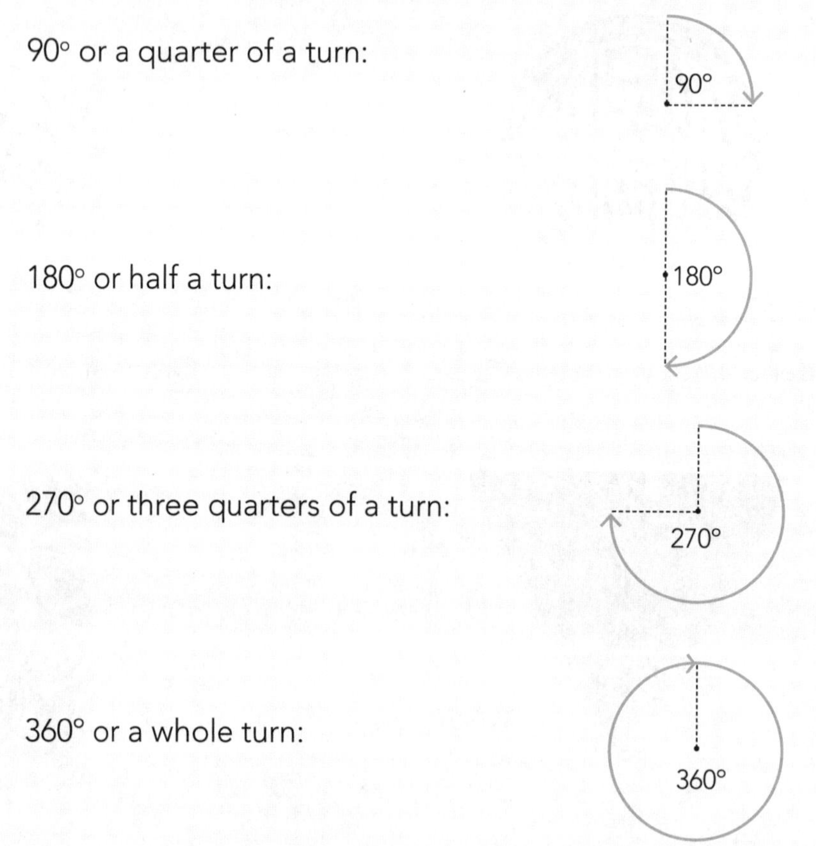

PHOTOCOPYING OF THIS PAGE IS RESTRICTED UNDER LAW. ISBN: 9780170447539

Using angles of rotation

Examples: Write the angle of rotation for each of the following.

Remember: 1 The **green** figure is the **original**, so **start** your angle there.
2 The **grey** figure is the **image**.
3 Rotations are in a **clockwise** direction.

Remember: Unless you are told otherwise, angles are always measured in a **clockwise** direction.

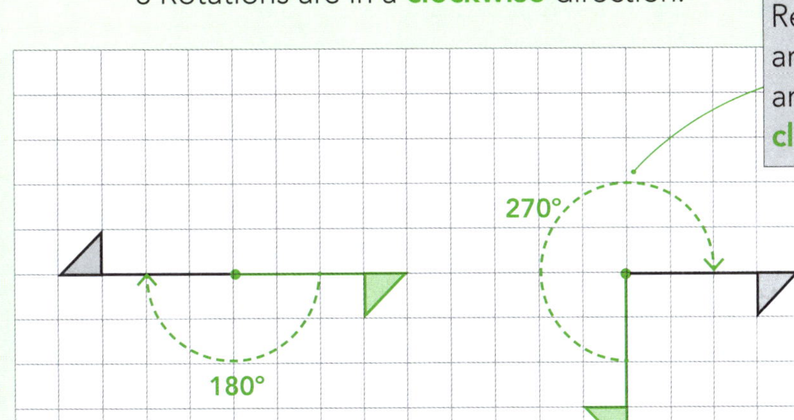

Write the angle of rotation for each of the following.

1

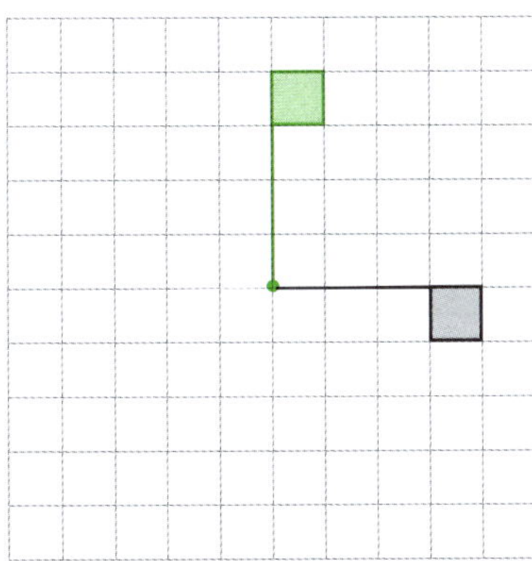

Angle = ________°

2

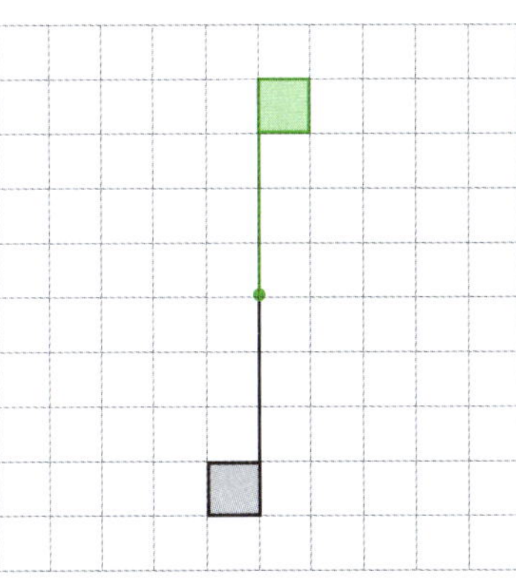

Angle = ________°

3

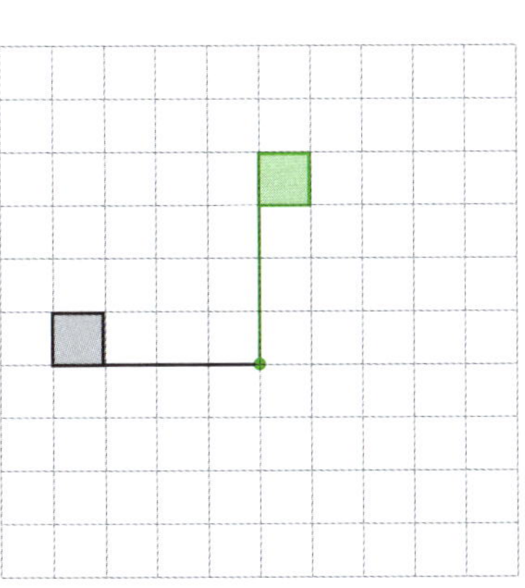

Angle = ________°

4

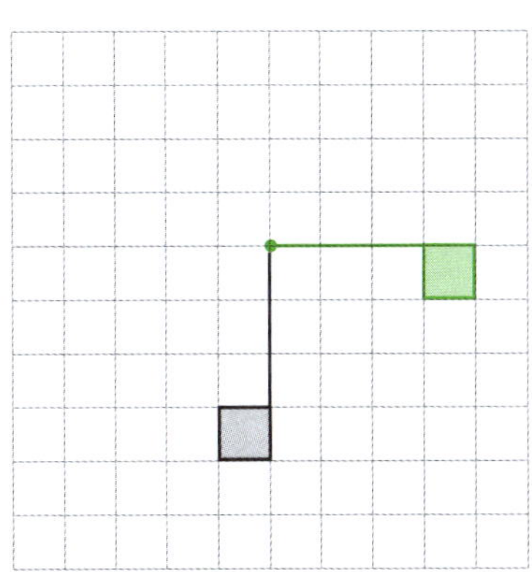

Angle = ________°

ISBN: 9780170447539
PHOTOCOPYING OF THIS PAGE IS RESTRICTED UNDER LAW.

Drawing rotations

- Remember that unless you are told otherwise, rotations are **always clockwise**.
- It is really helpful to have a pin and tracing paper for this.

Rotate this figure 90° clockwise around the point.

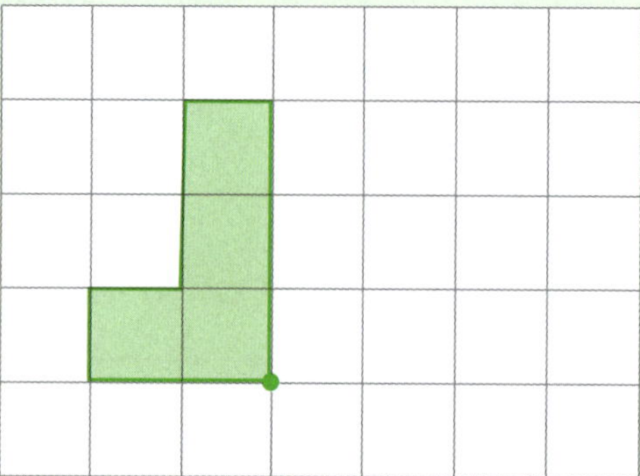

Step 1
Find a line on the shape which passes through the centre of rotation.

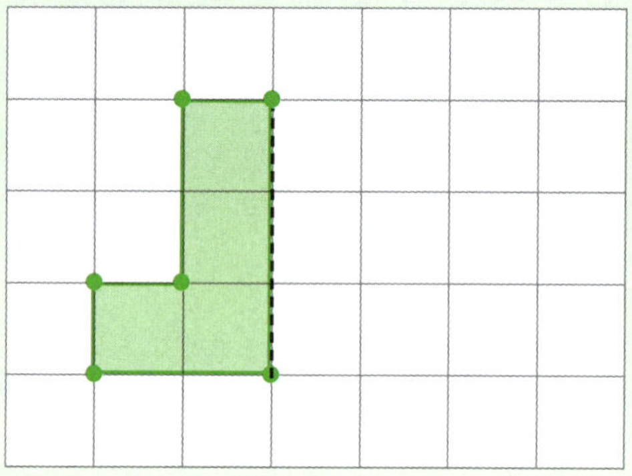

Step 2
Rotate the line by the required amount.

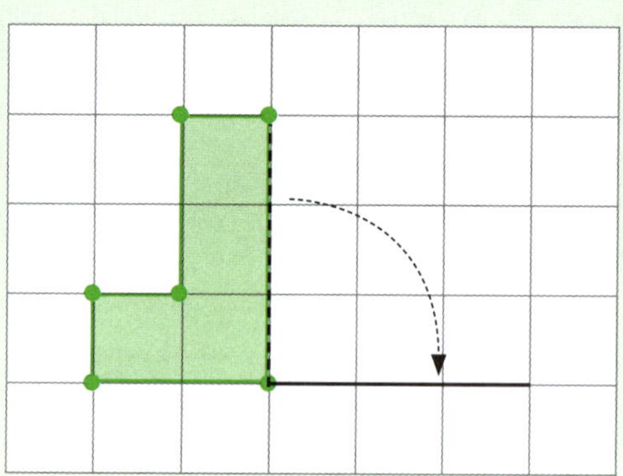

Step 3
Plot the remaining points in relation to this line.

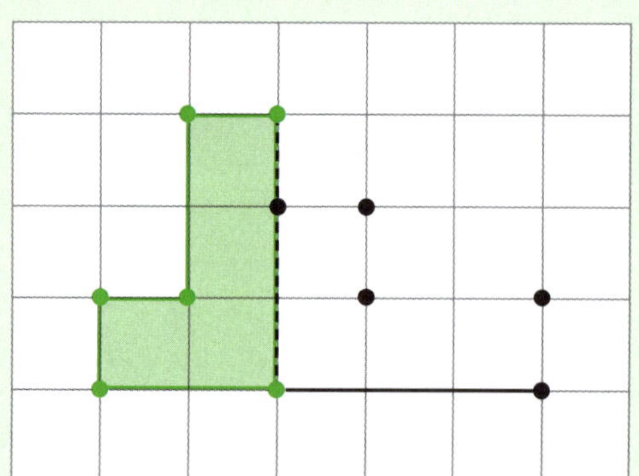

Step 4
Join the points.

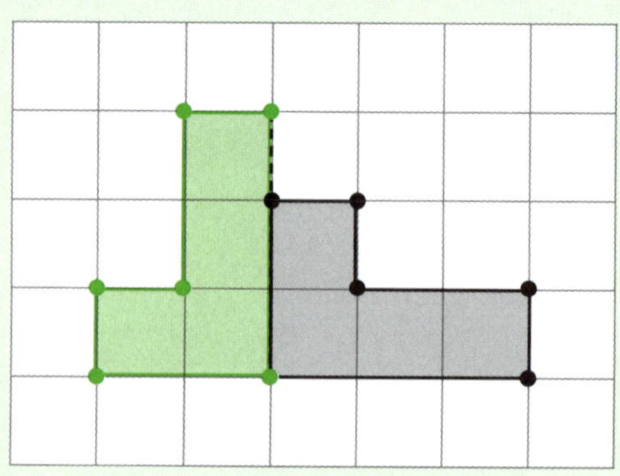

PHOTOCOPYING OF THIS PAGE IS RESTRICTED UNDER LAW. ISBN: 9780170447539

Draw the images of these figures after they have been rotated.

1 Rotate this figure 90° clockwise about the point.

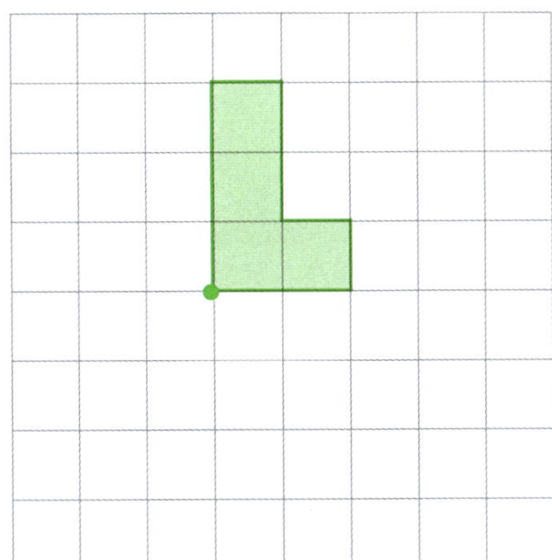

2 Rotate this figure 180° clockwise about the point.

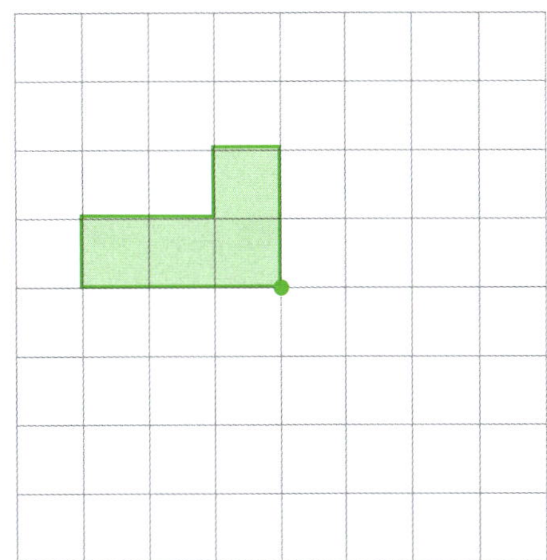

3 Rotate this figure 270° clockwise about the point.

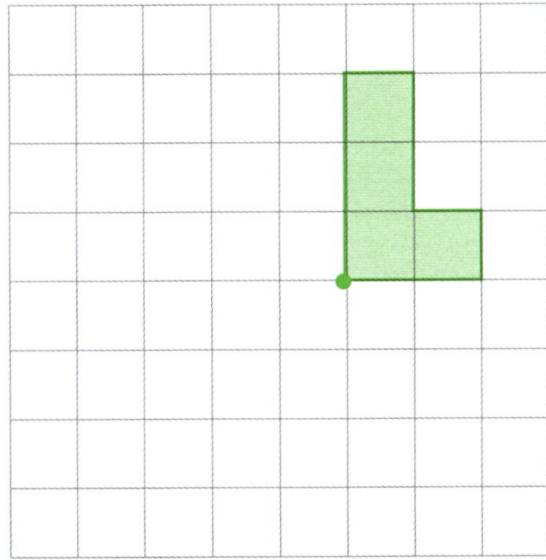

4 Rotate this figure 90° clockwise about the point.

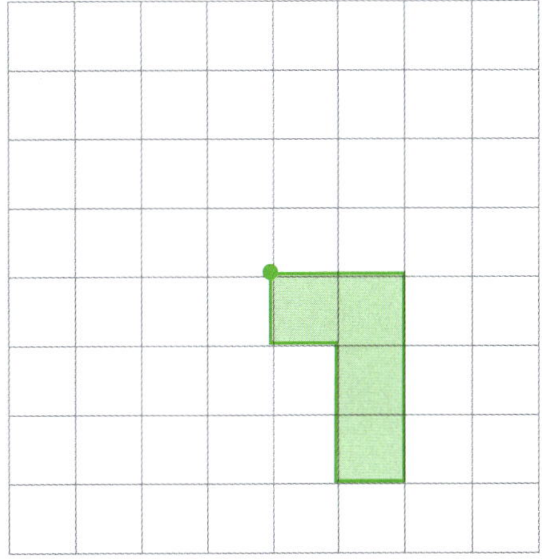

5 Rotate this figure 270° clockwise about the point.

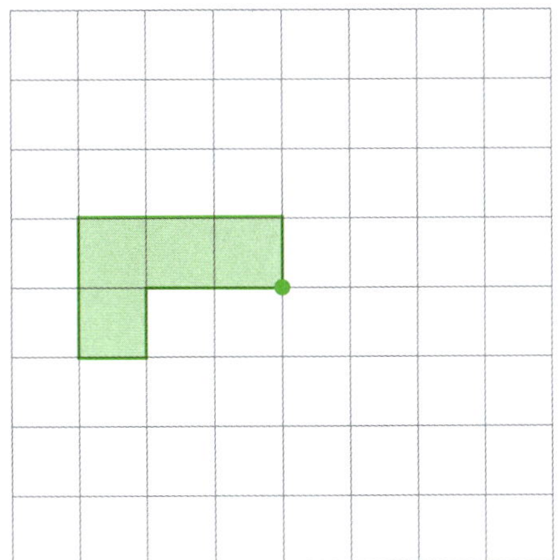

6 Rotate this figure 270° anticlockwise about the point.

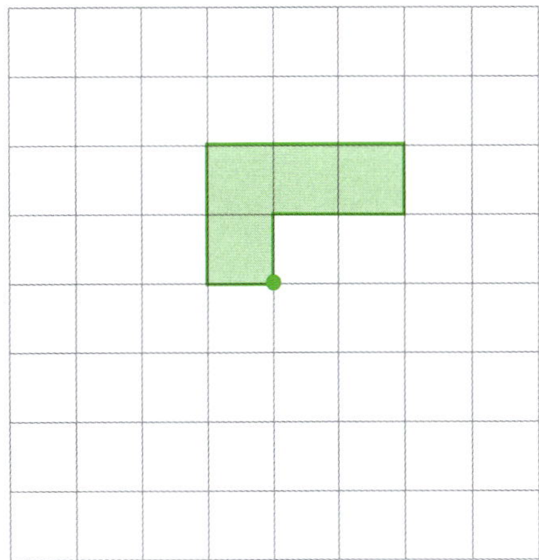

ISBN: 9780170447539 PHOTOCOPYING OF THIS PAGE IS RESTRICTED UNDER LAW.

Rotational symmetry

- All figures can be rotated so they map onto themselves.
- All figures have at least one order of **rotational symmetry**; some have more than one.
- The **order of rotational symmetry** is the **number of times a figure looks the same** (maps onto itself) during a full rotation (360°).

This figure looks the same **once** during a full rotation.
This means that its order of rotational symmetry is **one**.

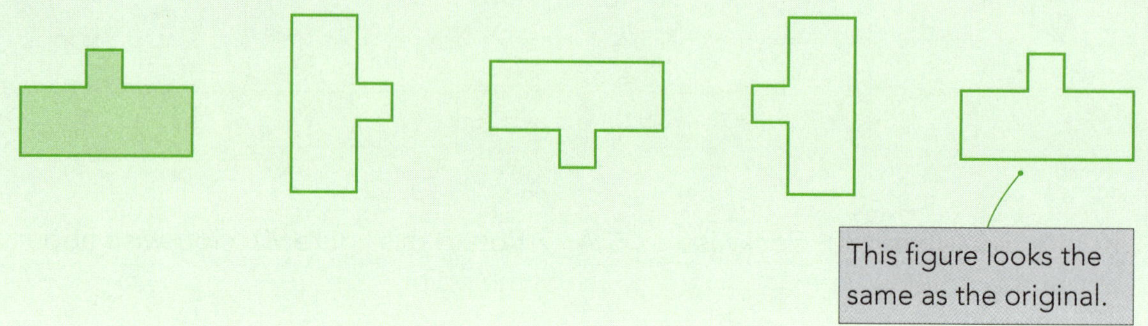

This figure looks the same **twice** during a full rotation.
This means that its order of rotational symmetry is **two**.

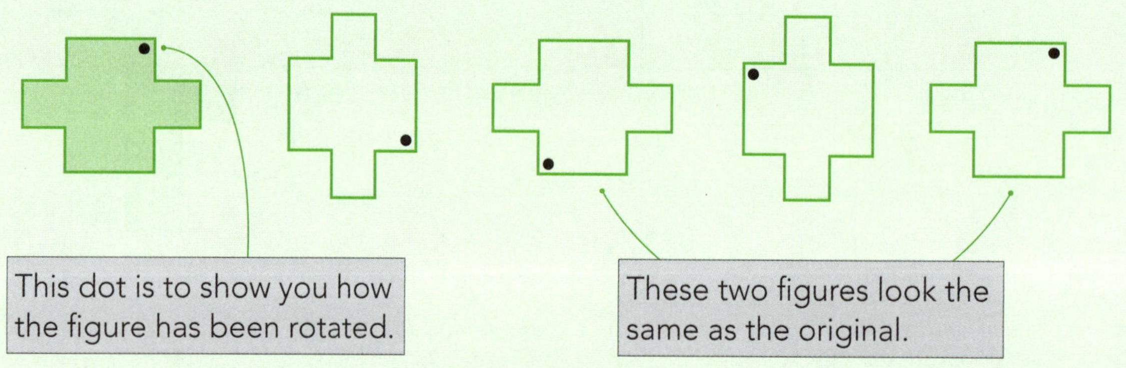

State the order of rotational symmetry for these images.

1

Order of rotational symmetry = ________

2

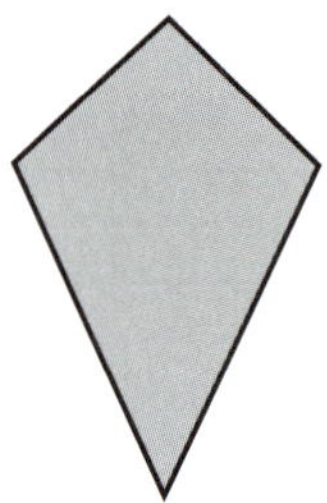

Order of rotational symmetry = ________

PHOTOCOPYING OF THIS PAGE IS RESTRICTED UNDER LAW.
ISBN: 9780170447539

3

Order of rotational symmetry = ________

4

Order of rotational symmetry = ________

5

Order of rotational symmetry = ________

6

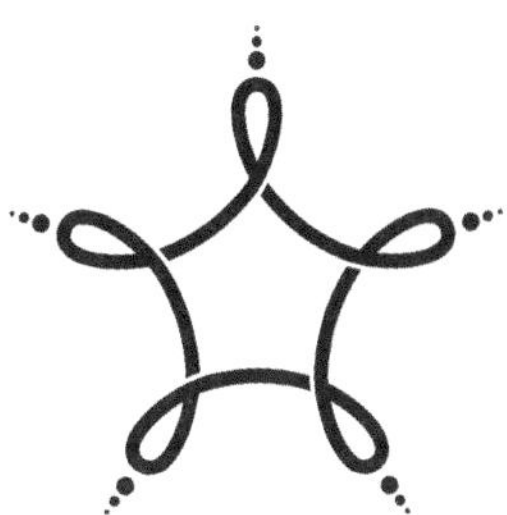

Order of rotational symmetry = ________

7

Order of rotational symmetry = ________

8

Order of rotational symmetry = ________

9

Order of rotational symmetry = ________

10

Order of rotational symmetry = ________

ISBN: 9780170447539 PHOTOCOPYING OF THIS PAGE IS RESTRICTED UNDER LAW.

Enlargement

- The figure **gets bigger or smaller**.
- The **scale factor** tells us how much larger or smaller the lines in the figure become.

$$\text{scale factor} = \frac{\text{length of image}}{\text{length of original figure}}$$

Examples:

The lines in the image are **three times** as long as those in the original. The image has a scale factor of **3**.

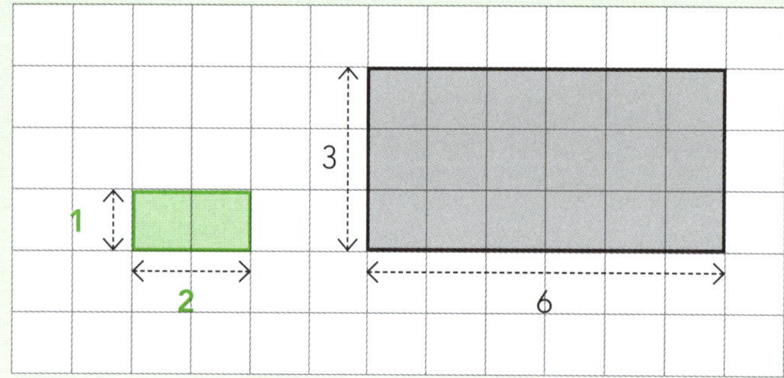

$$\text{scale factor} = \frac{3}{1} = \frac{6}{2} = 3$$

The lines in the image are **half** as long as those in the original. The image has a scale factor of **half** or **0.5**.

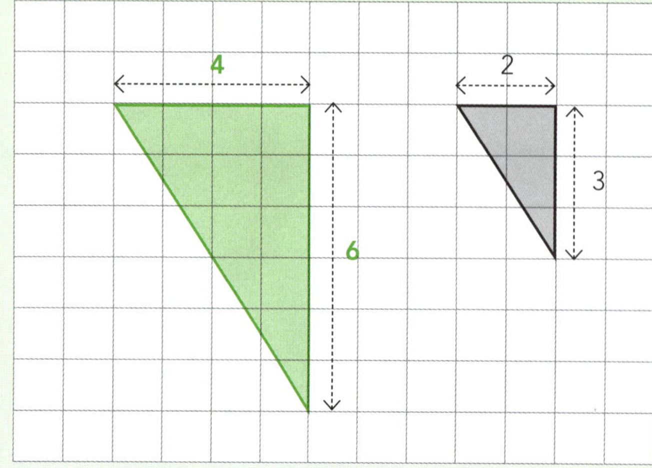

$$\text{scale factor} = \frac{2}{4} = \frac{3}{6} = \frac{1}{2}$$

PHOTOCOPYING OF THIS PAGE IS RESTRICTED UNDER LAW.
ISBN: 9780170447539

Write the scale factor for these enlargements.

1

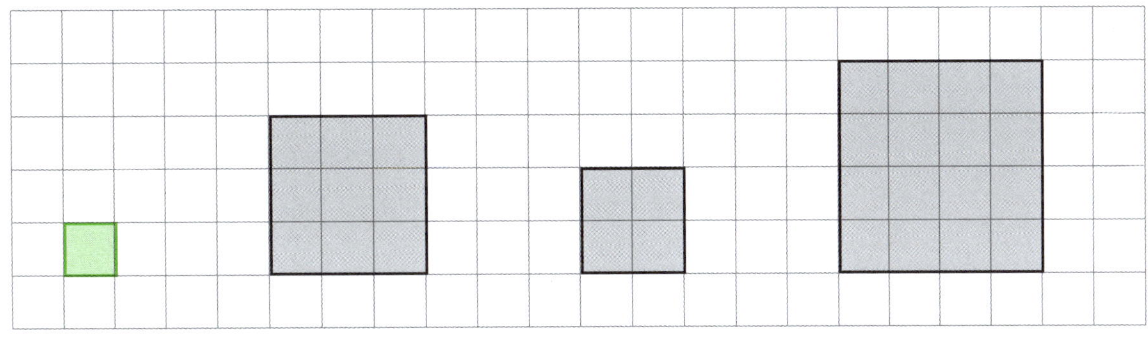

scale factor = ______

scale factor = ______

scale factor = ______

2

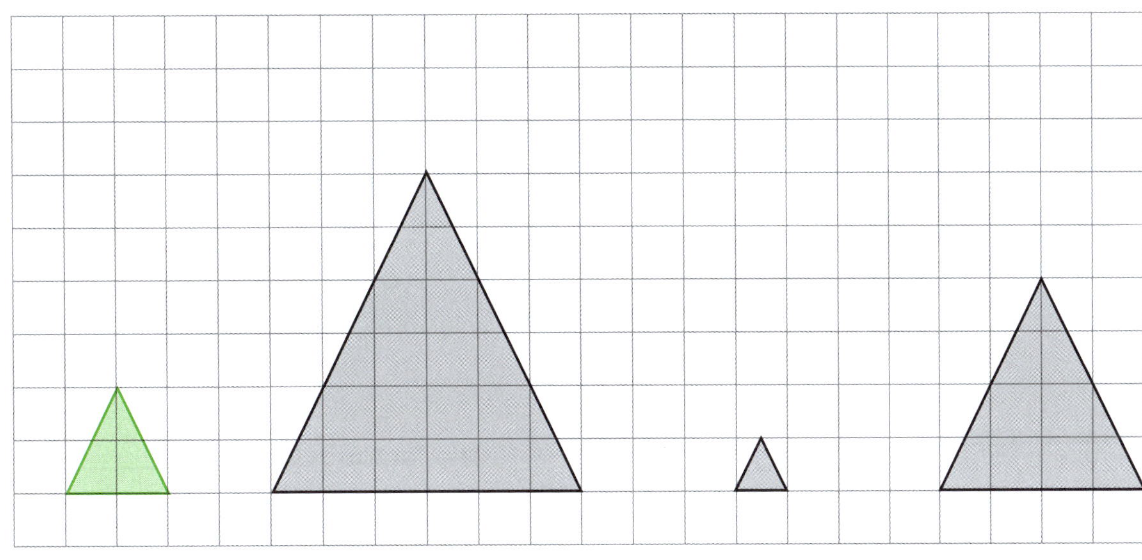

scale factor = ______

scale factor = ______

scale factor = ______

3

scale factor = ______

scale factor = ______

scale factor = ______

scale factor = ______

ISBN: 9780170447539 PHOTOCOPYING OF THIS PAGE IS RESTRICTED UNDER LAW.

Draw the image of these originals with the given scale factor.

4 Scale factor of 2

5 Scale factor of 3

6 Scale factor of ½

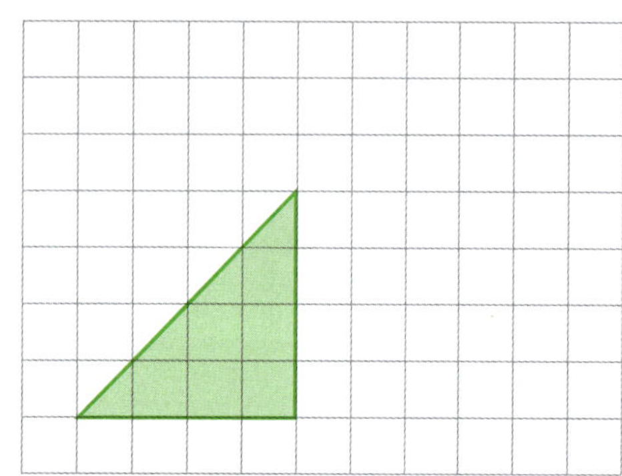

7 Scale factor of 2

8 Scale factor of 4

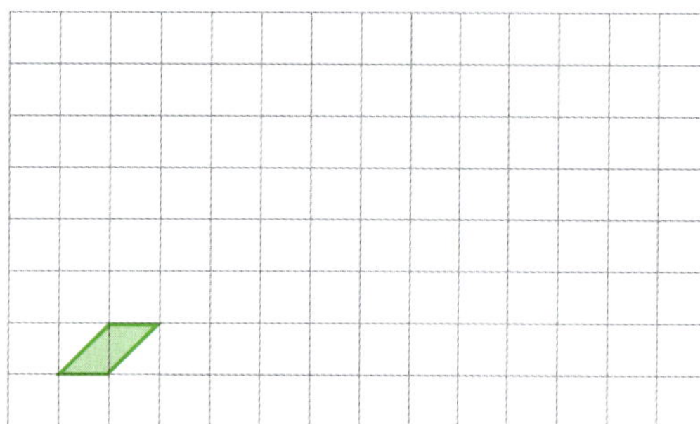

9 Scale factor of 0.5

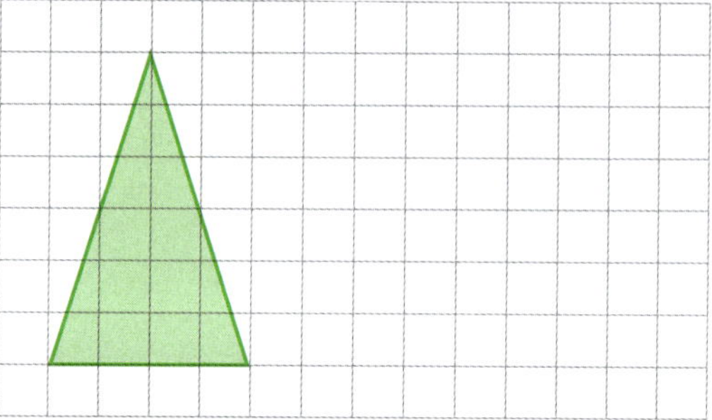

10 Scale factor of 2

PHOTOCOPYING OF THIS PAGE IS RESTRICTED UNDER LAW. ISBN: 9780170447539

Revision 1

1 Highlight the word(s) that can be used to describe this shape.

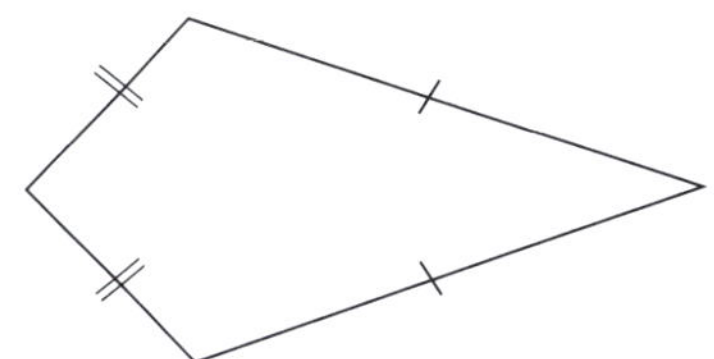

polygon regular symmetrical quadrilateral

2 Select the *best* term to describe each of the following figures.

Irregular quadrilateral	Regular hexagon	Triangle	Regular triangle
Isosceles triangle	Regular quadrilateral	Hexagon	Parallelogram

a

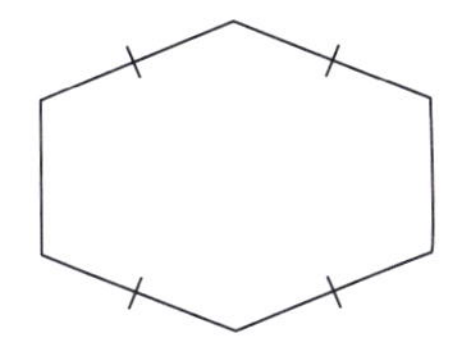

b

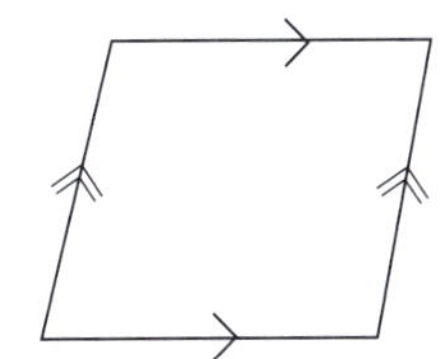

c

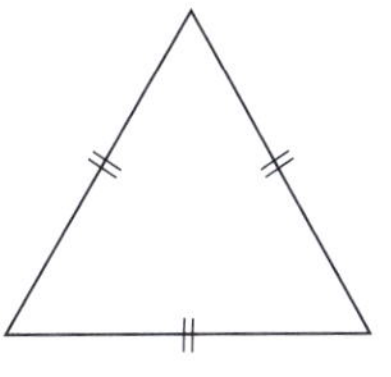

3 **a** Name the marked angle. ∠ ________

b What type of angle is this? ________

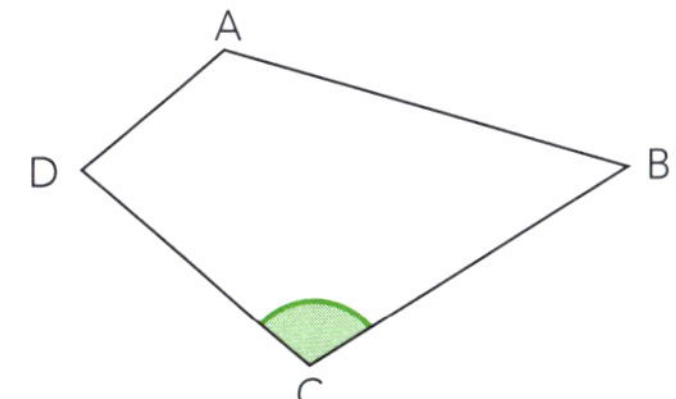

4 Write down the size of this angle.

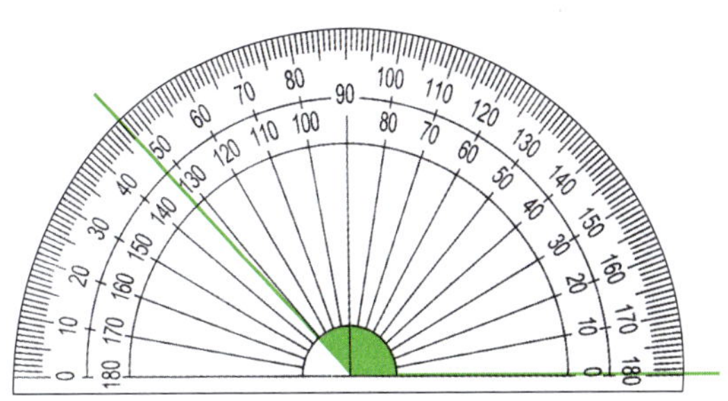

5 Calculate the size of the marked angles.

a

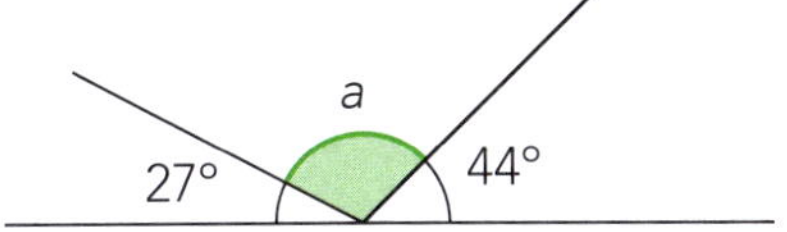

b

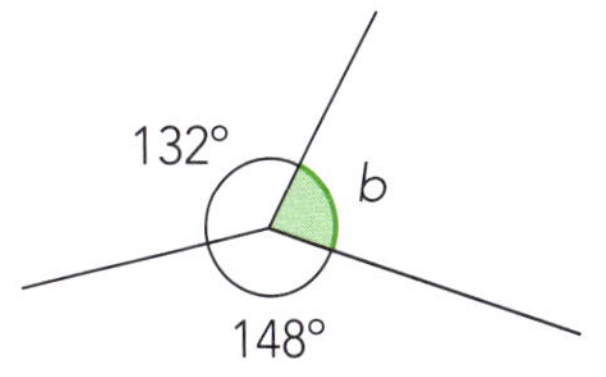

ISBN: 9780170447539 PHOTOCOPYING OF THIS PAGE IS RESTRICTED UNDER LAW.

c

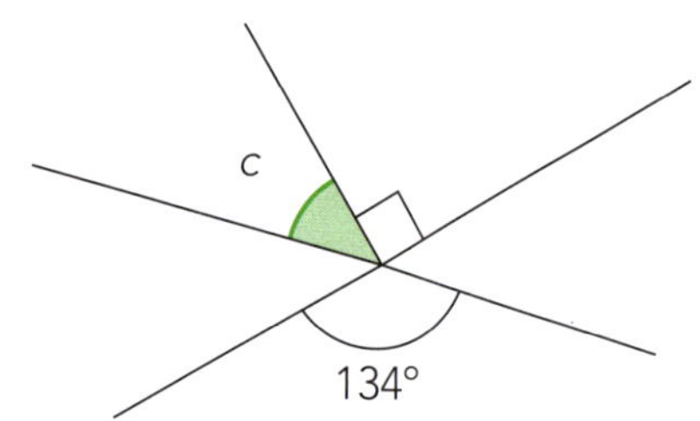

d

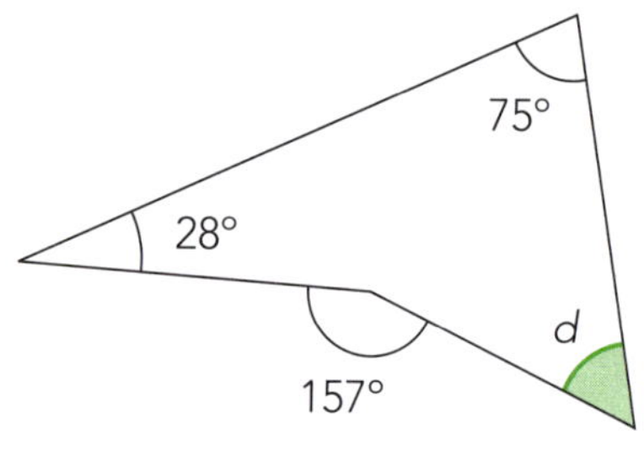

6 Write down the numbers of vertices, edges and faces this 3D shape has.

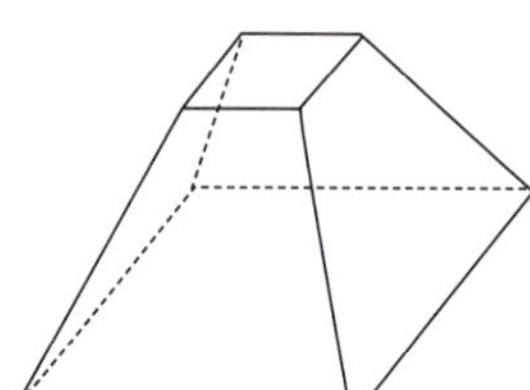

Vertices ________

Edges ________

Faces ________

This figure is/is not a prism.

7

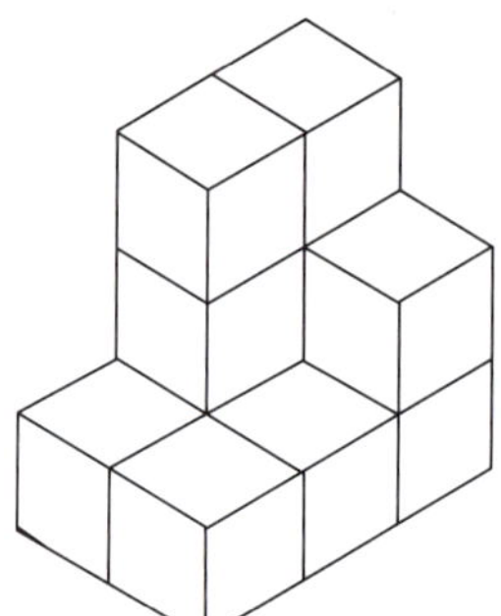

a Draw this shape on the isometric grid, but without showing the junctions between blocks.

b Write the number of blocks in each column.

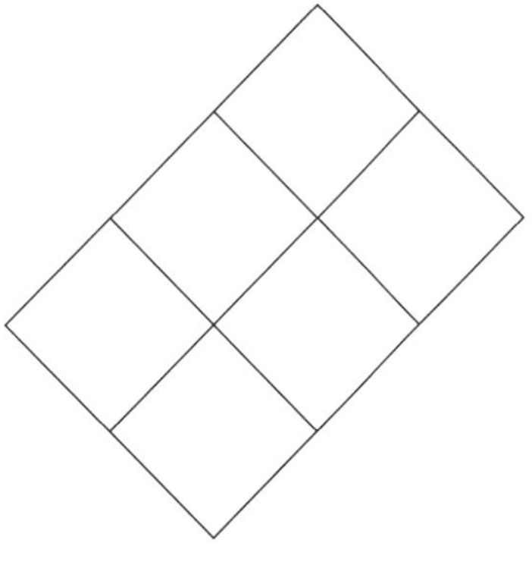

c Draw the top, left and front views of this shape.

Top Left Front

PHOTOCOPYING OF THIS PAGE IS RESTRICTED UNDER LAW. ISBN: 9780170447539

8 Use this map to answer the following questions. Scale: 1 cm = 2 km.

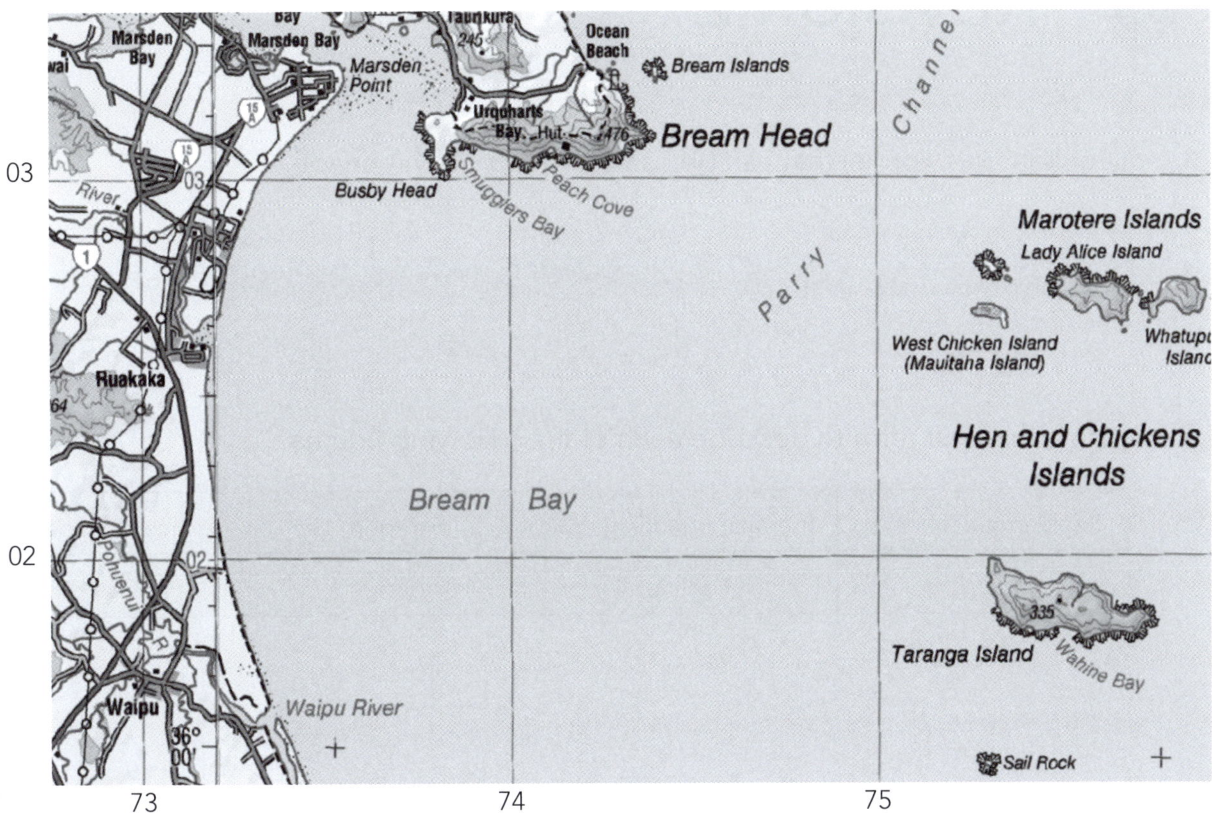

a Circle the direction and bearing for a line from the centre of Wahine Bay on Taranga Island to the Bream Islands.

SE SW NE NW

045° 225° 315° 135°

b What would you find at at 744032? ________________

c Write the grid reference for Busby Head. ________________

d Estimate the distance between Marsden Point and the northern tip of Taranga Island. ________________

9 Rotate the figure by 270° around the green dot, and then translate the resulting figure by the vector $\begin{pmatrix} 4 \\ -3 \end{pmatrix}$.

ISBN: 9780170447539 PHOTOCOPYING OF THIS PAGE IS RESTRICTED UNDER LAW.

Revision 2

1 Highlight the word(s) that can be used to describe this shape.

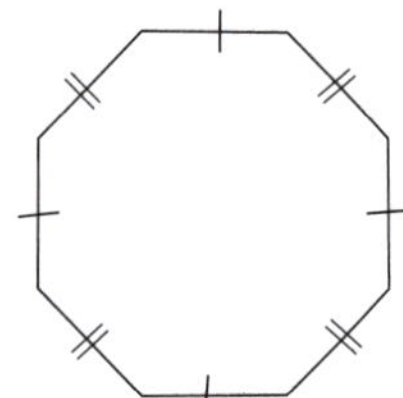

octagon   regular   symmetrical   parallelogram

2 Select the *best* term to describe each of the following figures.

Regular quadrilateral	Irregular quadrilateral	Polygon	Isosceles trapezium
Trapezium	Quadrilateral	Arrowhead	Parallelogram

a

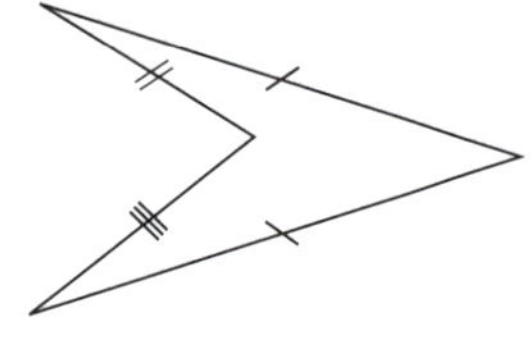

____

b

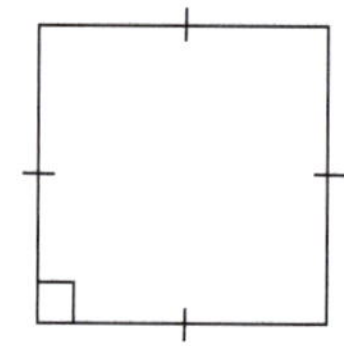

____

c

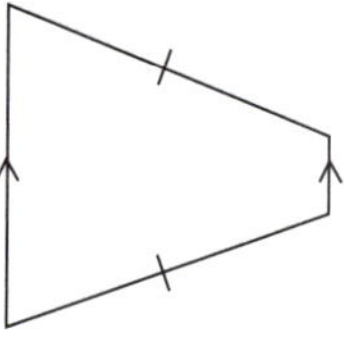

____

3 **a** Name the marked angle. ∠ ________

b What type of angle is this? ______________

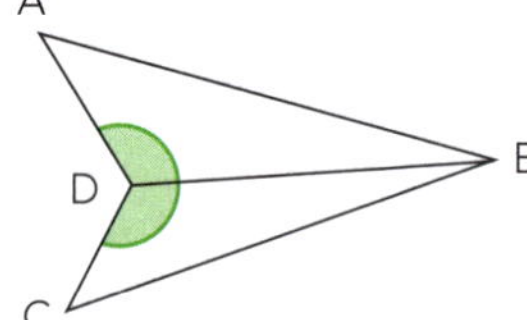

4 Write down the size of this angle.

____

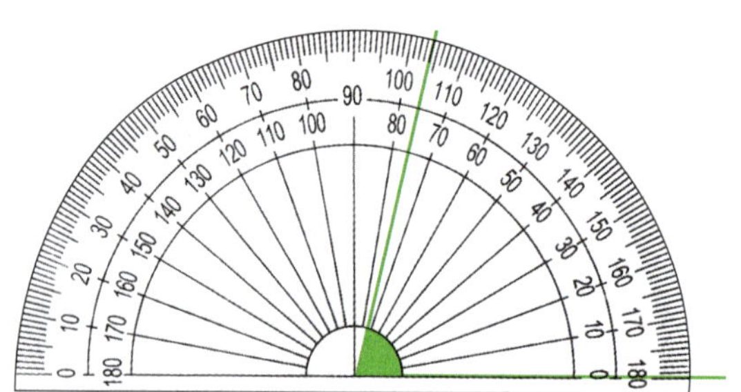

5 Calculate the size of the marked angles.

a

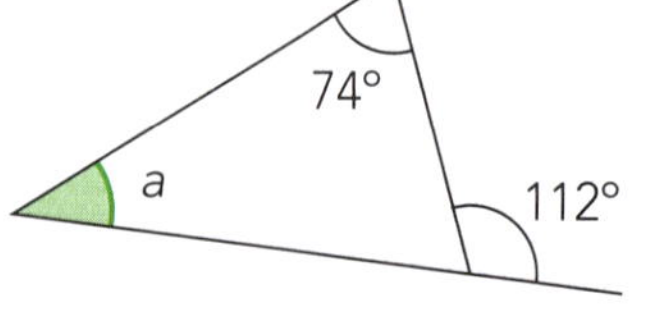

____

____

b

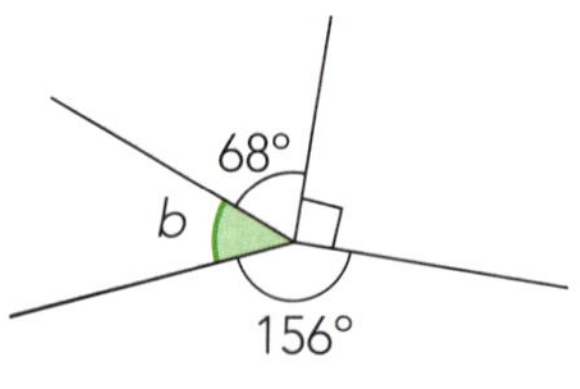

____

____

PHOTOCOPYING OF THIS PAGE IS RESTRICTED UNDER LAW. ISBN: 9780170447539

c

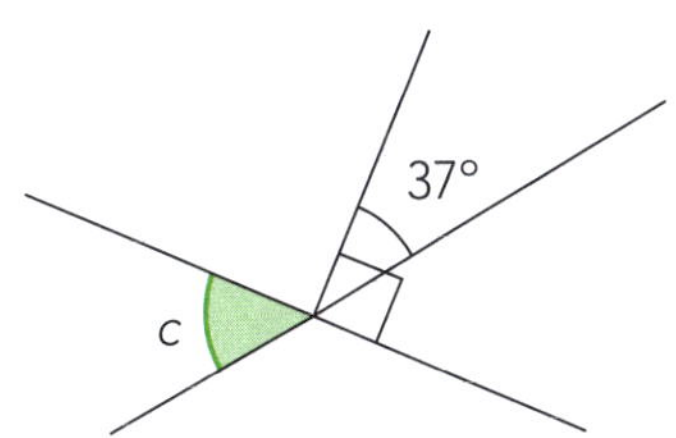

d

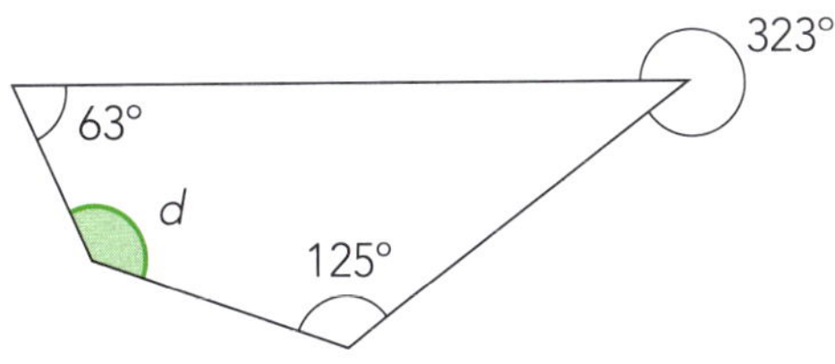

6 Write down the numbers of vertices, edges and faces this 3D shape has.

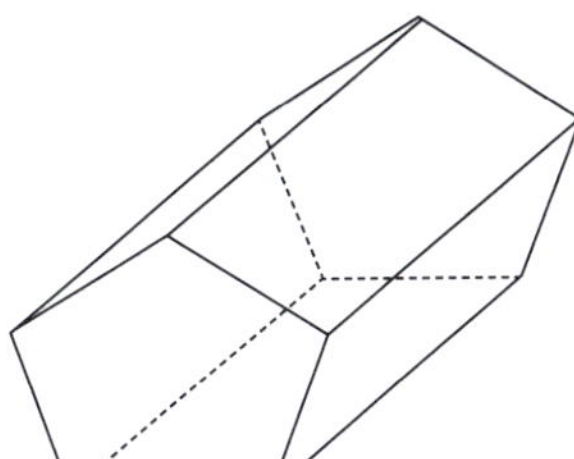

Vertices ________

Edges ________

Faces ________

This figure is/is not a prism.

7

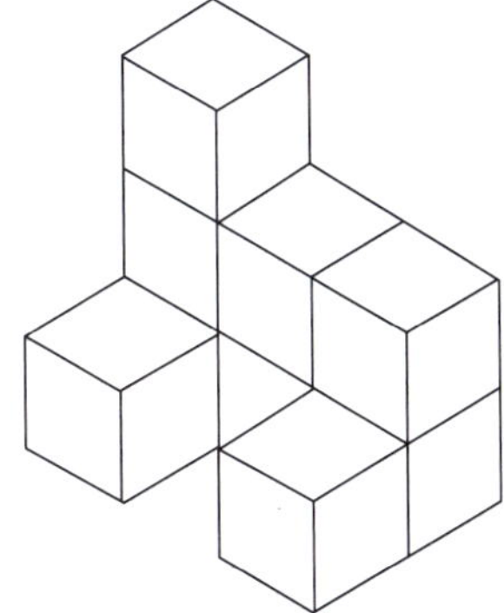

a Draw this shape on the isometric grid, but without showing the junctions between blocks.

b Write the number of blocks in each column.

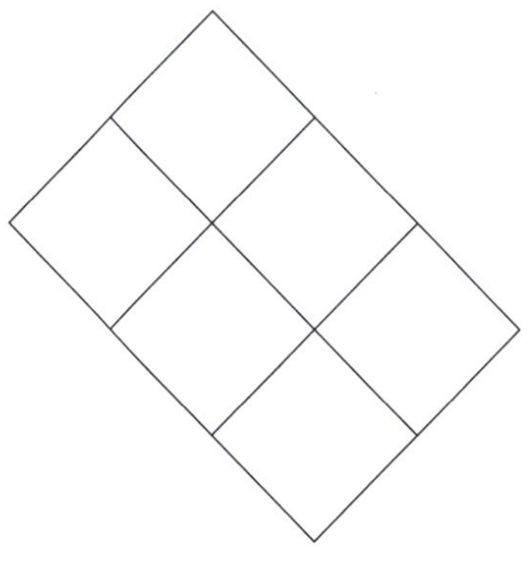

c Draw the top, left and front views of this shape.

Top Left Front

8 Use this map to answer the following questions. Scale: 1 cm = 2 km.

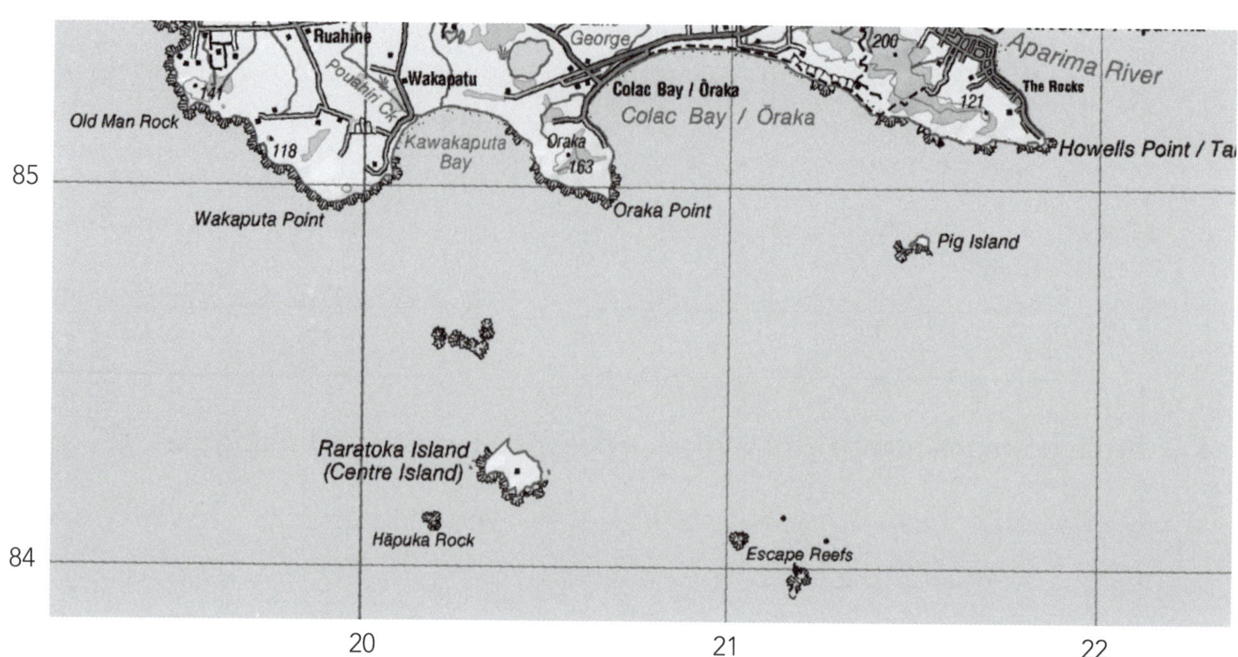

a Circle the direction and bearing for a line from the mouth of the Aparima River to the point on Raratoka Island.

NE NW SE SW

045° 225° 315° 135°

b What would you find at at 215848? ________________

c Write the grid reference for Oraka Point. ________________

d Estimate the distance between Old Man Rock and Hapuka Rock. ________________

9 Reflect the image in the mirror line, and then draw an enlargement of the reflected image, using a scale factor of 2.

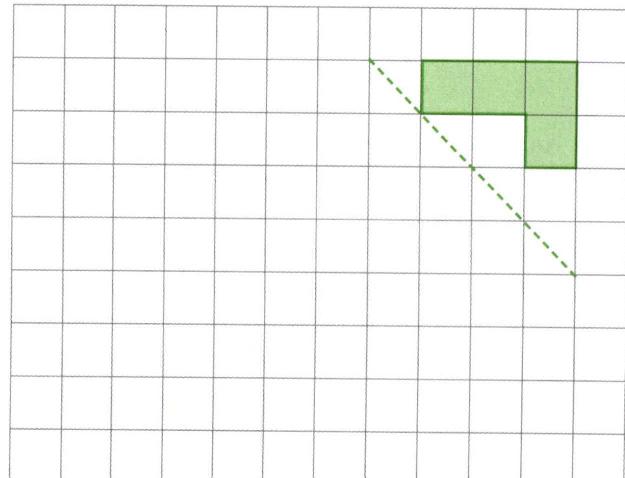

PHOTOCOPYING OF THIS PAGE IS RESTRICTED UNDER LAW. ISBN: 9780170447539

Answers

Shapes (pp. 6–12)

Polygons (p. 6)

1 Polygon
2 Not a polygon
3 Not a polygon
4 Not a polygon
5 Polygon
6 Polygon
7

Number of sides	Name	Diagram
3	Triangle	
4	Quadrilateral	
5	Pentagon	
6	Hexagon	
7	Heptagon	
8	Octagon	
9	Nonagon	
10	Decagon	

Shape language (pp. 8–9)

1 symmetrical 2D
2 polygon regular quadrilateral
3 2D polygon
4 polygon quadrilateral
5 pentagon irregular
6 polygon symmetrical hexagon
7 heptagon 2D polygon
8 hexagon, polygon, regular, symmetrical, 2D
9 hexagon, polygon, symmetrical, 2D
10 octagon, polygon, symmetrical, 2D
11 heptagon, polygon, 2D

Naming 2D shapes (pp. 10–11)

1 circle
2 pentagon
3 isosceles triangle
4 square
5 parallelogram
6 oval
7 heptagon
8 right-angled triangle
9 trapezium
10 semicircle
11 octagon
12 equilateral triangle
13 isosceles trapezium
14 rectangle
15 right-angled isosceles triangle
16 nonagon
17 kite
18 decagon
19 rhombus
20 hexagon
21 pentagon

Challenge 1 (p. 12)

Square size	Number
1 x 1	6
2 x 2	5
3 x 3	4
4 x 4	6
5 x 5	0
6 x 6	1
7 x 7	0
8 x 8	1
Total:	23

Triangle shape	Number
Total:	24

Angles (pp. 13–32)

Types of angles (pp. 13–14)

1 Acute
2 Reflex
3 Right
4 Obtuse
5 Straight
6 Acute
7 Reflex
8 Reflex
9 Acute
10 Right

Naming angles (p. 15)

1 ∠BCA
2 ∠CBA
3 ∠a
4 ∠DAB
5 ∠CDA
6 ∠b

Measuring acute and obtuse angles (pp. 16–17)

1 65°
2 85°
3 155°
4 103°
5 15°

Measuring reflex angles (pp. 18–19)

1 215°
2 285°
3 196°
4 332°
5 340°

ISBN: 9780170447539 PHOTOCOPYING OF THIS PAGE IS RESTRICTED UNDER LAW.

Estimating angles (p. 20)

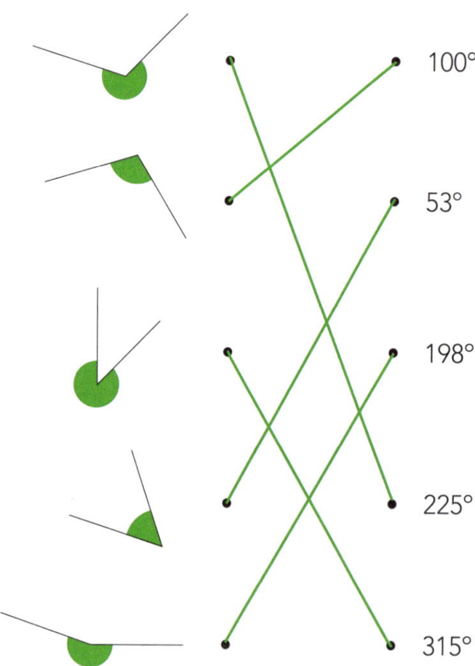

Angles on a line (pp. 21–22)

1 $y = 45°$
2 $z = 56°$
3 $x = 130°$
4 $a = 39°$
5 $y = 107°$
6 $z = 97°$
7 $x = 34°$
8 $b = 59°$
9 ∠AEB = 50°
10 ∠PTQ = 29°

Angles at a point (pp. 23–24)

1 $x = 89°$
2 $y = 198°$
3 $a = 270°$
4 $z = 315°$
5 $x = 127°$
6 $y = 72°$
7 ∠PSR = 245°
8 ∠WZX = 148°
9 $x = 128°$
10 $x = 62°$

Vertically opposite angles (pp. 25–26)

1 $y = 124°$
2 $b = 93°$
3 $b = 49°$
4 $c = 45°$
5 $p = 112°$
6 $c = 51°$
7 $e = 26°$
8 $x = 52°$
9 ∠JNK = 38°
10 ∠RVS = 64°

Angles in a triangle (pp. 27–28)

1 $y = 47°$
2 $z = 54°$
3 $x = 32°$
4 $b = 39°$
5 $x = 63°$
6 $z = 60°$
7 $a = 47°$
8 $z = 53°$
9 ∠DGF = 112°
10 ∠XZY = 43°

Angles in a quadrilateral (pp. 29–30)

1 $x = 124°$
2 $y = 68°$
3 $z = 63°$
4 $a = 99°$
5 $x = 46°$
6 $b = 52°$
7 $z = 97°$
8 $y = 82°$
9 ∠FIH = 95°
10 ∠QPS = 65°

Mixing it up (pp. 31–32)

1 $x = 104°$
2 $x = 63°$
3 $y = 136°$
4 $a = 41°$
5 $g = 102°$
6 $x = 75°$
7 $k = 122°$
8 $x = 36°$
9 $z = 66°$
10 $m = 52°$
11 $x = 63.5°$
12 $x = 47°$

2D and 3D shapes (pp. 33–38)

2D and 3D language (pp. 33–34)

1 Vertices 6
Edges 9
Faces 5

2 Vertices 4
Edges 6
Faces 4

3 Vertices 10
Edges 15
Faces 7

4 Vertices 12
Edges 18
Faces 8

5

6 faces, 8 vertices and 12 edges

7 faces, 7 vertices and 12 edges

8 faces, 12 vertices and 18 edges

8 faces, 6 vertices and 12 edges

5 faces, 6 vertices and 9 edges

5 faces, 5 vertices and 8 edges

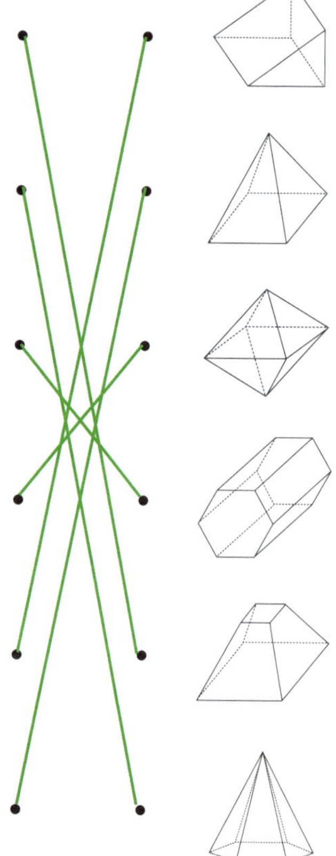

Prisms (p. 35)

1 ✓
2 × Curved sides
3 × End shapes are different
4 ✓
5 ✓
6 × End shapes are different

Naming 3D shapes (p. 36)

1 Sphere
2 Cone
3 Square-based pyramid

PHOTOCOPYING OF THIS PAGE IS RESTRICTED UNDER LAW.
ISBN: 9780170447539

4 Cylinder
5 Triangular-based pyramid
6 Cube
7 Hemisphere
8 Pentagonal prism
9 Triangular prism
10 Octahedron
11 Hexagonal prism
12 Cuboid

Nets (pp. 37–38)

1

2

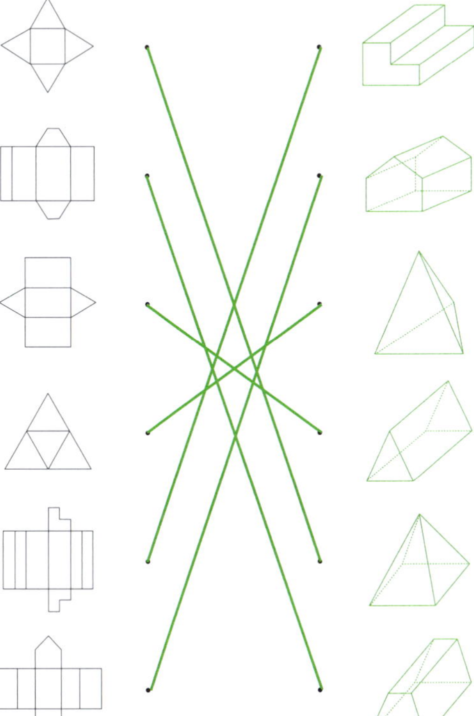

Isometrics (pp. 39–49)

1

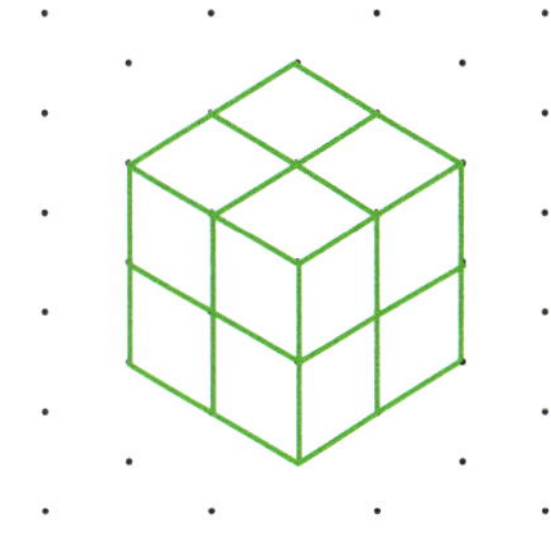

2

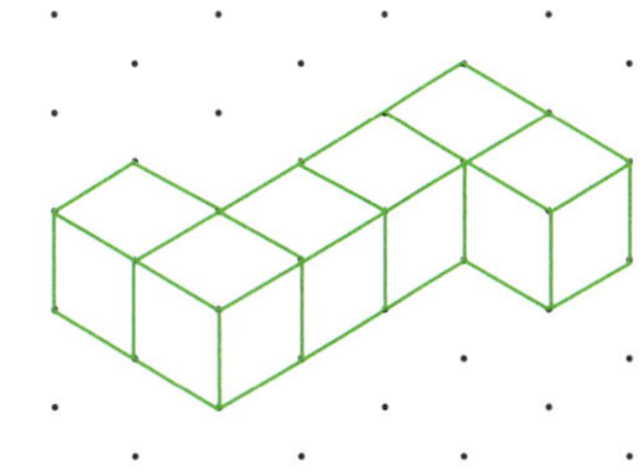

3

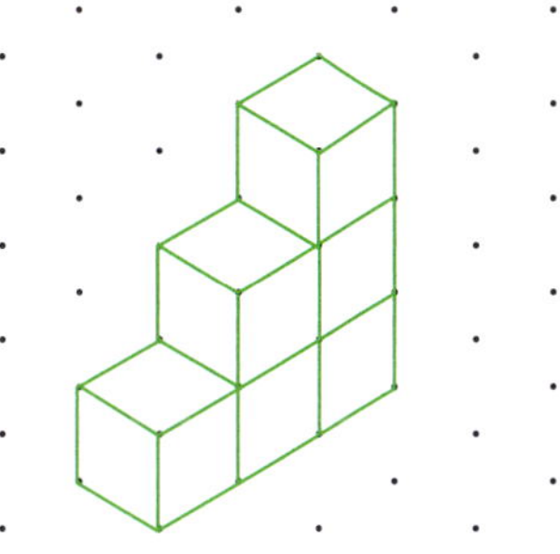

4

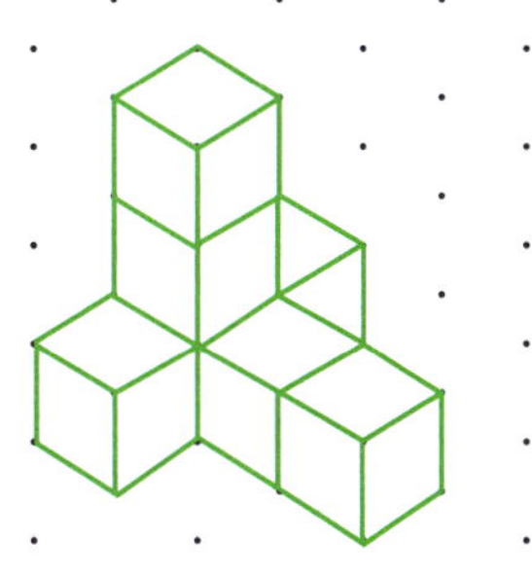

5

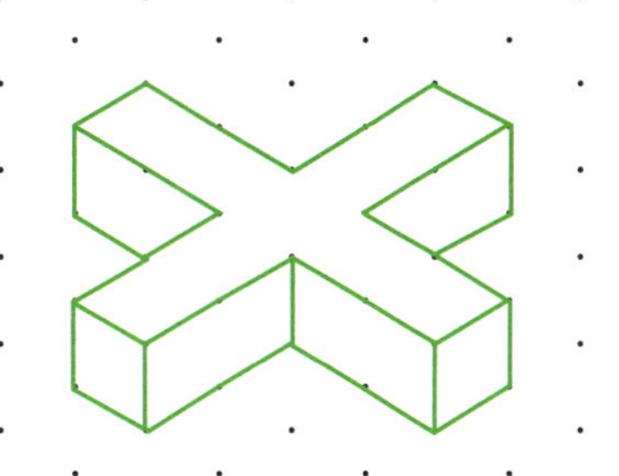

ISBN: 9780170447539 PHOTOCOPYING OF THIS PAGE IS RESTRICTED UNDER LAW.

6

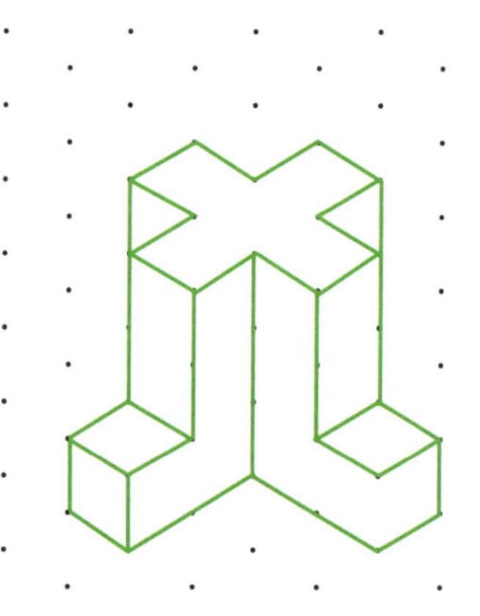

7

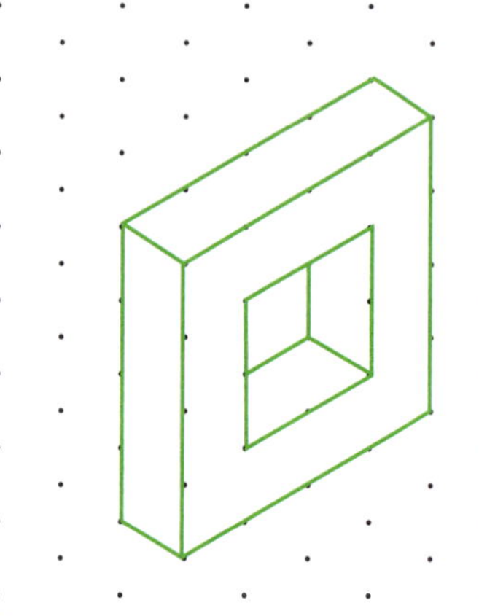

Drawing isometric shapes from numbers in each column (pp. 42–45)

1

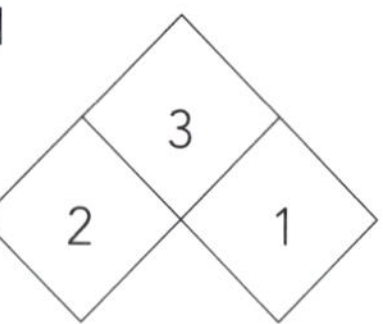

2

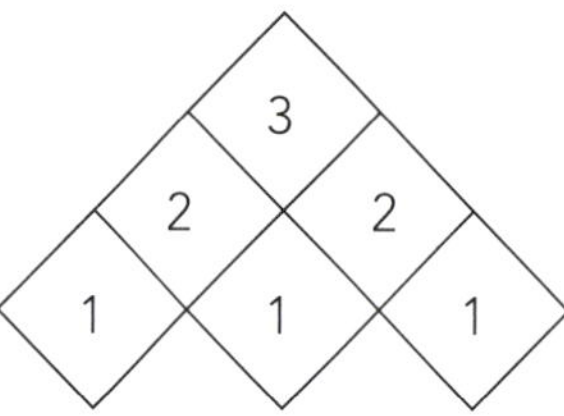

3

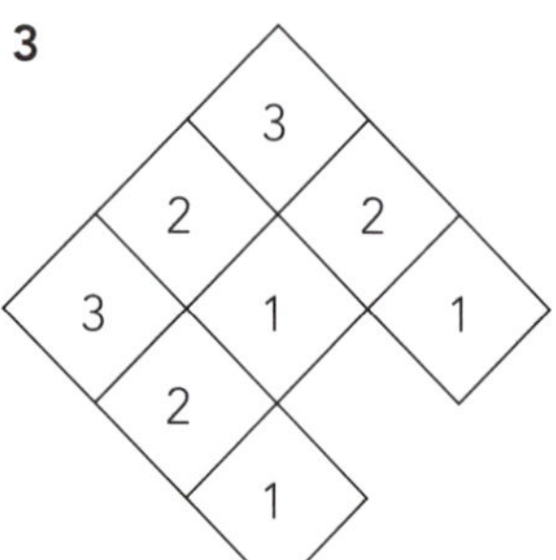

4

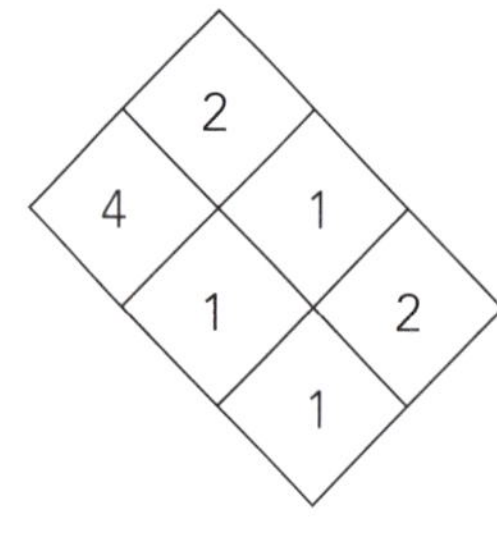

5

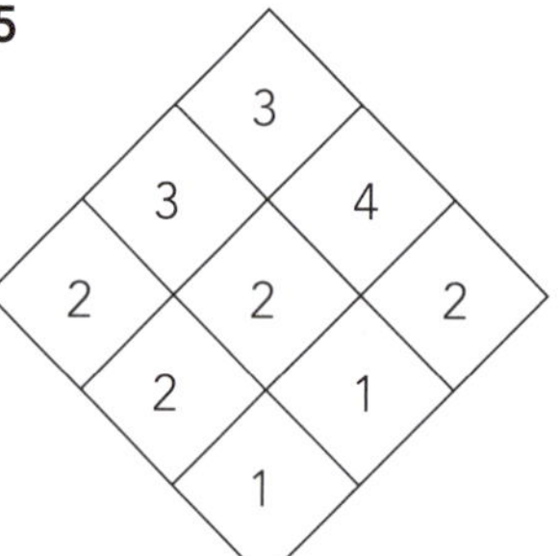

6

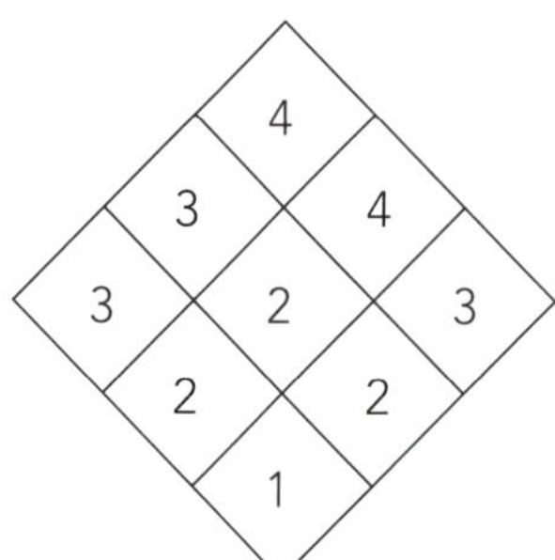

7

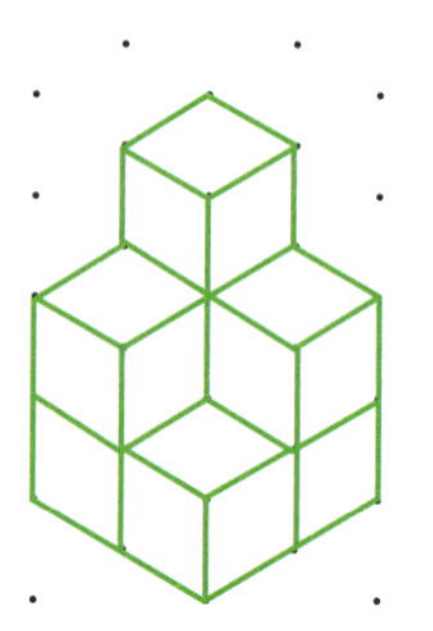

8

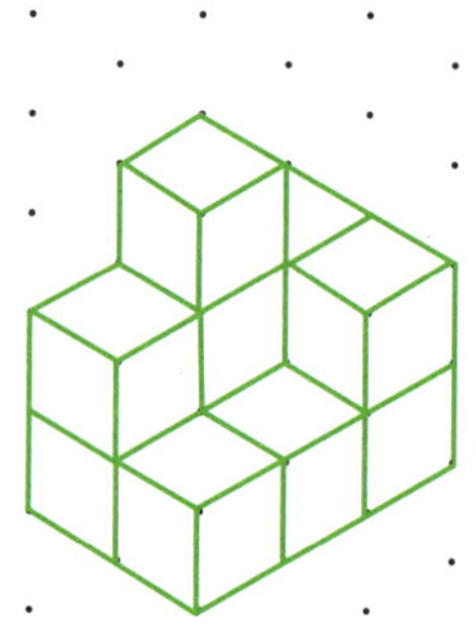

9

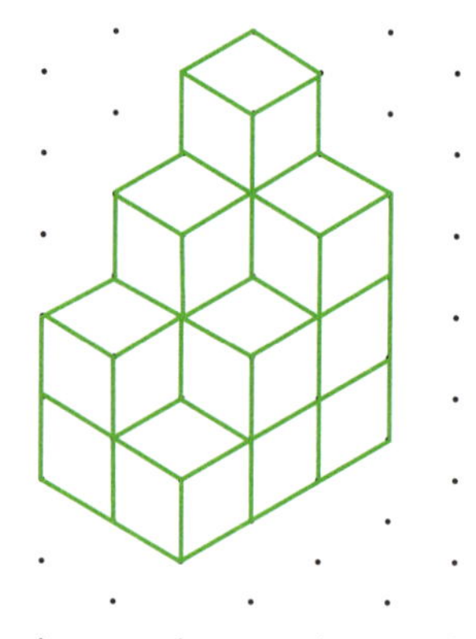

PHOTOCOPYING OF THIS PAGE IS RESTRICTED UNDER LAW. ISBN: 9780170447539

10

11

12

Different views of isometric diagrams (pp. 46–48)

1 D

2 C

3 B

4 A

5 F

6 E

7

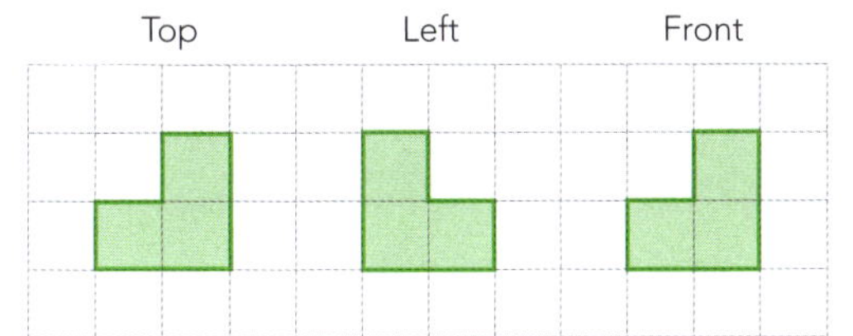

8

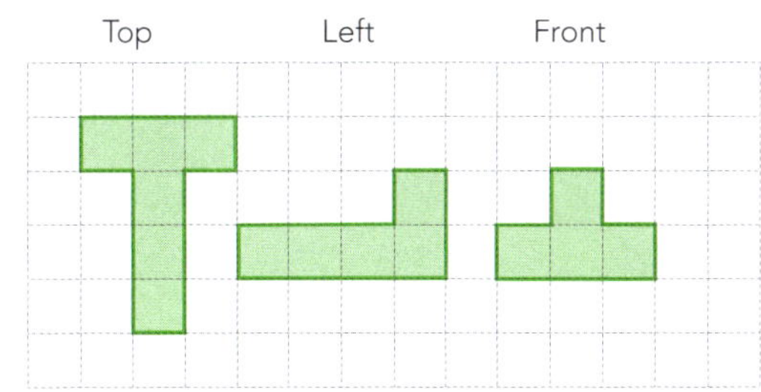

9

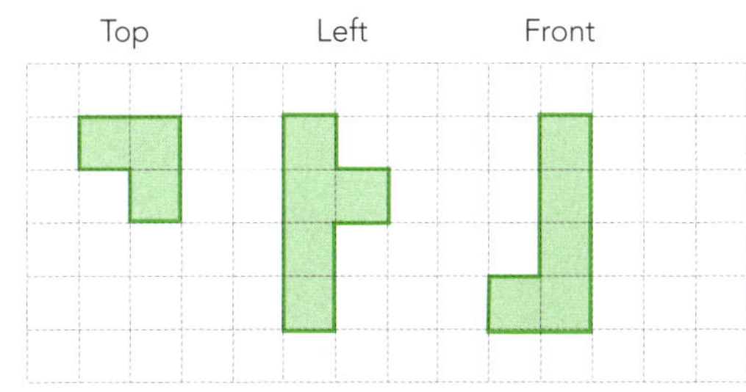

10

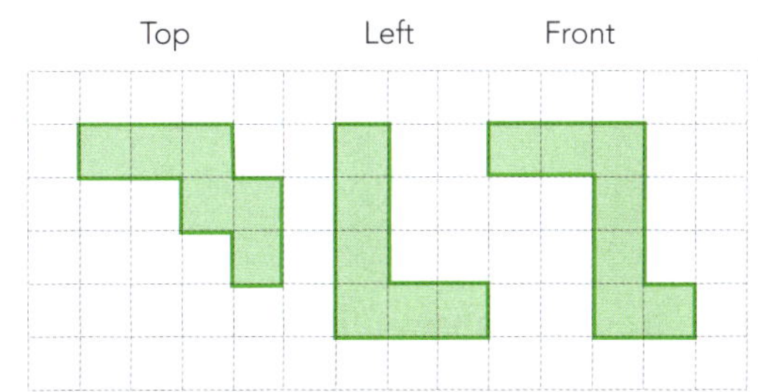

Challenge 2 (p. 49)

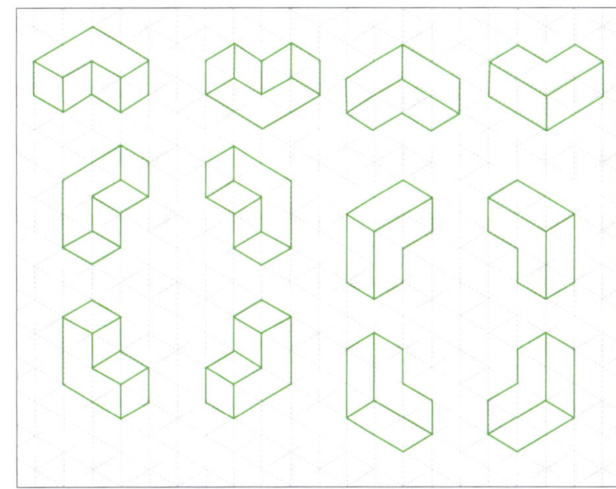

Position and orientation (pp. 50–61)

Directions and bearings (pp. 50–52)

1 270° W

2 135° SE

3 180° S

4 315° NW

5 090° E

6 045° NE

7 000° or 360° N

8 225° SW

ISBN: 9780170447539 PHOTOCOPYING OF THIS PAGE IS RESTRICTED UNDER LAW.

9

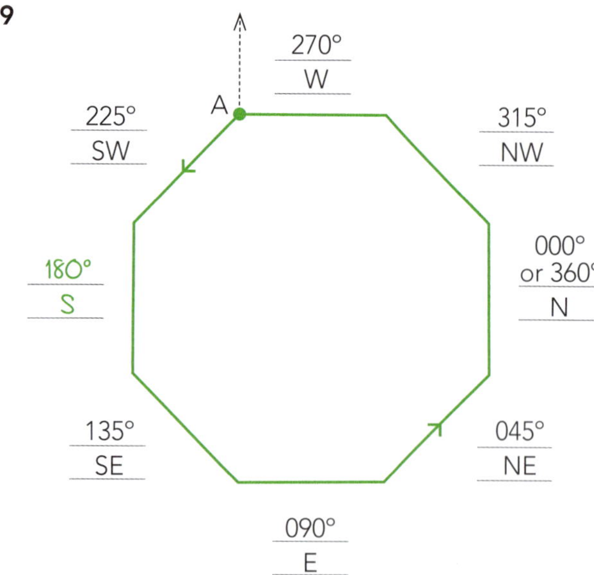

10

	Bearing	Direction
a	135°	SE
b	315°	NW
c	090°	E

Location: grid references (pp. 53–57)

Your answers in this section may vary. If so, check with your teacher.

4-point grid references

1 The Entry/Exit point
2 Rhinoceros
3 Alligator
4 The watering hole cafe
5 A rest stop
6 The cheetah
7 5254
8 2442 or 2443
9 1565
10 2326 or 2226
11 4943 or 4944
12 3966

6-point grid references

16 The Brothers Point
17 Hut
18 Stuarts
19 The Sisters
20 Chaslands
21 Makati

Note: for Q**22**–**25** allow 1 point either side of the third and sixth digits.

22 327833
23 326835
24 318829
25 311838
26 6 km
27 9 km
28 4 km
29 2 km
30 S
31 NE
32 W
33 SW

Paths and directions (pp. 58–61)

Your distances may differ slightly from these – if so, check with your teacher.

1 From A, go **220** m at a bearing of **090°** to B.
From B, go **250** m at a bearing of **135°** to C.
From C, go **360** m at a bearing of **270°** to D.
From D, go **150** m at a bearing of **225°** to E.

2 From A, go **200** m at a bearing of **045°** to B.
From B, go **190** m at a bearing of **090°** to C.
From C, go **210** m at a bearing of **315°** to D.
From D, go **110** m at a bearing of **000°** or **360°** to E.

3 From A, go **120** m at a bearing of **225°** to B.
From B, go **210** m at a bearing of **135°** to C.
From C, go **380** m at a bearing of **270°** to D.
From D, go **310** m at a bearing of **315°** to E.

4 From A, go **120** m at a bearing of **180°** to B.
From B, go **480** m at a bearing of **315°** to C.
From C, go **310** m at a bearing of **215°** to D.
From D, go **330** m at a bearing of **090°** to E.

5 From A, go **340** m at a bearing of **045°** to B.
From B, go **200** m at a bearing of **180°** to C.
From C, go **240** m at a bearing of **135°** to D.
From D, go **580** m at a bearing of **270°** to E.

6 From A, go **450** m at a bearing of **090°** to B.
From B, go **340** m at a bearing of **135°** to C.
From C, go **140** m at a bearing of **270°** to D.
From D, go **250** m at a bearing of **315°** to E.

7 The Victoria Clock Tower
8 The Margaret Mahy Family Playground
9 The Hare Krishna Temple
10 Walk about 635 m on a bearing of 000° (or 360°), then about 440 m on a bearing of 270°, then about 70 m on a bearing of 180°.
11 Walk about 200 m on a bearing of 270°, then about 90 m on a bearing of 180°, then about 80 m on a bearing of 270°.

Transformation geometry (pp. 62–80)

Translation (pp. 63–66)

1 $\begin{pmatrix} 2 \\ 5 \end{pmatrix}$
2 $\begin{pmatrix} 3 \\ 1 \end{pmatrix}$
3 $\begin{pmatrix} -4 \\ 2 \end{pmatrix}$
4 $\begin{pmatrix} -1 \\ -5 \end{pmatrix}$
5 $\begin{pmatrix} 4 \\ -2 \end{pmatrix}$
6 $\begin{pmatrix} -2 \\ 5 \end{pmatrix}$
7 $\begin{pmatrix} -3 \\ 1 \end{pmatrix}$
8 $\begin{pmatrix} 1 \\ -5 \end{pmatrix}$
9 **Right** two and **up** three
10 **Right** four and **down** one
11 **Left** three and **up** five
12 **Left** one and **down** six
13 Left two and up four
14 Right six and down three

PHOTOCOPYING OF THIS PAGE IS RESTRICTED UNDER LAW.
ISBN: 9780170447539

15

$\begin{pmatrix}-3\\0\end{pmatrix}$	$\begin{pmatrix}-4\\-1\end{pmatrix}$	$\begin{pmatrix}-2\\-4\end{pmatrix}$	$\begin{pmatrix}-4\\2\end{pmatrix}$	$\begin{pmatrix}3\\-1\end{pmatrix}$	$\begin{pmatrix}0\\-2\end{pmatrix}$	$\begin{pmatrix}2\\5\end{pmatrix}$	$\begin{pmatrix}2\\2\end{pmatrix}$	$\begin{pmatrix}2\\-3\end{pmatrix}$	$\begin{pmatrix}-5\\1\end{pmatrix}$
f	c	e	h	a	g	j	d	b	i

16

$\begin{pmatrix}3\\2\end{pmatrix}$	$\begin{pmatrix}4\\-1\end{pmatrix}$	$\begin{pmatrix}-2\\-1\end{pmatrix}$	$\begin{pmatrix}1\\-3\end{pmatrix}$	$\begin{pmatrix}-4\\0\end{pmatrix}$	$\begin{pmatrix}-3\\3\end{pmatrix}$	$\begin{pmatrix}3\\1\end{pmatrix}$	$\begin{pmatrix}0\\3\end{pmatrix}$	$\begin{pmatrix}-5\\-3\end{pmatrix}$	$\begin{pmatrix}-5\\3\end{pmatrix}$
a	b	c	d	e	f	g	h	i	j

17 $\begin{pmatrix}4\\3\end{pmatrix}$ **18** $\begin{pmatrix}4\\-3\end{pmatrix}$

19 $\begin{pmatrix}-5\\2\end{pmatrix}$ **20** $\begin{pmatrix}-5\\-1\end{pmatrix}$

21 $\begin{pmatrix}3\\1\end{pmatrix}$ **22** $\begin{pmatrix}-5\\-3\end{pmatrix}$

23 $\begin{pmatrix}4\\0\end{pmatrix}$ **24** $\begin{pmatrix}0\\-4\end{pmatrix}$

Reflection (pp. 67–69)

1

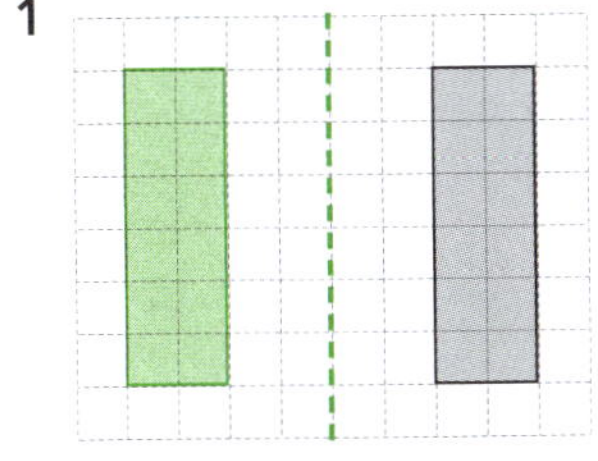

2

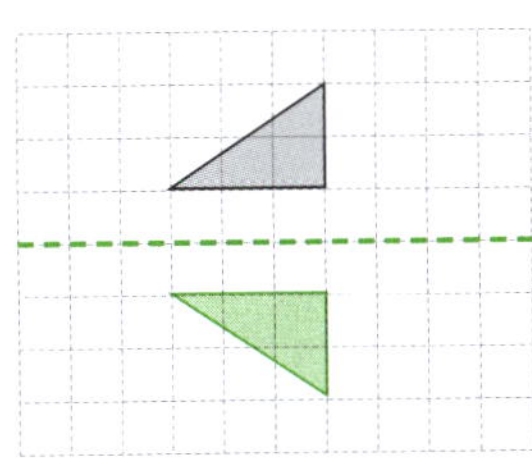

3

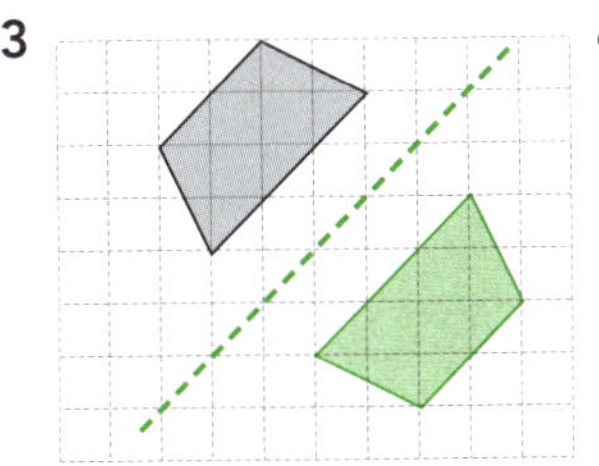

4

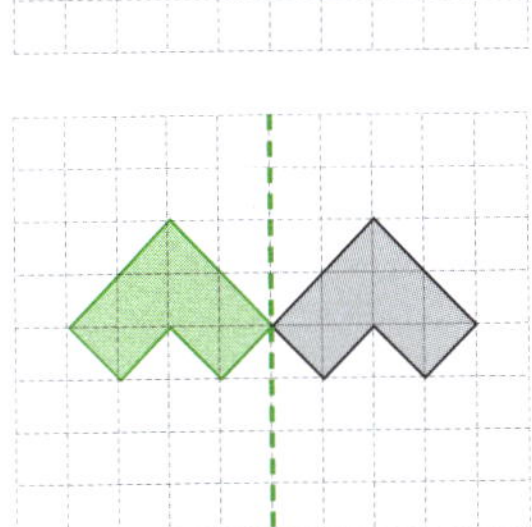

5

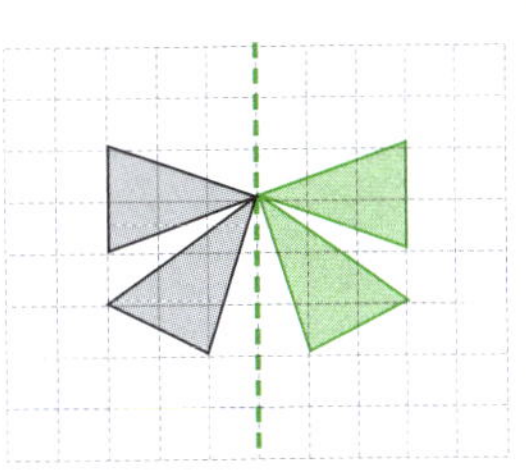

6

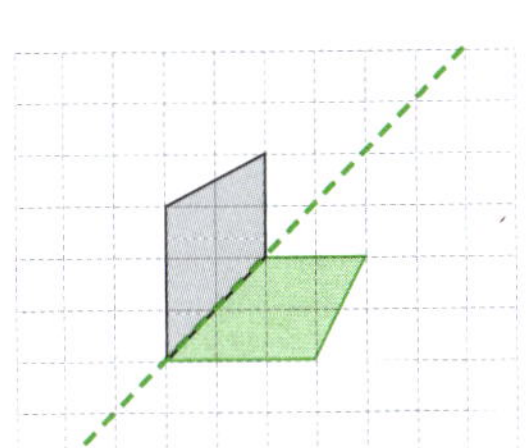

Drawing reflections

1

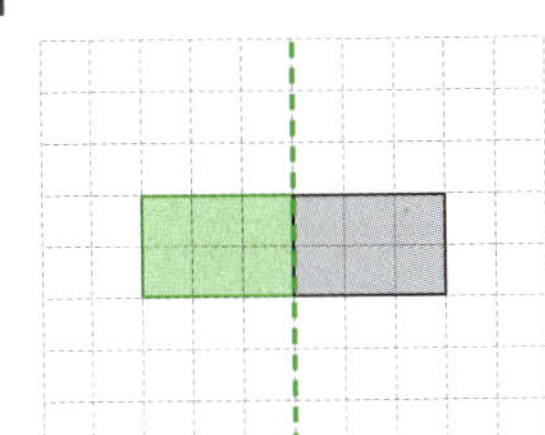

2

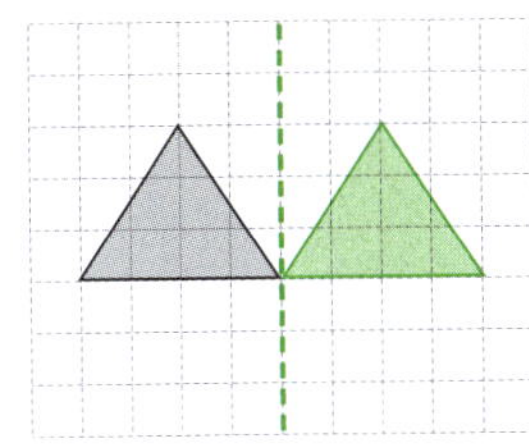

3

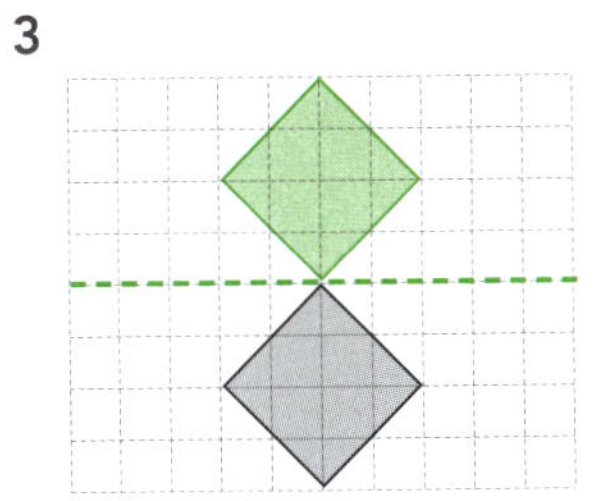

4

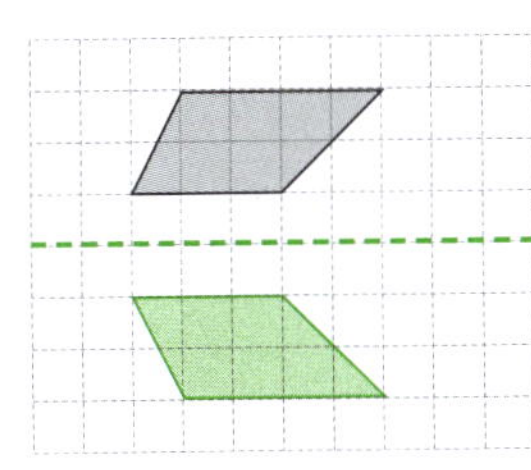

Line symmetry (pp. 70–71)

1

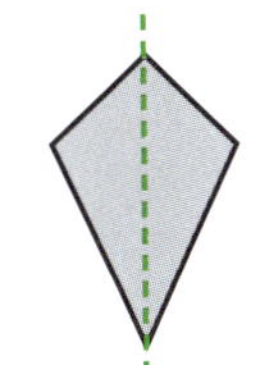

Order of line symmetry = 1

2

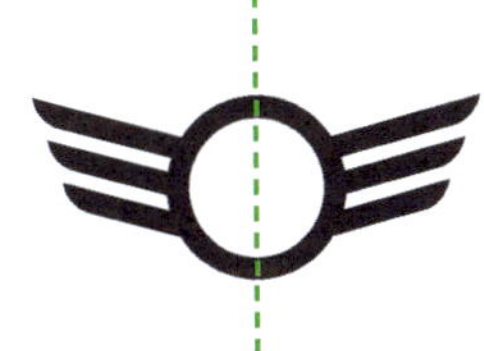

Order of line symmetry = 1

3

Order of line symmetry = 1

4

Order of line symmetry = 1

5

Order of line symmetry = 1

6

Order of line symmetry = 2

7

Order of line symmetry = 1

8

Order of line symmetry = 3

9

Order of line symmetry = 2

10

Order of line symmetry = 1

ISBN: 9780170447539 PHOTOCOPYING OF THIS PAGE IS RESTRICTED UNDER LAW.

11 

Order of line symmetry = 1

12 

Order of line symmetry = 4

Rotation (pp.72–75)

Using angles of rotation

1 Angle = 90°
2 Angle = 180°
3 Angle = 270°
4 Angle = 90°

Drawing rotations

1 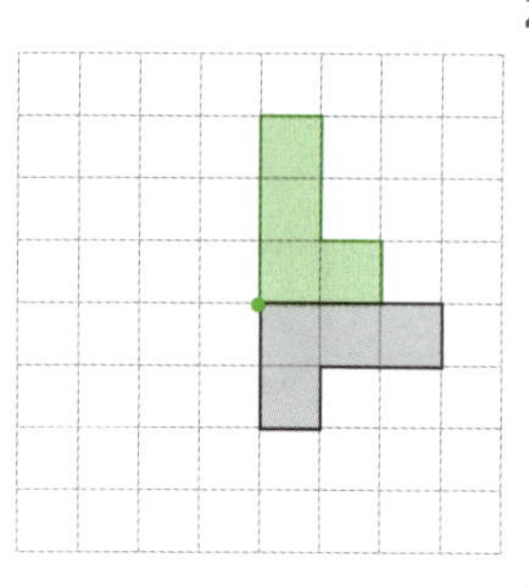

2 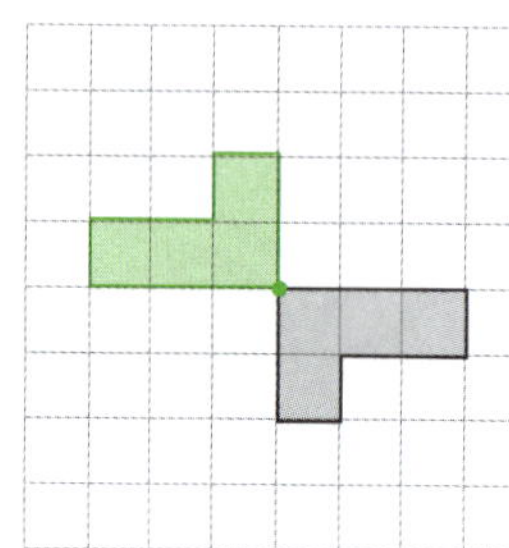

3 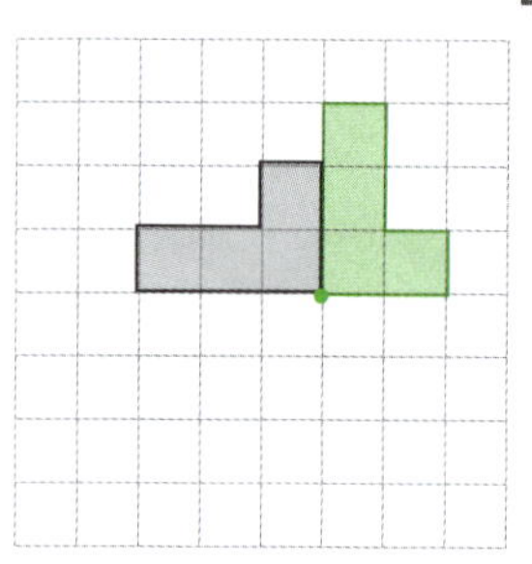

4 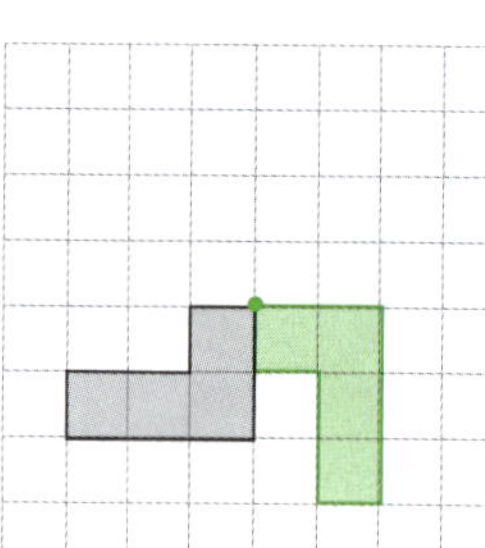

5 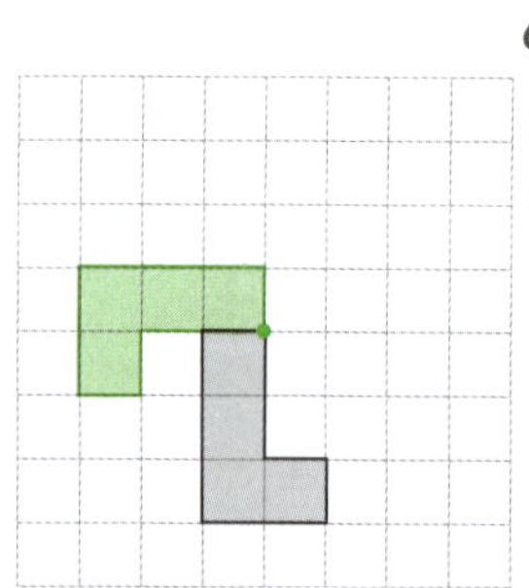

6 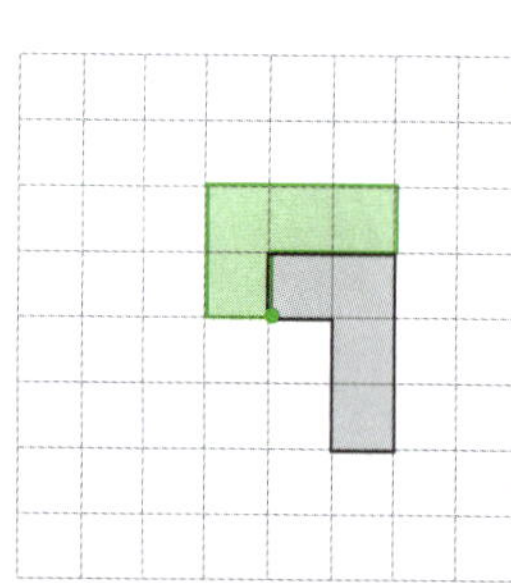

Rotational symmetry (pp. 76–77)

1 Order of rotational symmetry = 2
2 Order of rotational symmetry = 1
3 Order of rotational symmetry = 2
4 Order of rotational symmetry = 3
5 Order of rotational symmetry = 3
6 Order of rotational symmetry = 5
7 Order of rotational symmetry = 6
8 Order of rotational symmetry = 4
9 Order of rotational symmetry = 9
10 Order of rotational symmetry = 18

Enlargement (pp 78–80)

1 scale factor = 3
scale factor = 2
scale factor = 4
2 scale factor = 3
scale factor = 0.5
scale factor = 2
3 scale factor = 4
scale factor = 2
scale factor = 3
scale factor = 0.5

4 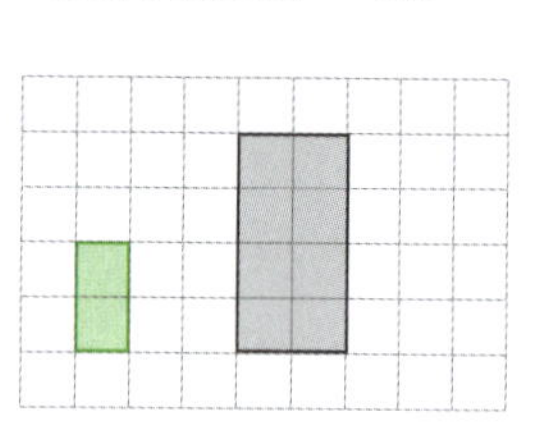

5 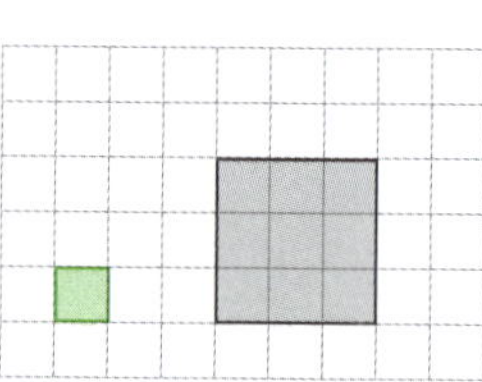

6 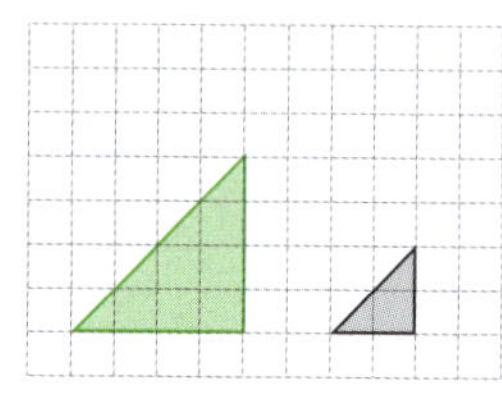

7 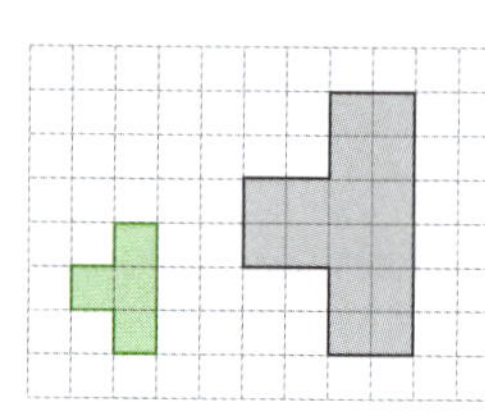

8 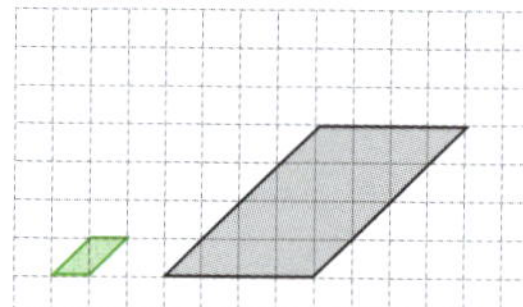

9 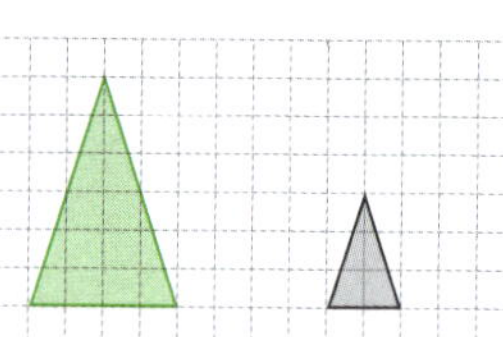

10 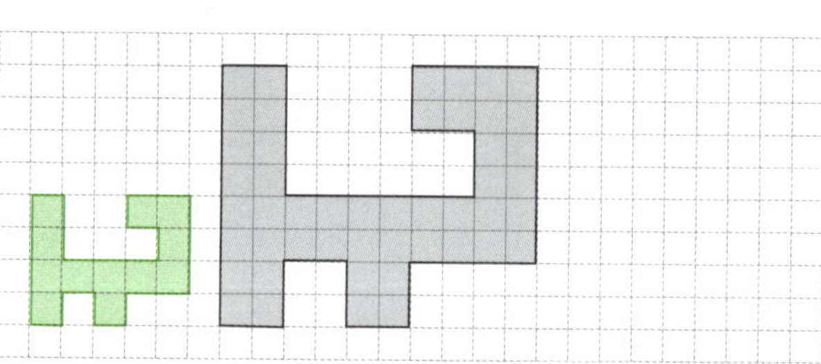

Revision 1 (pp. 81–83)

1 polygon symmetrical quadrilateral
2 a Hexagon b Parallelogram
c Regular triange
3 a ∠DCB or ∠BCD
b Obtuse
4 133°
5 a $a = 109°$ b $b = 80°$
c $c = 44°$ d $d = 54°$
6 Vertices 8
Edges 12
Faces 6
This figure ~~is~~/is not a prism.

PHOTOCOPYING OF THIS PAGE IS RESTRICTED UNDER LAW. ISBN: 9780170447539

7 a

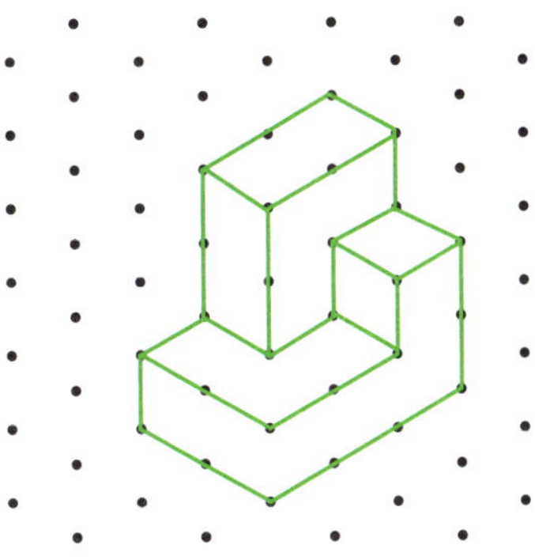

b

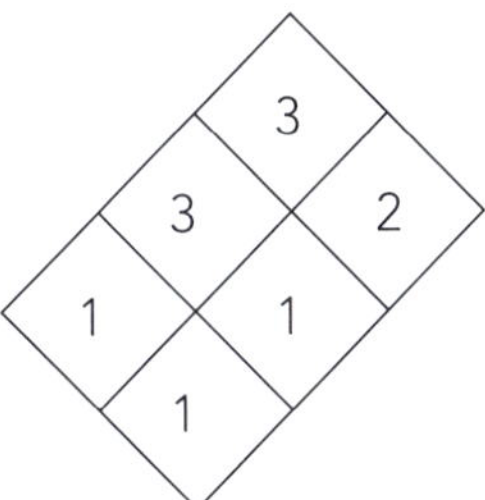

c

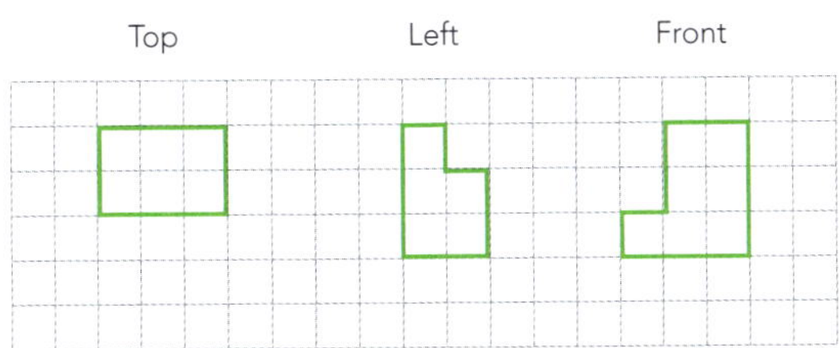

8 a NW 315°
b Bream Head
c 738030
d 21 km

9

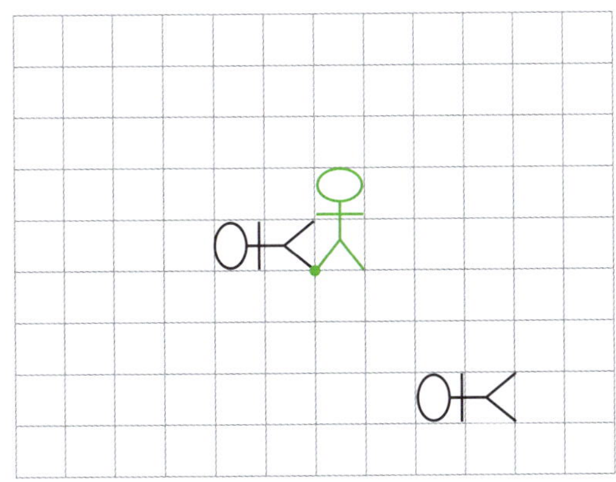

Revision 2 (pp. 84–86)

1 octagon symmetrical
2 a Arrowhead b Regular quadrilateral
c Isosceles trapezium
3 a ∠ADC or ∠CDA
b Reflex
4 76°
5 a $a = 38°$ b $b = 46°$
c $c = 53°$ d $d = 135°$
6 Vertices 10
Edges 15
Faces 7
This figure is/~~is not~~ a prism.
7 a

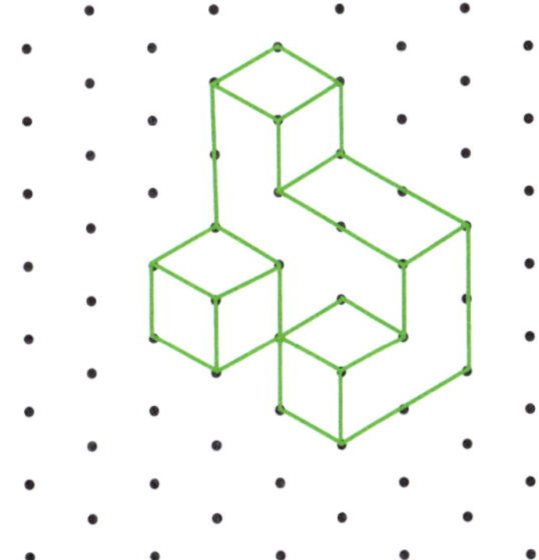

b

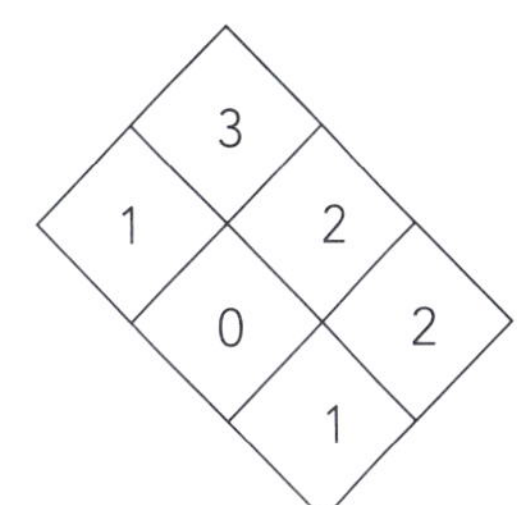

c

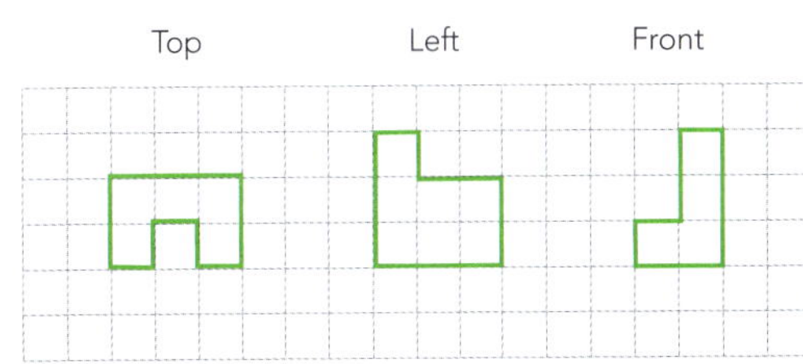

8 a SW 225°
b Pig Island
c 207849
d 13 km
9 Note: the position of your enlargement doesn't matter.

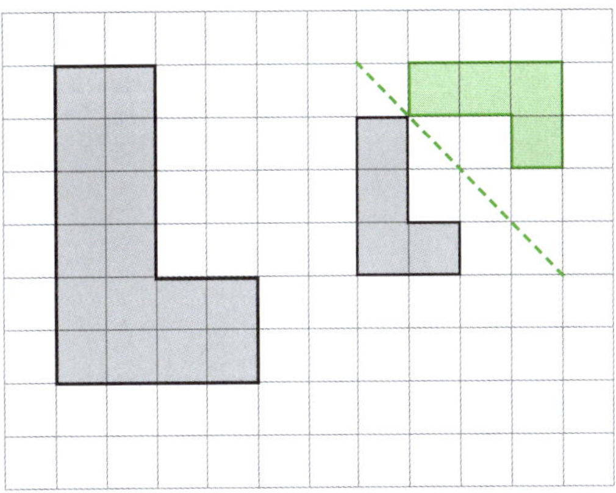

ISBN: 9780170447539 PHOTOCOPYING OF THIS PAGE IS RESTRICTED UNDER LAW.